Social Networks and Social Influences in Adolescence

Social Networks and Social Influences in Adolescence charts the inter-actions of young people both in and out of school and the role of peers and friends in strengthening social attachments and in establishing social identities. It describes how social identities are worked out in the different settings which comprise the adolescent's world and how these experiences differ for those who are shy, popular, aggressive or antisocial.

The book is in three parts. Part I describes how the social ties between friends link young people to various kinds of peer group structure, in-cluding friendship cliques, the peer crowd and classroom groups, as well as antisocial groups and gangs. Part II explores young people's behaviour in the wider social environment and the implications of social acceptance or rejection for academic motivation, aggression and health risk behaviour. Finally, Part III describes how professionals can support adolescents in building social attachments, giving practical examples of how this is being done in various communities. *Social Networks and Social Influences in Adolescence* will prove invaluable for students and professionals working with young people.

John Cotterell is a senior lecturer in the Graduate School of Education at Queensland University, where he teaches courses on adolescence and edu-cational environments. He has worked as a teacher, researcher and youth leadership trainer and has written extensively on adolescence.

Adolescence and Society
Series editor: John C. Coleman
The Trust for the Study of Adolescence

The general aim of the series is to make accessible to a wide readership the growing evidence relating to adolescent development. Much of this material is published in relatively inaccessible professional journals, and the goals of the books in this series will be to summarise, review and place in context current work in the field so as to interest and engage both an undergraduate and a professional audience.

The intention of the authors is to raise the profile of adolescent studies among professionals and in institutes of higher education. By publishing relatively short, readable books on interesting topics to do with youth and society, the series will make people more aware of the relevance of the subject of adolescence to a wide range of social concerns.

The books will not put forward any one theoretical viewpoint. The authors will outline the most prominent theories in the field and will include a balanced and critical assessment of each of these. Whilst some of the books may have a clinical or applied slant, the majority will concentrate on normal development.

The readership will rest primarily in two major areas: the undergraduate market, particularly in the fields of psychology, sociology and education; and the professional training market, with particular emphasis on social work, clinical and educational psychology, counselling, youth work, nursing and teacher training.

Social Networks and Social Influences in Adolescence

John Cotterell

London and New York

To Sue, Liz, Dave and Andrew

First published 1996
by Routledge
11 New Fetter Lane, London EC4P 4EE

Simultaneously published in the USA and Canada
by Routledge
29 West 35th Street, New York, NY 10001

Routledge is an International Thomson Publishing company

© 1996 John Cotterell

Typeset in Times by LaserScript, Mitcham, Surrey
Printed and bound in Great Britain by
Clays Ltd, St Ives PLC

British Library Cataloguing in Publication Data
A catalogue record for this book is available from the British Library

Library of Congress Cataloguing in Publication Data
Cotterell, John, 1941–
    Social networks and social influences in adolescence/John
    Cotterell.
        p. cm. – (Adolescence in society)
    Includes bibliographical references and index.
    1. Teenagers – Social networks. 2. Group identity. 3. Peer
    pressure. 4. Friendship in adolescence. 5. Adolescent psychology.
    I. Series.
HQ796.C8218 1996
305.23'5 – dc20   95-42130
                                                                  CIP

ISBN 0–415–10973–6 (hbk)
ISBN 0–415–10974–4 (pbk)

Contents

Illustrations

1 Introduction

Adolescent relations: themes and theories

Relations with others lie at the heart of the adolescent experience. Young people are concerned with making and keeping friends, and they invest a great deal of energy in group social life in order to do so. They place a lot of importance on belonging, on being included, and on being part of a group; group affiliation not only supplies emotional security, but also is a source of status and reputation with motivational properties. Thus the group context of social relations assumes a centrally important place in personality development during the adolescent years.

This book represents the prospecting activities of an educator interested in young people's social development. The terrain which is travelled in the following chapters is concerned with face-to-face relationships, intergroup relations, and group social influence. Our present knowledge of social relations in adolescence is scattered, like 'shows' of gold, across the ridges and dry gullies of psychology, sociology, criminology, youth work, social work, and education. Sometimes the findings obtained from those fossicking in one of these areas are not reported to others who share similar interests, but who may adopt different methods of search and enquiry. A wide range of knowledge is relevant to the discussion of adolescent relations and the influences on social behaviour. It includes the practical experience of the youth worker and observer in the field, who, like the prospector, have the benefit of local knowledge of real 'workings'; but there is also a place for the researcher, who, like the geologist, draws upon wider knowledge of patterns and trends in determining the value of the find.

RELATIONS IN ADOLESCENCE

Social behaviour is always in a context, and mediates between the structure of that social situation and the psychological states of the participants. In the adolescent years, the formal contexts of schools and youth organisations provide settings which structure roles and relationships in quite different ways from the informal leisure settings that are frequented by young people. What is of interest for this book is how social relations are expressed and worked out in the different social settings and institutional contexts which comprise the adolescent's social world, and the implications of these social experiences for individual development. Much of the material deals with what young people do and say to each other, and the specific ways in which their behaviour is influenced by others around them.

The prime concern in these pages is 'horizontal' social relations – those which occur between people possessing similar social power and having similar life experiences. Such peer group relations are generally described as reciprocal and egalitarian. Different structures of adolescent group life are described, and the distinctive social relations associated with them. The friendship cliques and peer groups to which the adolescent belongs are primary groups, which not only contribute support to the adolescent in coping with the wider world, but are sources of group identity which help to endorse the emerging personal identity. Reference is made to other relations of a vertical kind as well, between for example adolescents and teachers, but these are seen in these pages as secondary to the relations which adolescents establish with their own age group and on their own terms.

The theoretical frameworks which are employed to explain the patterns observed are relational in kind; that is, they refer to properties in the social relations rather than to attributes of the individual actors. This is more properly social-psychological than psychological, and is a view similar to that adopted by La Gaipa and Wood (1981, p. 170) in their study of friendship among disturbed adolescents, which locates emotional disturbance not in the make-up of the individual, but instead in 'the nature of the interaction strains'. The significance of friendship and belonging to a group is explored, and linked with the power of group acceptance and rejection to influence behavioural conformity. Attention is also given to what motivates youth to demonstrate initiative and exercise social responsibility, and the contexts and settings where the social development of young people may be fostered. There is motivational force in social relations. People do not just die for love; they also kill out of jealousy, cheat to maintain a reputation, and get into fights because their friend is attacked; and career ladders are not only corporate structures but also pathways for achievers through their changing relations with workmates. It is of great practical value to bring together current knowledge on adolescent relations and to consider them from a motivational perspective; for example, the supportive properties of group affiliation, and what motivates adolescents to conform to their peers, to hang around in groups, or to behave in antisocial ways. When social relations are viewed in terms of a person's needs and motivation, the scope of social influence extends enormously.

In discussing social relations in adolescence in these chapters, a distinction which seems useful is that between 'evolutionary' and 'contingent' explanations of behaviour. Developmentally oriented researchers seek evidence of continuities between the adolescent's present behaviour and her/his behaviour during childhood. The pervasiveness of this evolutionary perspective within developmental psychology leads researchers to measure and monitor variables rather than response patterns, to expect and find evidence of gradual rather than dramatic change, and to seek comparisons across similar rather than dissimilar environments. The model of development in the social sciences is individual, moving inexorably forward from infant to child, child to adolescent, adolescent to adult; thus it is easy to assume that as the physical and cognitive structures unfold in a progression from immaturity to reach an advanced stage, similarly the manifestation of adolescent social competencies can be predicted from traces found in childhood, and explained by childhood processes. However, adolescent relations with others are, at least in some respects, qualitatively different from those in childhood, and not merely their upward extension. Clearly, not all adult behaviour has its origins in childhood. If it did, what place would culture and socialisation play in the acquisition of socially skilled behaviour?

For several of the topics discussed, it is necessary to draw on literature on adult social relations and group behaviour, simply because there is insufficient youth research into important areas of young people's social experience. Just as child psychology stretches upward in an attempt to extend the reach of its 'laws' over the adolescent landscape, so there are theories of social action and group influence based on studies of adults which can justifiably be extended downward as useful bridges to an understanding of the world of youth. Research on adult friendship, bereavement, crowds, and collective behaviour all offer information on social processes relevant to the study of adolescent relations.

Adolescence is viewed as very similar in so-called Western societies. As a consequence, behaviour, as adaptation to the place rules and roles in social environments, is seen to follow similar lawful paths. This seems to overlook the subtle but real cultural differences in behaviour which exist between, for example, Australians, Britons, US Americans, and Canadians. Because a large number of the publications concerning adolescence come from American sources, the picture of youth which is portrayed in the academic literature may not accurately reflect the different meanings contained in the social worlds of youth in more distant countries influenced by British culture, such as Australia, New Zealand, and South Africa, although the broad patterns of cognitive and social development may be very similar. Within a particular country, there are further class, ethnic, and regional differences which are expressed in the contexts of school, work, and neighbourhood. These differences are not merely matters of style; they affect the ways of coping among young people from different cultures, and point up the salience of certain social influences on behaviour. Dating, for example, seems to occur much earlier for American adolescents than it does for their counterparts in Australia and Britain; parenting styles and expectations for behaviour also seem to differ between countries. These subtle differences in behaviour are of real importance at the interactional and relational level, and may explain much about the differences, for example, in the expression of dissent and modes of coping with frustration between youth from Sydney, Southampton, or San Francisco.

From an historical perspective, the theoretical advances in the field of adolescent social behaviour can be marked off, like the ice ages, with periods of advance and retreat, but with each period of advance being located in a different region of the field of adolescence. Thus the work on group influence and reference group theory, the research on the status attainment process, the study of youth gangs, and the investigations of adolescent friendship may each be thought of as belonging to a different era of theoretical development, not in the sense of progression and revision but, like an ice age glacier, independently leaving its imprint on the landscape for others to interpret and derive implications from. Moreover, the insularity of the adolescent research field has meant limited application to adolescence of important theoretical work on social relations and social influence which is well known in research on adults. At other times, earlier concepts have become mixed in with later ones, like the debris at the foot of a glacier, so that their origins have become obscure and something of their relevance lost in transportation. My approach is to revisit those earlier theories where relevant, and seek out the original bedrock of research and observation from which the concepts were derived, so as to describe them in a way which is faithful to the original understandings given by the authors. Of course, this venture is not always geological; some of the ideas I wish to include in the discussions are very recent, but may be located in literature seldom visited by those who work with adolescents. The plan which is adopted presents the major theories in this chapter, but reserves discussion of relevant details of the theories to appropriate points in other chapters, thus embedding theoretical insights into a topical approach.

CENTRAL THEORIES

Concepts associated with two major psychological theories are interwoven in the chapters: *attachment theory* and *social identity theory*. Neither theory has been developed specifically for the adolescent age period, but their heuristic value extends beyond their original boundaries. The concept of attachment provides a framework for discussing the emotional basis of relations with others and with groups, and the way security and belongingness needs operate as motivational forces on individual behaviour. The concept of social identity addresses the role of group identifications as a source of identity, and offers a means of linking the social and societal forces in group phenomena with individual actions. In addition to these major theory frames, the structures of relations are considered in terms of *social networks*, and the contents of those relations in terms of social support. This view of social networks as tools of analysis rather than as a metaphor reflects current thinking, and offers a means of determining the boundaries between groups, and of describing the social world of individuals by the specific ties of obligation and affection which link them with other people.

Adolescence as a period of identity development

Adolescent development may be characterised in social psychological terms as a period when individuals resolve two key relational processes: attachment and identity. Attachment refers to the emotional bond between an individual and another person, group, or institution. Although the concept of attachment is not employed in identical ways by psychiatrists and psychologists on the one hand, and criminologists on the other, there is sufficient commonality of meaning for us to describe the relational ties between adolescents and others in their social field, including institutions like schools, from an attachment perspective.

Identity refers to the person's sense of self-definition in relation to others whom s/he is like in some ways and not like in other ways. Achievement of a personal identity is based upon processes of self-categorisation and group identification. Newman and Newman (1986) suggested that in developing a sense of personal identity, the major psychosocial task for young people at secondary school, particularly in the years from 12 to 16, is resolving the crisis of group identity versus alienation. In these years, adolescents experience rapid physical and cognitive changes, and become increasingly sensitive to the approval and acceptance of their peers. Later, these concerns with group identity subside, so that by the age of 18 or so, questions of individual identity and future goals become more central. What the Newmans propose is that adolescents must first resolve questions about their relations to the peer group and decide on a group identity before they can properly define their relations to their family or achieve a sense of personal identity.

ATTACHMENT PROCESSES IN ADOLESCENCE

Attachment theory (Bowlby, 1969, 1974, 1984) provides a broad framework for understanding personality development and adjustment across the lifespan. An attachment is an affectional bond between two people which promotes a sense of psychological security. The child's sense of security is derived from the presence (either physical or psychological) of a protective adult; and when the child feels secure, it is able to explore and learn. In psychological terms, the child appropriates to itself the sense of being valued by a significant other, derived from experiences of comfort and security.

A central tenet of Bowlby's theory is the continuity of attachment. He reviewed a dozen longitudinal studies on personality development (Bowlby, 1974) to conclude cautiously that the patterns visible in the first twelve months of life resemble those seen much later. On the basis of these studies, Bowlby listed three propositions:

1 Confidence in the availability of an attachment figure diminishes the person's anxieties and fears;
2 This confidence is built up slowly across the period of infancy and childhood and persists relatively unchanged throughout life.
3 Expectations concerning the accessibility and responsiveness of attachment figures reflect the individual's experiences, and are not fantasies but models of the world.

Attachment and personality development are thus linked to the child's model of self via the representational concept a child develops of the attachment figure. Healthy personality development is vested in healthy social relations.

Adolescence has been regarded as a period of development when the growing person detaches from parents, 'cuts the apron strings', and begins acting independently of them. The bond which was established in infancy with the caregiver as a trusted other has widened by adolescence to include emotional closeness with, and confidence in, the responsiveness and availability of several trusted others outside the family. Through these multiple attachments, youth experience trust, acceptance, understanding, and respect for individuality (e.g., Kenny, 1987; Offer and Offer, 1975). Armsden and Greenberg (1987, p. 428) apply this argument in stating that 'human beings at any age are most well-adjusted when they have confidence in the accessibility and responsiveness of a trusted other'. A study of college-age adolescents by Kobak and Sceery (1988) contrasted the ego development of students who held qualitatively different 'working models of attachment'. Securely attached students were found to display less anxiety, lower hostility, and greater ego resiliency (which they described as the ability to modulate negative feelings constructively).

Conceptually, there is a strong similarity between social support and the concept of social attachment, which has been noted by several writers interested in adolescence and lifespan research (e.g., Hill and Holmbeck, 1986; Kahn and Antonucci, 1980; Weinraub *et al.*, 1977), and is elaborated in the notion of the 'provisions of social relations' (Weiss, 1974). Companionship is a pleasurable experience of social interaction which is particularly associated with the informal contacts and leisure activities popular among young people. It is an aspect of social relations which tends to have been overlooked in empirical studies of social support. Several of the provisions of social relations described by Weiss, such as reliable alliance, social integration, reassurance of worth, and attachment, are detectable in companionship. Many of these provisions occur through no special effort or deliberate actions on an individual's part: the links between persons occur naturally, through the social exchanges which are pursued every day in countless social situations. Individuals share in common pursuits for their own sake, for the enjoyment of one another's company. They experience a sense of belonging, acceptance, solidarity, and social affirmation simply from being together.

Rook (1987) shows that lack of stimulation from companions in shared activities makes people vulnerable to loneliness and psychological distress. She further suggests that whereas support may alleviate distress and return a person to an 'even keel', companionship provides more positive benefits, such as affection, humour, and relaxation from tension. The interactions between a person and members of the network of others provide the social provisions which create community, confirm identity, and prevent loneliness. Patterns of contact with others in the neighbourhood, school, and local groups become formed over time into social ties which embed each person into a community.

Weiss (1973, 1982, 1989) has suggested that our understanding of emotional loneliness might be profitably enriched by the study of the attachment system and how it develops. Following Bowlby, Weiss interprets the loneliness of emotional isolation as an adult form of disruption to the attachment system which links the child to parent figures. When lonely people were asked by Schultz and Moore (1989) to imagine a solution to their loneliness, they did so unhesitatingly, and surprised not only the authors but themselves with the nature of their responses. These were images of close body contact and comfort, often retrieved from vivid childhood experiences and captured in the notion of 'snuggling up to someone'. They emphasised physically tangible forms of reassurance, in a highly familiar setting with trusted others. The picture they gave of security, acceptance, and affirmation in an intimate relationship is strongly reminiscent of close parent–child relations, which suggests that emotional loneliness may be a developmental extension of attachment anxiety. The relation to loneliness in adulthood is straightforward; Weiss (1989, p. 11) states it thus: 'Loneliness occurs among those without attachment figures when there is vulnerability to threat.'

Attachment and social control

Social control theory views attachments to parents and social ties to community institutions as social bonds which embed the person into conventional society. Hirschi (1969) suggested that persons engage in delinquent activity because the social controls over their behaviour have lost their force, as a consequence of weakened bonds between the young person and societal institutions. Their weak bonding into these institutions renders the social controls contained in them ineffective as a means of constraint on deviant behaviour. These controls exist as values and beliefs about socially appropriate forms of behaviour, as well as inhibitions against acting in particular socially deviant ways. They are the products of socialisation experiences imposed on a person from infancy by society, through numerous agents such as parents, siblings, teachers, youth leaders, neighbours, church members, and so on.

Attachment is the basis for internalising norms and developing a conscience. Antisocial youth are those who manifest in their beliefs, values, and behaviour a lack of attachment to family, school, church, and community. Hirschi does not explicitly define attachment; the closest he gets to a definition is a notion of emotional attachment, as in the following remark: 'If a person feels no emotional attachment to a person or an institution, the rules of [that institution] tend to be denied legitimacy' (Hirschi, 1969, p. 127). There is also the notion of valuing the opinion of a person in authority as an indication of the existence of a social bond. Hirschi shows that delinquent behaviour is not simply a reaction to unfair treatment by authority figures. Among boys who said that they were 'picked on' by their teacher, those who reported engaging in delinquent behaviour were also found to have expressed no concern for what teachers think. Not all boys who were picked on were found to be delinquent. Boys who expressed concern for their teacher's opinion of them, regardless of how they were treated, had a lower incidence of delinquent behaviour than boys who were treated similarly, but who did not care what the teacher thought. Valuing the teacher's opinion indicated the presence of some desire for attachment to the teacher, or to the school.

Attachment to peers is discussed in Hirschi's theory in terms of differential association and subsequent group conformity. 'Most delinquent acts are committed with companions', claims Hirschi (1969, p. 135); 'most delinquents have delinquent friends'. This statement is not intended to imply a notion of apprenticeship in delinquency, which others have argued, where membership of a cohesive antisocial group provides an environment for the learning of skills in performing delinquent acts. Hirschi's theory is about association and commitment, rather than about direct instruction in car theft or graffiti writing. For Hirschi, delinquent friends are a convoy towards a youngster's delinquency. He states, 'the boy takes up with delinquents and commits delinquent acts because he has lost his stake in conformity' (p. 138).

Attachment is likely to be reflected in a person's involvement in conventional activities, and the acceptance of, and commitment to, conventional norms of behaviour. Social control is implicit in the philosophy of the major youth organisations. It is expressed in their concern with the development of character and citizenship, which are seen as achieved through commitment to its principles and authority, and through participation in its activities. These are socialisation concerns rather than social relations concerns. Less acknowledgment is made of the influence of explicit social ties on notions of group identity or processes of identification, but it is clear that the informal social exchanges between members of the organisation are key elements in communicating to individuals that they belong and that they matter to others in the group. These social ties are literally the bonds of attachment by which individuals become integrated into the membership of the organisation.

SOCIAL IDENTITY THEORY

Social identity theory (Tajfel, 1978) views group processes and interpersonal processes as being fundamentally distinct from one another, and asserts that group phenomena must be understood in their own right, and not simply as an averaging of individual processes. Such a view is a reaction in some ways to the highly individualistic approach found in modern psychology and a return to the earlier group-focused concerns of social psychology expressed in the writings of Sherif (1936), which argued that individual behaviour cannot always be explained from knowledge of the individual, because belonging to a group has psychological effects which can change the nature of the individual. The words echo a viewpoint propounded earlier, namely that 'the laws of group life . . . are not the laws of individual life' (McDougall, 1921, p. 13). Group behaviour requires its own analysis. When people act as a group, their behaviour is best understood not as different members of the group acting in terms of their personal identities, but as 'individuals acting in terms of a shared identity' (Turner, 1991, p. 155) and a shared cognition of themselves.

Social identity theory is essentially concerned with the social construction of group membership, and the consequences of finding a place in society for the individual's self-definition. Initially the theory arose from Tajfel's interest in prejudice, and his conviction that the study of social stereotypes by social psychologists required that 'the term "social" is taken seriously as the fulcrum of our work' (Tajfel, 1981, p. 4). Social identity was defined as 'that part of an individual's self-concept which derives from his knowledge of his membership of a group (or groups) together with the value and emotional significance attached to the membership' (Tajfel, 1978, p. 63). Using illustrations of racial, ethnic, and economic disadvantage, Tajfel was able to show that value differentiations between groups are not far below the surface at any time. Turner *et al.* (1987) assert that group images and stereotypes are valid aspects of personal definition, because they delineate a shared psychological field. In these respects, social identity theory is more closely linked to sociological than psychological perspectives on behaviour. Hogg and Abrams (1988, p. 17) describe it as an approach which examines 'the group in the individual'.

Major concepts

There are four linked concepts in social identity theory: *social categorisation, social identity, social comparison,* and *psychological group distinctiveness*. The social experience of belonging to a group or a community and participating in its activities is linked with psychological experiences, through the cognitive processes of social categorisation and social comparison, in a path which begins with group definition and moves to self-definition. Social identity is the product of social knowledge, whereby society, and definable communities in the wider society, form the psychology of their members to pursue social goals and give meaning to everyday existence. The process of social identifications is captured by Turner *et al.* (1987) in their description of social identity as 'a socially structured field within the human mind'.

Self-categorisation processes

Self-categorisation refers to the tendency of people to form opinions which agree with what they believe to be the viewpoints of others who are in some way important to them. Turner *et al.* (1987) refer to 'referential informational influence' to describe the process by which the individual, through observing the behaviour of others, derives information about others' attitudes and values which serves as reference group norms. The process of influence is voluntary and originates within the person seeking the information, influenceability being dependent upon some mutuality of identity. Any collectivity of individuals constitutes a group if the members of that collectivity perceive themselves to fit into the same social category, and if they also 'share some emotional involvement in this common definition of themselves and achieve some degree of consensus about the evaluation of their group and of their membership of it' (Tajfel and Turner, 1979, p. 40). A person's behaviour appears to be influenced by social category membership to different degrees according to the extent to which s/he identifies with the social type. These stages or levels are displayed in Box 1.1 and illustrated with examples from football supporters.

Associated processes

The contribution of self-categorisation to social influence is seen in the phenomenom of *group polarisation*, where people who share a particular value position endorse that value more strongly following the opportunity to discuss it. Group cohesion and conformity to group norms are thus explained as 'an effect of the mutually perceived similarity between self and ingroup others, produced by the formation and salience of shared social category memberships' (Turner, 1991, p. 160). Closely allied with the processes of social categorising are those of *social comparison*, because the person is engaged in evaluating her/his attitudes, opinions, beliefs, etc., against those of others, including those in other social groups. Tajfel suggests that the psychological value of belonging to a group is derived from its status relative to that of other groups. The effects of social categorisation, in segmenting the individual's social environment into her/his own

Box 1.1 Social identification with Chelsea Football Club

---

1 The person recognises that the social category 'Chelsea' applies to her/him, but views belonging to the social group neutrally, and not as particularly important (e.g., equated with living in the Chelsea area).
2 The person loosely identifies with the social category 'Chelsea' and adopts some of the norms and behaviours of Chelsea supporters (e.g., follows the fortunes of Chelsea club, and knows names of players).
3 The person is psychologically invested in the social category 'Chelsea' (e.g., goes to all the games, wears a supporters' scarf, sings the song) and introjects so that it becomes central to her/his definition of self, to the extent that the successes and defeats of the team are experienced personally.

groups and other groups, provide a basis for broader social comparison than merely comparing oneself with other individuals; and this form of comparison contributes to *social identity* by noting the positive characteristics of one's ingroup and its distinctiveness from the outgroup.

Some environmental conditions assist the process of social categorisation by what is termed *meta-contrast*, the tendency in certain situations for group differences to become accentuated and for differences between individuals who belong to the same groups to be ignored. For example, where people share a common neighbourhood but have markedly different customs or religious practices, as in the Gaza Strip or in the Shankill Road area of Belfast, the adjacency of groups contributes contrast which makes the social categories more salient; and people are perceived more as members of distinct social groups than as individual persons. The close proximity of different schools may accentuate the features of difference between them so that intergroup hostility develops, as is presently the case in high schools in parts of south Jakarta, where intergroup fighting is of major concern.

Clearly, each person has multiple social identities, based upon membership of different social groups. The existence of a social category also does not mean that those who fit the category must accept it. Some national or regional categorisations are denied, and others may remain dormant until they are 'switched on' by the situation, such as the Commonwealth Games, the Falklands war (e.g., Cutts-Dougherty *et al.*, 1992), or change in government economic policy which particularly disadvantages people in a particular region (e.g., Abrams and Emler, 1992). Other social identities, for instance ethnic group identity, may be continually in an active state rather than 'switched on' by a polarising event. For example, in situations which contain intergroup conflict (often related to ethnic or religious differences) people are more conscious of their membership of a particular group (e.g., Hunter *et al.*, 1991; Waddell and Cairns, 1986). In their study of Northern Ireland, Waddell and Cairns (1986) show the extent to which two 'arbitrary national identities', loyalist and Irish republican, depend on the 'less arbitrary' religious ones, Catholic and Protestant, and how these take on the force which is associated with ethnic differences.

Applicability to adolescent relations

Does social identity theory have heuristic value? Is it useful for explaining social relations between groups, including conflict between religious and ethnic groups? Social identity theory offers generally superior explanations of the way groups exert influences upon conformity and attitude polarisation, and offers a plausible explanation for intergroup relations such as group cohesion, social stereotyping, and crowd behaviour (Van Knippenberg, 1991, p. 271). However, it must be acknowledged that a large part of the research associated with the theory is experimental, and may not generalise to the social groups and situations common to the adolescent world. The very nature of such social reference theories makes proof difficult to establish when studies are conducted in the field, where the social identities under scrutiny are empirically derived from the participants' real-world experience. Several studies which have attempted to apply the theory conclude that there is support for some of its key assumptions but note that it has a similar difficulty to reference group theory; namely, establishing which group identity is 'switched on' (e.g., Gaskell and Smith, 1986; Verkuyten, 1991). However, there is sufficient evidence from research on adolescent group relations to suggest the value of this theory perspective, and some of these studies are reported below.

Identification with the peer group is associated with adolescents' descriptions of themselves and their evaluations of outgroups. Palmonari *et al.* (1990) found that the type of group Italian young people belonged to was unimportant in their evaluations of other youth, but what was significant in terms of attitudes to others was the *extent of identification* with their group. Those whose attitudes and values were closely aligned with those of their peer group viewed themselves and members of their own group as well as outgroup members more favourably than did adolescents who lacked strong group identifications. Group identification was also related to adolescents' difficulty in coping with various developmental tasks. Adolescents highly identified with their group reported that their group focused on the same developmental tasks which they saw as challenging, and devoted less attention to matters which they considered less important. It appears that those adolescents more attuned to the attitudes and values of their peer group were more able to obtain understanding and support from their group, and were able to recognise positive aspects of their own group and also of other groups.

Social identity may hamper an adolescent's ability to benefit from some educational experiences, particularly where racist attitudes are strongly present in a community, leading ethnic minority youth to develop an 'oppositional social identity' (Clark, 1991). In the scenario which Clark portrays, some African-American youths may rebel against the school's attempts at socialising them for achievement in mainstream society; they may deliberately resist the teacher, perform poorly at school, and view non-cooperation and work avoidance as 'cool'. In short they may seek to prolong their sense of marginalisation as a means of claiming a group identity, albeit a negative and oppositional one, which has already been held by some members of the wider community.

Social identifications may be a means of social mobility. Gaskell and Smith's (1986) study of London male school leavers reported that their respondents had no difficulty in describing themselves according to broad social categories. However, only a small proportion of the black respondents identified with an ethnic group as a social category. The majority chose a different category for themselves, and assigned higher status to this membership group than to black young people as a group in general. These findings are consistent with the claim in the theory that people strive for a positive social identity from their membership group, as a means of enhancing their self-concept.

Social identity may also have a self-preserving function, providing stability and certainty in the arena most important to young people – the self in social relations. And group structure contributes to social identity. Abrams and Emler (1992) examined the role of regional social identity among youth attitudes in four regions of England and Scotland, and the way it may relate to young people's unwillingness to move far in search of employment opportunities. Commitment to their locality was evident, even when its economic disadvantages were acknowledged. Reflecting on their Scottish sample, where regional identification is more clear cut, and assisted by history as well, the authors suggest that regional identification among young people reduces the likelihood of movement out of the region, even where such a move could lead to personal advancement. They note that 'the social networks or ties in an individual's social environment represent powerful anchors . . . Departures from the group may be regarded as treachery or betrayal, and may attract more hostility even than is usually directed towards outgroup members' (Abrams and Emler, 1992, p. 292).

SOCIAL RELATIONS AND SOCIAL NETWORKS

The concept of social networks is useful for describing the structures and sets of relations found in an individual's social landscape. It encourages thinking about persons as being linked to others by various kinds of social tie, and provides a useful means of identifying key figures and groups in a person's social field. Social network analysis directs us to consider human behaviour in terms of its immediate social context, and as Salzinger (1982, p. 118) puts it, 'to a great extent, this context is created by the people surrounding us'. Friendships are seen to be embedded in a broader system of relations through the social ties of each friend with others. The degree of overlap between the social network of one person and that person's friends is critical in determining their access to new people. As a tool of social analysis, network analysis deals with the geography, as it were, of social relations.

The earliest studies of social networks, undertaken by Barnes (1954) on a Norwegian island, traced the ties of friendship and acquaintance which bound the people into a community. They enabled Barnes to describe how people were linked to one another, through the clusters and cliques he could identify in the community, and to observe how these became transformed into organised groups. Others, like Mitchell (1969), were more interested in the effects of social ties in anchoring the individual in the community. Mitchell documented the hundreds of different social contacts which an African villager was seen to make with others in the course of his everyday activities. A psychological sense of community, as well as role definition, is derived from social exchanges of this kind, which repeatedly occur between the actor and members of her/his social network.

Networks may be described in terms of strength of ties linking members of the network with one another, as well as in overall terms of network structure and density (see Salzinger, 1982; Wellman, 1981). Social ties with others, and with groups, vary in strength; that is, they vary in the intensity of the emotions which link the participants. Social influences are seen to vary depending on the level of intimacy within the relevant sector of the social network. The stronger the tie, the more likely it is to be supportive and able to exert influence on the participants. Ties which are maintained through contact across different social settings tend to be stronger than 'uniplex' ties, which are limited to a specific type of relationship. Networks which are composed of many overlapping ties among members tend to become self-sufficient and insular, directing members' energies towards maintaining the structure and constraining them from investing in new relationships. In such tightly knit or dense networks, relationships within the cluster become more important than other relationships. Loose-knit structures are less stable, but more open to new members, and more able to provide bridges to other groups. These different network structures supply different kinds of support: in times of emotional crisis, dense networks respond faster, and more comprehensively; in times of transition and uncertainty, loose networks are more appropriate, because they contain more diverse resources and contacts.

Social provisions through network relations

The significance of the social network for human development thus goes well beyond a mapping of social contacts to allow us to appreciate the quality of the relationships themselves. The value of network analysis is apparent when it is linked with discussion of the social processes within relationship ties and the benefits of these relationships. Hobfoll and Stokes (1988, p. 506) suggest that it may 'provide a kind of social X-ray that yields process information'. The social network operates as a miniature social system or 'soziotype', structuring the individual's social opportunities, and linking her/him to others who can provide various social resources. Through the transactions which occur between a young person and members of her/his social network, the person becomes bound into a community that 'embeds and supports critical identities' (Hirsch, 1981, p. 161).

Extending the social network

Adolescence is a period when growth in the social network is needed for the young person to develop the social competencies required for participation in adult society. Accordingly, attention needs to be given to methods of widening an adolescent's network. Apart from the influence of personality on the ease with which young people make friends and utilise their existing network ties, accessibility of settings is important for network growth. Social environments are important in providing opportunities to people to meet new friends and build on existing ones. They also provide a means of widening one's social network. Non-kin adults, older siblings, and casual friends or acquaintances are important as bridges to different social fields. Social network ties comprise not only individual contacts but also links to clusters of network members: friends in the church choir, the guys who work at the local garage, the members of the basketball team. These network clusters occur in specific settings in the social-ecological environment (e.g., Cotterell and Schoggen, 1986), and these settings contain general roles for participants which are appropriate to the 'place rules' of the particular setting (Canter, 1986). The rules and roles are generally best specified in organised groups, where there are structures provided for making new friends and where social conventions exist enabling newcomers to establish network ties without difficulty.

Different environments promote different adolescent peer groups. The principle was noted by Montemayor and van Komen (1980), who observed adolescent contacts with others both at school and in seven different kinds of out-of-school setting, including two church ones as well as the kinds of leisure setting we have already listed. The groups (which included pairs) were also interviewed. The groups containing adolescents in out-of-school settings were found to be much less age segregated than those in schools, although friendship groups were age segregated similarly to the in-school groups. Over one-third of the groups contained adult companions. Adolescent girls of all ages were more likely than boys to be in the company of their parents, and it was very rare for boys over the age of 16 years to be seen with parents.

In summary, social networks are not just metaphors; they are active social arrangements. 'People belong to networks as well as to categories', says Wellman (1988, p. 32), and membership categories reflect underlying structural relationships. Social networks reflect the regularities of the way adolescents and groups or collectivities actually interact, as distinct from how they believe they ought to interact. Although social networks may be anchored on an individual and are a means of describing the individual's social world or personal network, they can also portray the structure within groups and the relations between groups, including the changing nature of group boundaries. The chapters which follow contrast the different kinds of peer group structures found in adolescent society, and describe the processes of friendship formation, intimate communication, and group inclusion and exclusion.

The convoy model

Network ties link the person to others via the activity of establishing and maintaining social relations. The social network structures thus formed become the delivery system for social support; thus proximity-seeking behaviour is expressed in the activity of maintaining social network ties, visiting friends, writing letters, making phone calls. As a person moves through the life cycle, s/he is part of a network of supportive ties. Kahn and Antonucci (1980, p. 269) liken this network to a convoy, which changes over time but which contains resources of value to the individual's functioning and well-being at each life-stage. What is interesting about this concept is that it recognises the changing contexts and situations encountered by the developing person across the lifespan; for example changes in neighbourhood, the transition from school to work, marriage, etc. A person's social network changes in response to geographical, historical, and cultural influences (see Weinraub *et al.*, 1977), but it remains a personal network, unique to that person, with its boundaries defined by relations to that person. Furthermore, since the convoy is the delivery system for support, successful convoys are those which are appropriate to the person's support needs. For example, in geographical or role transitions, a person may lack appropriate convoys because the members of the network are unable to bridge the changing settings or circumstances so as to provide support. The convoy model is helpful to those who are concerned with designing supportive environments for youth, or who seek to encourage young people in their own self-determined social niches, in that it directs our focus to *group relational structures* and the settings which adolescents inhabit, as distinct from individual characteristics.

ORGANISATION OF THE BOOK

The text is organised into three parts. Part I describes the different sets of
relations which exist in the adolescent's social world and the personal
content of these relationships, using the concept of the social network to
distinguish between friends, mates, and acquaintances, and the way the
social ties between friends link them together in various kinds of peer
cluster. Part II looks outward from the relations between friends and peers
to influences on young people's behaviour in the wider social environment.
It is concerned with problem issues in the contexts of school, health, and
public leisure domains, and reviews evidence on the influences of friends
and acquaintances in shaping antisocial behaviour such as vandalism and
aggression, and inducing health risk behaviours which cause community
concern. Part III describes the role of schools and youth organisations as
key supportive contexts for establishing broad forms of attachment and
commitment, and integrating youth into society. It revisits the theories of
attachment and identity, and suggests ways and means by which young
people may gain access to others who can assist their social development.

Part I
Social relations

Introduction

Understanding the nature of friendship and peer relations is of central importance to the issues explored in these pages. Together with family, friends are the primary bonding materials in the edifice we call community. In the adolescent years, friendships take root and flower. A great deal of time is taken up in making and keeping friends, in talking with friends and talking about them, and, through these transactions, in individuals understanding the nature of social relations as well as understanding themselves. Moreover, friendships made in adolescence often endure into adult life. The school chums who remain lifelong friends, the teen romances that blossom into marriage, the siblings that prove that blood is thicker than water, all testify to the powerful experiences of friendship building which began in adolescence. Friendship is not an optional extra in adolescence: it is crucial to achieving many developmental tasks. There is also a personal urge to socialise; Douvan and Adelson (1966, p. 178) put it in these words: 'The adolescent does not choose friendship, but is driven into it.'

Surprisingly, our scientific knowledge of adolescent relations is relatively meagre. One review lamented the fact that 'Friendship, which looms so large in the life of the teenager . . . remains essentially unexplored in psychology' (Adelson and Doehrman, 1980, p. 107). The neglect has continued, according to Hirsch and Renders (1986), despite the fact that it would be difficult to understand adolescence if the domain of friendship were to be ignored. Research has been directed more at the study of children's friendships than at those of adolescents. But social relations in adolescence are unlike those of childhood in fundamental ways, and much more like those in adult life. Thus we find in the mid-1990s that we still have quite limited understandings of the nature of friendship experiences across the years from 12 to 20, in important aspects such as friendship stability, gender differences in friendship, friends' support in times of trouble, and friends' influence on deviant behaviour.

What is distinctive about the adolescent years, compared with those of childhood, is the widened social landscape, which makes the adolescent's behaviour system more accessible to social influence processes arising from encounters with others in group settings different from the home. The chapters in Part I discuss the structures of social relations in adolescence, and the connections between the psychological features of personal relationships and the structural characteristics of the settings in which these are embedded. The social world of adolescents is varied, and extends well beyond close friends to include different kinds of peer groups and cliques, and alliances with older youth and adults. These different kinds of friendship structure find expression in the diverse settings and organisations to which adolescents have access.

The three chapters in this section are concerned with describing the nature of social relations in face-to-face groups: close friendships, friendship cliques, and other peer groups such as the adolescent crowd. The term *relations* is employed when the social and structural characteristics of interactions are of concern, for example in peer group and clique interactions both within and between groups. *Relationships* is reserved for interpersonal interactions and for situations where the concern is for personal exchanges between a trusted other. Thus 'relations' captures the broader features of network interaction, and the way these are patterned by group contexts; and 'relationships' directs our attention to the content of social exchanges, the provisions of social relations, and the quality of support which is experienced in interaction with others.

Social relations are seen to vary depending on the level of intimacy within the relevant sector of the social network. Drawing on the work of Milardo (1992), we note that exchange processes as well as their contents differ within significant other (intimate) networks, exchange networks, and interactional networks. Chapter 2 on peer groups is directed at intergroup relations in exchange networks and the way the group context contributes to these. It discusses the relation between group life and group identity, and the way peer pressure is expressed through the mechanisms of group maintenance. Chapter 3 examines the nature of friendship, including opposite-sex friendship, in adolescence, and describes the processes of self-disclosure and supportiveness in intimate friendships. The chapter on loneliness and rejection (Chapter 4) describes emotional loneliness in intimate networks, and social loneliness and rejection in exchange networks of the broader world of peers.

2 Peer group structures and group life

A distinguishing characteristic of adolescence is the amount of time which young people spend in public places in groups of their peers. The groups vary in size from small cliques to peer crowds; and in the course of one evening these groups grow, split up, and form again as larger groupings, in ways which are distinctive to youth. Being part of a group, and deriving one's identity from the group, are among the benefits which young people seek from associating with others of their own age. Peer groups and relations between groups are the major concern of this chapter. Its purpose is to identify the various peer group structures both in and out of school, and to describe how the structures are related to one another, as well as to discuss their functions in adolescent social development.

The distinction may be drawn between three broad types of adolescent peer group: *cliques*, *crowds*, and *gangs*. All are based on face-to-face interaction, voluntary association, and mutual cooperation. All are types of peer group, but differ in size, structure, and stability. Each conforms to the generally accepted understanding of a group as 'a collective of individuals who have relationships to one another that make them interdependent to some degree' (Cartwright and Zander, 1968, p. 46). It is not uncommon, however, for the term 'peer group' to be employed in a more general sense as well, to refer to young people who do not represent a face-to-face group, but with whom a person may feel identified in some way. These are *reputation-based peer groups* (e.g., Brown, 1989), in contrast to the interaction-based groups identified before. There is a practical limit to the size of interaction-based groups, but no such limit applies to crowd types based on reputation. The distinction between actual groups of which one is a member and reference groups with which one may identify is an important one for understanding the nature of peer influence. As later discussions will show, peer group influence is not dependent on one's participation in a group; affiliation with a group is sufficient to affect a person's attitudes, beliefs, and behaviour.

ADOLESCENT CLIQUES

The basic adolescent peer group is the clique, which is a small group of friends of similar age, and generally of the same sex. Cliques are the building blocks of peer society, the anchor for social activities, and the access route for making new friends. When an adolescent speaks of 'my friends', 'my mates', 'the girls', 'the lads', or uses some other collective noun of this kind, s/he is usually referring to a friendship clique, an interaction-based grouping of peers who 'hang around together' and may be either close friends or 'just friends'. Clique members communicate easily with one another, and spend a great deal of their time together simply talking and enjoying each other's company. They vary in the extent of closeness or intimacy, ranging from coalitions of mates whose association is confined to a particular context, and does not extend into other contexts, to clusters of close friends who are inseparable. The clique is a natural extension into the adolescent years of the groups and gangs of childhood. Associating in cliques is distinctively an activity which has importance in early adolescence, with studies reporting a steeply rising proportion of young people who become attached to a clique in the years from age 10 to age 14. In this chapter, we look at the relationship of the clique to the wider social network of peers, particularly the adolescent crowd and the inter-actional network of acquaintances which lies beyond it.

Cliques are natural groupings of peers. The earliest work on group formation and the development of social norms in peer groups was conducted in camp settings, where small numbers of adolescents were carefully observed over several weeks (Sherif, 1936), and the tradition has been continued by others, like Savin-Williams (1980). However, this approach is unable to capture the ebb and flow of clique relations because the population available for group formation is fixed by the camp and its accommodation rules. To understand the changing clique structures in the broader social world of adolescents, investigations must be conducted in the locales of adolescent group life where informal relations may develop, free from adult surveillance and regulation.

Distinguishing features of some cliques

Adolescent cliques and crowds have been observed for some years by my students and me across a range of public settings, including suburban shopping malls and entertainment venues in the city and also in major seaside resorts. The methods employed favour the identification of peer group structures, including cliques and their merging into crowds. Box 2.1 shows that cliques could be identified by their similar clothing and appearance

Box 2.1 Characteristics of cliques in a shopping mall

Size	Sex	Ages	Clothing Style	Activities
5	3 male 2 female	14–16	Upper middle class, trendy. Boys in jeans and shirts, girls in skirts with shirt out and belted.	Eating: talking, joking, mucking about. Shopping: girls look at clothes, boys chase each other.
4	4 male	17–18	Jeans, striped shirts, deck shoes, hair jelled, earrings.	Eating at café: throwing paper napkins at each other, discussing girls.
6	6 female	12–13	Short skirts, with shirts out, with belts around waist.	Window-shopping, rushing from shop to shop, and laughing loudly.
3	3 male	14–15	Black jeans, T-shirts with emblems, pointy shoes, greasy hair.	Smoking, nudging each other about girls nearby and laughing.
5	5 male	16–17	Jeans, T-shirts, sneakers, untidy hair.	Leaning on railing, and pushing, shoving. Loud comments on nearby girls.
5	5 female	15	Preppie appearance: slim with long blonde hair, casual skirts and blouses. Fashionable.	Horsing around, chasing and laughing. Much physical contact and jostling.

as well as by their leisure preferences and styles of hanging out. Clothing differences are minor rather than dramatic (no punks or Gothics were seen, and only one skinhead group), but they are none the less badges of group membership. The adolescents we observed appeared to go to great pains to wear clothing which was similar to that of their friends, suggesting that group identity for both males and females is partly derived from clothing, shoes, and hairstyle.

An adolescent may belong to several cliques containing different friends in the course of a day: for example, team-mates at basketball practice before school, pals in science class, 'the guys' at the party, the after-school 'kids' in the local neighbourhood. Some of these cliques are located in specific settings: e.g., the basketball court and the local street corner, and the relationship is one of companionship confined to this particular context, whereas close friendships are not restricted to a given setting. Thus the

Box 2.2 Schematic pattern of an adolescent's clique memberships

CLIQUE 1 →	CLIQUE 2 →	CLIQUE 3 →	CLIQUE 4
(Sport)	(Science)	(Party)	(Street corner)

adolescent may have several different groups of friends, with little overlap from one clique to another (Box 2.2).

Interaction between cliques

When adolescents 'hang out' in shopping malls, friendship cliques appear to adopt sex-differentiated roles: girls in female cliques move through the mall window-shopping, occasionally entering a store to riffle through the racks of clothes and argue the merits of the style or colour; boys in male cliques stand or sit at a vantage point and watch 'the passing parade' of girls. Both sexes are found near and inside the takeaway food outlets and eateries. Within the clique there is a constant stream of social interchange, chatting or conspiratorial whispering, which often breaks out into boisterous loud talking, joking, and laughter. While the clique members are chatting, they are also observing the scene around them. The casual way in which clique members chat and watch almost suggests that they seek to camouflage the goal of seeing and being seen by others beneath the ostensible activity of talking with their friends.

The pedestrian mall, shopping mall, or eatery provides a place for youth to meet as groups and confirm their group solidarity, while observing the scene around them 'from a safe distance', within their own clique. From the safety of the group the members can make contact with other cliques, including cliques of the opposite sex. Intergroup contact follows a pattern of social signals, ranging from single glances from one member of the clique or nudges between pairs, followed by group glances, through to calls and taunts directed at a girls' clique by a group of boys. Groups who were seated in takeaway food outlets often engaged in idle forms of play and teasing, directed at adjacent opposite-sex groups. For example, a group of four girls threw chips at one another, and another group of four older boys threw rolled-up paper napkins.

When contacts are achieved, the members of the respective cliques interact in a nonchalant, almost uninterested way, which stands in sharp contrast to the loud and vigorous attention-seeking behaviour exhibited within the clique prior to the contact being made. Within the groups, touching and jostling is common among same-sex peers, but physical contact between the sexes is more subtle and covert. For example, the fieldnotes on a clique of two boys and two girls aged 15 to 16 years report that 'there was no overt boy–girl contact, but one boy frequently walked past the girls and nudged them when making a joke. The girls seemed to enjoy this.' There were exceptions to this pattern, perhaps reflecting failure to make contact. For example, we observed a group of five boys aged 16 to 17 standing outside a McDonalds, smoking. Two of the group pretended to have a fight. When the group recognised two girls who had been to McDonalds, there was increased pushing and shoving as the boys called out to them. The girls made a sarcastic remark and walked off, followed by further shouts from the boys.

ADOLESCENT CROWDS

While the bonds of friendship may be forged through clique relationships, they also flow over into adjacent cliques and friendship pairs. When Dunphy (1969) undertook his pioneering fieldwork on some forty peer groups in Sydney across a period of two years, he called the larger groups 'crowds', a term he borrowed from Hollingshead (1949) to describe a 'type of peer group' which was an amalgamation of several cliques of young people. Dunphy was interested in examining at first hand the relationship between cliques and crowds and whether they performed different functions. For example, is the crowd just a large clique, or is its morphology different?

From his observations, Dunphy (1969) concluded that the adolescent crowd had a distinctly different function from that of the cliques, in that it offered a means for developing the social skills of adolescents in interacting with members of the opposite sex. Others at the time (e.g., Smith, 1963) were also recognising the role of the crowd in providing a social environment within which youth could experimentally test and practise their social skills, particularly in relation to contacts with the opposite sex.

Cliques and crowds observed

A casual observation of adolescent peer groups points up the difficulties in determining who is in the group, because membership appears to be quite fluid. However, the boundaries of cliques and crowds become apparent when observations are conducted on the same group of young people over time, and when numbers of groups can be observed in the same area at the same time. Pedestrian malls in the city on Friday or Saturday night provide these opportunities. Observers reported that the cliques found in open areas such as plazas and pedestrian street malls were larger than those found inside shopping malls and adjacent settings. They often numbered up to fifteen persons, and were usually same-sex, whereas those in shopping malls ranged in size from three to six persons in both mixed and single-sex groupings. Eateries such as McDonalds and Hungry Jack's contained small single-sex cliques of three and four young people, as well as larger mixed groups of ten and twelve, suggesting that the latter may have been composites of single-sex cliques. Some adolescents who were observed in mixed-sex groups in one setting were seen to separate into single-sex cliques upon leaving the setting.

Early in the evening, the pedestrian malls are crowded with young people standing around in cliques, which appear to have two different goals. The cliques of younger adolescents are single-sex groups, intent on forming into crowds before going off to some activity or event. The larger single-sex groups seen in the open plazas and pedestrian malls were characterised by much coming and going. Smaller groups would break away from the others, and then rejoin the main group, suggesting the existence of substructures to the cliques, such as friendship pairs and triples. What the observers may have been witnessing is a peer marshalling arena where peer crowds assemble. The separate friendship cliques meet and gather up their membership before proceeding to an activity such as watching a movie or going to a disco. The process of assembling the crowd is often accompanied by displays of affection (hugging between girls, slapping and punching among boys), but evidence that this is not entirely pre-arranged is attested by the shouts and squeals of surprise when members see other friends or acquaintances, some of whom are persuaded to join the group.

For the cliques of mid-adolescents, their main purpose seems to be to 'hang around' and 'check out the talent'. This involves much talking and glancing around, and appraising nearby groups of the opposite sex. A group of ten boys about 15 to 16 years of age were observed chatting together, but with their attention focused on a nearby group of five girls who were also chatting and glancing over at the boys. The numbers in the boys' group grew with the addition of several new arrivals. The glances between the groups continued, accompanied by smiles from the girls, which seemed 'flirtatious' to the female observer. She reported how the body language of the two groups 'became intense', with the glancing looks becoming bolder, and accompanied by shuffling and jostling among group members. Eventually one of the boys walked over to the girls and began talking to them. The groups had been observed standing in the same area for half an hour. Observations later in the evening found smaller sub-groups formed within these larger crowds, and these were composed of members of both sexes.

This pattern of intergroup contact between single-sex cliques, with the high-status members making contact with the opposite-sex group, and later forming a sub-group, fits the model of crowd development proposed earlier by Dunphy (1963). The crowd provides adolescents with a more varied group, which generally includes girls and boys (whereas the clique may be single-sex) and is more activity-based than the clique. Its larger size and greater social mix are ideal for leisure outings such as going to a dance or to the cinema, playing or watching sport, and having a party. As a coalition of several cliques, the crowd is not dependent on the presence of all cliques or all clique members in order for it to function. Thus if some clique members are unavailable at the time, the crowd is still sufficiently large and diverse to pursue its agenda.

The size and structures of adolescent groups obey what can be called 'the principle of critical size'. Larger groups are found eating out and going to the movies, discos, and parties, with the crowd often progressing from one venue to another. These are unstructured, easily planned activities with high arousal potential, where enjoyment within the crowd bubbles up and sometimes seems to generate an internal echo effect through the audience available, which further heightens members' enjoyment of the activities. Small groups lack this echo effect, and thus smaller single-sex cliques attempt to enlist other cliques to join up with them, so that the crowd experience can be achieved. Mixed-sex cliques operate with a smaller group size, because their goals are focused on specific relationships with one or two others, and acceptance within the group is sought through conversation and sharing experiences, not through more boisterous acting out and attention seeking.

The structures and interactions noted among Brisbane youth are largely in agreement with Dunphy's (1963) five-stage model of peer group formation, which traces the development of groups from single-sex cliques (Stage I) to their amalgamation into a crowd (Stage III) and their eventual disintegration into opposite-sex pairs (Stage V), but the processes of social exchange and group inclusion/exclusion are more dynamic and volatile than may appear to be the case in that report. The most volatile stages are Stage II (single-sex cliques in contact with other cliques) and Stage III (mixed-sex crowd). Most of the behaviour described in this section refers to these two stages. They are poorly understood and infrequently described in the research literature, probably because their noisy bustle and apparent disorganisation seems to lack the coherence of more definitely bounded groups.

ADOLESCENT STREET GROUPS OR GANGS

Where does the adolescent gang fit into these group types? Is a gang a group, or something less than a group? I include the teenage gang in the discussion, first, because the gang is an important peer group for some adolescents; second, because it is a peer group which gets attention from the media; and third, because an understanding of social relations should include the full range of adolescent groups found in the community.

A definition of the American-style delinquent gang has been given by Miller (1975, p. 9) as follows: 'a group of recurrently associating individuals with identifiable leadership and internal organisation, identifying with or claiming control over territory in the community, and engaging either individually or collectively in violent or other forms of illegal behaviour'. What most people have in mind when they refer to gangs is somewhat less dramatic than this image of the violent juvenile gang, if still a touch unsavoury. It is captured by the notion of a congregation of youths, usually male, who gather in a particular set of locations and have a propensity to be antisocial. Nevertheless, for us to speak of an adolescent gang, at least two criteria should be met: the group should be easily recognised by the community and agencies within it; and adolescent members of the group should consciously identify with it, through clothing, other key behaviour, and assigning the gang name to themselves.

Although the link between gangs and delinquency has become almost standard in American research, there is plenty of evidence that delinquent gangs are only a small proportion of what broadly comprises street-corner groups of youths who gather and 'hang out' to talk and while away the time. Indeed, the word 'gang' is often studiously avoided in many European countries, possibly to avoid this confusion. Gang members in Glasgow referred to themselves as a 'team' (see Patrick, 1973), while the preferred term for neighbourhood gangs of youth in Mexican-American communities in California is 'clubs' (see Horowitz and Schwartz, 1974). Berlin youth are described as youth 'bands', although in many respects, such as their territorial basis, marked with graffiti, and their use of gang names and uniforms, they resemble youth gangs found in America. Hagedorn (1990) is critical of the crime focus of gang research, when in his view 'the vast majority of gang members are likely to have very little connection to violent behaviour' (p. 246). He argues that evidence of what gangs as a whole do with their time, and how they function in their neighbourhood as primary sociality structures, would support his claim. A similar point is made by Aumair and Warren (1994) about Melbourne youth gangs, which have formed for the purpose of socialising, and, having little money, tend to congregate in public areas. This gives them high visibility, and leads people to the mistaken conclusion that gangs are increasing in number and that they pose a problem.

Gangs as groups or collectivities

The question of whether gangs are cohesive, regimented groups or loose collectivities with weak ties of allegiance like other adolescent crowds is a matter of continual debate. In his foreword to a recent American book on gangs, Cohen (1990) maintains his view that collectivity or aggregation is a more appropriate term to describe the typical street-corner gangs than words which suggest a cohesive group structure. This loose organisation fits the description of local street gangs in Australian cities (Aumair and Warren, 1994). Authorities like Schwendinger and Schwendinger (1985) see no resemblance between the loose association of youth in street gangs and the structure, rituals, and discipline of an organised youth group (e.g., the Scouts). They say that the distinction between gangs and other groups is a matter not only of organisational structure, but also of the relative involvement of adults and of property in defining the group's meetings and in imposing longer-range goals and history on the group. Street gangs lack such long-range perspectives. They are expressive groups rather than task groups, and for most purposes their organisation can remain loose because the goals of the group can be achieved by improvisation and by the delegation of particular tasks to members as and when this is required.

Ages of gang members

Klein (1971) called the adolescent years 'the gang age', which generally begins at about 11 or 12 years and continues into the early twenties. Such a view of gang association as an extension of youth implies that young boys enter gangs in early adolescence and move out of them when the responsibilities of adult life begin to bite. It is generally correct to argue that gang membership is largely an adolescent phenomenon, although some authors have commented on a pattern of continuing gang involvement into their adult years among Mexican-American youth in Los Angeles (Vigil, 1990) and black youth in Milwaukee (Hagedorn, 1988), perhaps because of the effects of economic deprivation within these cities in prolonging individual members' dependency on the gang. It is also not unusual for membership of bikie gangs to continue well beyond the period of youth, with some remaining active into middle age (e.g., Harvey and Simpson, 1989).

There is, however, considerable evidence that gangs are chiefly composed of teenagers in the mid-adolescent age group. Miller (1975) examined age-proneness to gang membership using data from arrest statistics in four major US cities. He found that the majority of gang-member arrests (82 per cent) fell in the 14–19 age range, and only 6 per cent were younger than 13 or older than 23 years. Lasley (1992) studied characteristics of gang membership among black and white youth drawn from thirty-six gangs in the greater Los Angeles area, and including middle-class as well as lower-class young males. About 5 per cent of the 435 boys contacted were 13 years or younger, and about 14 per cent 20 years or older, with the oldest gang members being 31 to 33 years; however, the peak ages for gang membership were 16 and 17 years, irrespective of class differences. This finding is very similar to those of Klein (1971) on Los Angeles youth and Dunphy (1969) on Sydney youth a generation earlier, and is mirrored in other studies. For example, Smith's (1975) study of an adolescent delinquent group in a housing estate in Brisbane estimated the modal ages of the membership at 15–17 years, with a range of 13–20.

Lasley (1992) concluded that following these peak ages of 16–17 years, gang membership 'tends to decline monotonically' (p. 443), apparently in response to group processes operating on senior members. For example, the emergence of 'a generation gap' in the gang hastens the departure of older members. According to an informant of Lasley's: 'Young gangsters coming up always seem to be a little tougher than the rest. By the time the "BG's" [baby gangsters] become "OG's" [original gangsters] the old guys leave on their own or get pushed out. Most of the guys leave on their own because they are not respected or just can't keep up anymore' (quoted in Lasley, 1992, p. 448). However, the role of economic factors in hastening or slowing structural changes in the gang also needs to be considered. To the extent that gangs are composed of early school leavers and marginalised youths from 'urban underclass environments', a decline in current job opportunities may make it less likely for them to 'mature out' of the gang upon reaching their twenties. They may continue to maintain contact because the gang fills a void in their lives.

Gang size and structure

Anyone who seeks precision in describing the structure of gangs is likely to encounter difficulties. O'Hagan (1976) wryly noted that 'the allegiance of young offenders to their juvenile gangs is not a subject which permits uncomplicated investigation' (p. 307). Yablonsky (1959) had earlier reported that some of the boys he interviewed about the size of the gang gave wildly fluctuating estimates, which led him to conclude that the gang was a near group or collectivity rather than a real entity. Where area or locality features prominently as the basis of gang recruitment, allegiance may be strong, and estimates of group size may be more reliable.

The study of boys from fifty urban gangs in the Strathclyde area of western Scotland conducted by O'Hagan (1976) found a range of gang types. Some gangs were similar to those previously described by Cohen

(1955), and were stable and cohesive organisations; others had fluctuating memberships but contained a group of core members. Others could more appropriately be described as loose collectivities rather than gangs, because the associations between the boys were too fleeting and inconsistent to constitute a clear structure. The picture which emerges from O'Hagan's observations and his discussions with gang members is of a hierarchical structure within many gangs. Rather than consisting of a single group, the gang is composed of several layers of membership: gang leaders, committed members of the gang, fringe members, and drifters. If the gang is defined as composed of the first two categories only, it may be as small as five members, whereas inclusion of the fringe members and those who drift in and out of the gang may swell its numbers to twenty or more. He suggests that the unreliability of informants concerning gang size, noted by most investigators, may reflect the respondents' difficulties in defining gang boundaries. Moreover, other groups may be associated with the gang proper, and form separate cliques through which members may progress to become part of the 'senior' gang.

O'Hagan's observations are helpful in resolving the issue of age as well as that of size. He proposes that the sub-groups or associated cliques on the fringes of the gang serve as gang nurseries, providing structures for apprenticeship into the gang activities. These contain boys who tend to be younger and less mature than those who are in the gang proper. In O'Hagan's scheme, these nurseries may include a pre-adolescent clique (under 12 years old), an early adolescent clique (12–14), and a mid-adolescent clique (14–16), with the real gang consisting of mature adolescents in their late teens or early twenties. Of course, members of the younger cliques will generally describe themselves as part of 'the gang', but they are using the term loosely, to describe affiliation rather than true membership. In reality, they are 'tagging along', performing such roles for the gang as those of runners and lookouts. At the same time, they come under the tutelage and role-modelling influence of older gang members. It is not uncommon for several brothers to be in the same gang, in its junior and senior ranks.

The description of gang structure offered by O'Hagan is very similar to that described by Vigil (1990) in the Barrio cholos in Los Angeles, and that documented by Dunphy (1969) in his study of delinquent groups in Australia in the late 1950s. Gangs appear to consist of an assemblage of peer cliques, but in a looser structure than that observed in other cliques and crowds. For example, gangs include 'nutters', who maintain an erratic membership in the gang. The relation between the cliques and the gang collectivity may be thought of as a series of changing microsystems. The individual joins one group for a time, then leaves and rejoins, or moves on to another, somewhat as one might follow a set of connected pools in a watercourse. In the case of the Barrio cholos in Los Angeles, boys appear to proceed through a series of such 'pools' in the form of boy gang, young teenage gang, adolescent gang, and youth gang, which also vary in terms of their violent character.

The changes in affiliation are shown in Box 2.3. Separate gang members, labelled with the letters A–D, join the gang at time I, and additional members join at time II and time III. Time IV shows the gang split into two separate groups, one of which does not continue to exist for long. Individual joining patterns are shown with letters. For example, member A joins up at time I, but soon leaves, only to rejoin the new gang at time IV and leave again at time V. Member F joins at time II and follows others into a splinter group at time IV, before rejoining the remnants of the original group at time V. If the gang is all of I–VI, given its variations in membership, Yablonsky was right to ask whether the gang is a group or a 'near-group'.

Fourteen successions were traced in one gang structure, and seventeen successions in another (see Vigil, 1990). Moreover, varied membership patterns were found, some young people being regular members and others irregular or peripheral. These latter boys may join up with the group for a short time on a particular evening, and then leave; or they may join in some group activities (e.g., parties) but not in others. These organisational variations and membership changes may reflect stages in gang consolidation or, alternatively, stages in the group's disintegration. Gangs are changing rather than static structures; members come and go, as their needs and interests change. Moreover, gang identification and loyalty may wax and wane, depending on changes in the local area; for example, in the face of threats from a hostile group invading its territory, a gang may expand its

Box 2.3 A model of variations in gang structure

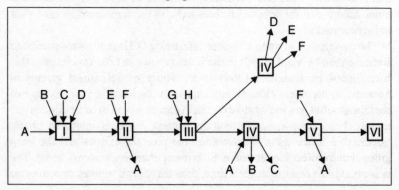

membership by accepting into the group those boys who are normally on the periphery of the gang and have been only loosely affiliated with it.

Girls in the gang

The predominance of males in gangs should not distract us from acknowledging the existence of female gang members as well as female gangs. Unfortunately, most writers have focused on the street-corner experiences of males and left the involvement of females as incidental to their concerns, and although they 'were involved somehow', as Patrick (1973, p. 20) puts it, few details are provided. While female gangs do exist, street kids are more likely to be male than female, because of gender differences in socialisation which affect girls' use of public space. An earlier report based on knowledge from street workers (Bernstein, 1964) suggested that some girls' groups appeared to exist as 'auxiliaries' to the boys' gangs, while others remained independent but in contact with various boys' gangs. Girls may form separate cliques on the periphery of the male gang (perhaps designated as distinct girls' gangs), and sometimes join in gang activities such as fighting and drinking; but according to Campbell (1984) the girls' relationship with male gang members and the gang as a whole continues to be 'a real factor' in girls' behaviour. Bessant (1994) adds some insight into all-girl gangs as meeting the needs for acceptance of their members. Her Melbourne informants saw their gang membership in positive terms: 'We looked after each other; it was like a support group'; and another said,' I felt good about it [getting into delinquent activity] because I belonged to a group' (Bessant, 1994, p. 49).

CROWD TYPES: PEER CROWDS AS SOCIAL CATEGORIES

The social-psychological processes of belonging to an actual group and interacting with members of it are not the same as perceiving oneself as belonging to a social category which may not ever find expression as a real group. Acceptance of a social category as applying to oneself can, however, be sufficient for *psychological group formation*. This phenomenon is frequently witnessed at sports events, where supporters of one team give a friendly greeting to fellow supporters who are total strangers, merely because of their identification with the same category (e.g., Chelsea supporters, English cricket supporters in Australia with their faces painted to represent the Union Jack, or Kiwis cheering for the All Blacks). Clearly the 'group' of interest in this process of ingroup formation is not a face-to-face group, but a collectivity or crowd of indeterminate size, whose 'groupness' is based on a social label. Similarly, minority groups employ distinctive clothing and hairstyles to assert their group identity. These peer groups are termed *crowd types*, to distinguish them from interaction-based crowds. They are a significant peer group in so far as they provide an identifiable reference group for linking the peer society and so-called peer group subculture to styles of behaviour adopted by young people, including behaviour in school.

Crowd types are characteristic of the tendency for adolescents to establish distinctive peer subcultural identities. These are generally based on 'style' (Brake, 1985), manifest in clothes, hairstyle, speech, and behaviour. These visible characteristics denote a collective identity in the public domain. Denholm *et al.* (1992) sought to create a profile of the major adolescent peer crowds recognised by young people in Tasmania. First, they enlisted the help of thirty adolescents from various parts of Tasmania in identifying the most common peer groups. Next, students from high schools in different parts of the state were given a list of the most frequently heard names for peer groups, with a request to describe them in terms of clothing, appearance, key activities, and the interests of members of such groups. Because the respondents were not asked if they actually belonged to any of these groups or knew any group members personally, the responses reflect at best adolescent social categorisation of peer groups. Seven of the ten common crowd types that were listed were widely recognisable across Tasmania, although they were known by many different names. These were bogans (or heavies), nerds (or squares), jocks (or sports), skeggs (or skates), surfies, hippies, and yuppies. Less commonly found groups included Gothics, arties (or trendies), and tecs (or dorks). Each group was seen to have its own ingroup words and phrases, and to wear clothes which distinguished them from other young people. Additionally, the adolescent respondents were able to distinguish between the kinds of music and leisure activities which the groups preferred. Examples of these are shown in Box 2.4.

Many of the features which distinguished these crowd types are associated with out-of-school behaviour, where the styles develop and attitudes are nurtured, before being transferred into the school context. This may help to explain the richness of the typology and the accompanying descriptions, although we cannot be certain about this, because the authors have reported composite portraits based on the information given by all their respondents. These composites may, in effect, describe the social categories within youth society at a more abstract level than these young people have experienced in dealings with their peers. The types are recognisable but not necessarily identical to those described in other countries. The bogans resemble the headbangers in American high schools; the jocks and the nerds are fairly universal (although 'nerd' is a less pejorative term

Box 2.4 Types of peer crowd reported in Tasmania

Group	Appearance	Activities	Music	Phrases
Bogans	Dirty, mainly black clothes, tight jeans, heavy boots, chains, chunky jewellery, long hair.	Vandalism, drinking, partying, fighting, driving in hotted-up cars.	Heavy metal and satanic	Get outa my face. Kick your head in!
Jocks	Sports clothes, tank tops, brand name sneakers, short haircuts, Bolle shades.	Jogging, working out, playing sport and talking about sport.	All kinds, especially high energy.	What's your PB? Wanna game?
Surfies	Ripped jeans, fluoro shorts, tank tops or T-shirts, thongs, dark shades.	Surfing, drinking, parties, hanging around.	Anything on the charts, rap, heavy metal.	Hang loose. Rad. Out the back. Amped. Cool rip.
Skeggs	Bright clothes, long-sleeved T-shirts, baggy shorts, caps on back to front.	Practising skate moves, bandaging up their cut legs, drinking, smoking.	Mostly rap, heavy metal thrash and satanic.	I did a little ollie! Kick flip. Chill out, dude. Good deck!
Nerds	Cords, skivvies (a kind of sweatshirt), wool jumpers, out-of-fashion shoes, short hair, glasses.	Debating, doing charity work, programming their IBM, playing Monopoly.	Classical, top 40, Country and Western	Terrific! I know the answer.

among Australian youth, I feel). The groups also reflect styles of coping with the demands of school and family. For example, one minor Australian type is called 'tryhards'. These kids keep trying to impress people, trying to act cool, trying to be popular and become accepted by the 'in' group. The implication is that they lack what it takes but do not realise it, and so will never be successful in gaining acceptance.

Crowd types as sources of social identity

American studies suggest that peer crowd labels function as social categories by which adolescents are able to locate themselves within the status
system of the school. Individuals develop a conceptual map of the types of
peer group found at school, and they use this to find their 'place' in the
social world of peers. Brown and his coworkers (e.g., Brown, 1989; Brown
and Lohr, 1987; Brown *et al.*, 1986b) have investigated the nature of peer
crowd types in the American high school, and the developmental consequences of crowd affiliation. This approach connects with social identity
theory and with the way adolescents perceive their status in relation to other
groups of young people.

There are various ways of determining the main peer crowds in adolescence. In the American studies, students are asked various questions
which pertain to 'the crowds at the school', a method similar to that
employed in the Tasmanian study. The procedure developed by
Schwendinger and Schwendinger (1985), known as the social type rating
method, goes a step further. It enlists students who are knowledgeable
about the peer society in their school as agents to describe the major peer
crowds, and then to act in pairs as raters concerning the actual crowd
membership of fellow students. Brown *et al.* (1986b) employed this technique to identify the peer crowds in two middle schools and a high school
in the Midwest of the United States. Despite some lack of clarity in the
questions asked, which may have blurred the distinction between crowds as
social types and crowds as real groups, the authors reported that the
adolescents in their research defined their peer group in terms of reputation
rather more than on the basis of social interaction; 'crowd names were
labels placed on individuals who were similar in attitudes or activity even
if they did not spend much time together' (Brown *et al.*, 1986b, pp. 92–93).
Three peer crowd types were common to all schools: the jock-populars, the
druggie-toughs, and the loners (presumably, the normal group was viewed
as the remainder). The social types were seen to hold different levels of
prestige. Adolescents who saw themselves as members of the highest-
status crowd (the jock-populars) also had higher self-esteem (Brown and
Lohr, 1987).

SECONDARY SCHOOLS AS A CONTEXT FOR CROWD TYPES

The tendency to categorise others into peer crowd types may also be
accelerated by certain social features of high schools which make
newcomers highly conscious of the mass society, which comprises large
numbers of other students, most of whom are unknown. It is at high school

that the dominance of peer crowd values has become a concern to educators. Identity at high school becomes a more complex concept, with the social categories assigned by the school system sometimes being at odds with those conferred (and valued) by one's peers. For example, being one of the brainy kids may have been acceptable to peers as well as parents and teachers at primary school, but may be viewed as a liability in the peer system at high school.

The presence of distinct crowd types, with their own territory within the school, may be a factor of school size; where the school is large, with several thousand students, identity is conferred through association with peers, rather than through assocation with classmates who are attached to a particular teacher. Moreover, when the student population is large, the need to be affiliated with a peer crowd may be greater. This conclusion was drawn by Smith and Gregory (1987), who compared a high school with about 1000 students and one with 175 students in the same American town. The large school was more rule-bound and departmentalised, with teachers distanced from students, whereas the small school had more informality and flexibility in its organisation and a stronger sense of community. Peer crowds were well established in the large high school, the major ones being the brains, the jocks and preppies, the hicks, and the heads. Each crowd dressed in distinctive ways and occupied its own territory within the school, with little interaction between students in the different crowds. Hostility between the groups seemed to be based on social class differences traced back to elementary school differences. In the small high school, by way of contrast, crowd boundaries were much more permeable; students described the peer group as 'more like groups of friends that decide they like each other'.

Organisation of a school into different streams or tracks also affects students' social relations. We see this in a study of a government high school in Queensland by Taylor (1980), who explored the development of different 'group perspectives' among students who had been allocated to different streams (academic, commercial/business, and general). She reports that students adopted distinctive ways of viewing themselves and others, which seemed to emphasise a division between the streams. Students were ready to portray other groups as holding distinctive attitudes and interests, often of a stereotyped form. The perceptions seemed to be consistent with the label of the stream which the respondent was describing. Adolescents in the less academic streams attributed to students in the academic stream attitudes of superiority and disdain for others, which appeared to reflect their own feelings of resentment and hostility towards an outgroup. The feelings expressed were 'They think they're much smarter'; 'They go round acting smarter.' Some statements were followed by self-labelling of their

own group as being 'dumbies', again attributed as a label by the outgroup.
What Taylor found disturbing about these attributions was that they had
crystallised after a mere six months in these streams, and that they were not
based on personal knowledge. The negative comments made by her respondents were frequently accompanied by admissions that 'I don't know
them very much'; 'I don't mix with them very much.'

Crowd identification as a means of adaptation

In our study of adolescents moving into secondary school (Power and
Cotterell, 1979, 1981), we found that crowd identification was part of the
process by which new students defined the situation at their new school.
The peer groups to which they assigned themselves, or were assigned by
others, indicated which value system they paid allegiance to. The classifi-
cations found in that study were simple: those in the pro-school subculture
were called 'the smart ones'; those in the counter-school subculture were
'the toughs'; and those in between, or at the fringe of either of these groups,
were termed 'average'. The students categorised as average were the majority.

These broad categories were employed by the students themselves,
although the toughs preferred to use more vivid labels when describing the
other groups. For example, the toughs disparagingly referred to the smart
ones as the 'goody-goodies'; the students who called themselves 'average'
were designated 'sheep' or 'nothings'. (In Australian slang, to be regarded
as a sheep is to be part of the 'mob', and lack individuality and personal
significance.) When asked about the defining characteristics of their own
group, the toughs resorted to physical appearance (long hair, jeans, tough
stance, emphasis on acting 'cool') and their tough behaviour (in the classroom: making smart remarks, standing up to teachers; in the schoolground:
fighting, harassing fellow students, asserting one's rights with older
students, associating with the opposite sex). They described the group
norms of toughs as follows:

You *have* to smoke and drink to be a tough.

When you are with someone tough, you have to act tough yourself.

To belong to our group you have to sort of want to hang around boys.
Mum doesn't like that, but I do; and I sort of enjoy myself in the lunch
hour.

(Power and Cotterell, 1979, p. 256)

Interestingly, these young adolescents made a distinction between 'being
tough' and 'acting tough'. Individuals who 'act tough' engage in
unacceptably aggressive behaviour, such as picking on smaller kids and

bashing them up, in order to gain acceptance by the real toughs. The latter had little sympathy for these 'posers', whose adoption of tough behaviour was too obvious and contrived, rather than natural. In their view, reputation supplies the ingredients of identity; an identity that has to be fought for and proven constantly is clearly not one which is based on a reputation readily accorded by one's peers. Coolness is all.

This discussion of processes of identity formation in the first year of secondary school, among adolescents who are 12 and 13 years of age, demonstrates how the broad social categories of jocks, nerds, smart ones, toughs, and sheep assign them to a provisional status and affiliation. However, while these labels help the adolescent know who s/he is in the eyes of her/his peers, the task of confirming or challenging the labels occurs at the clique level. The kinds of peer ridicule and criticism described in the preceding paragraphs must be defended, deflected, or dismissed, and it is the members of one's intimate clique who are involved in these inter-changes, reassuring the victim through the solidarity of the group that it will fend off all attackers.

The power of peer groups to determine the status of crowd types seems to wane by late adolescence. Crowd types appear to be more prominent concerns of younger adolescents than of older students; several studies report a decrease with age in the importance of affiliation with a particular crowd, as well as a decline in the extent to which crowd affiliations are viewed positively. This finding is consistent with the argument that older students are resolving the crisis of group identity versus alienation (Newman and Newman, 1976) and are consequently more reluctant to conform to crowd stereotypes. Several observers have noted that adolescents in their senior year become a more cohesive group, 'the seniors', and there is 'a curious dissipation of crowd boundaries' (Brown, 1989, p. 199). The social categories which had served as prototypes for identification in earlier years are no longer so appealing or so necessary for status. A change is occurring in the relevance of the school status system for their current social identi-fication. Being a senior who will soon graduate and be looking to a future beyond the high school is taking hold; the adolescent society no longer 'switches on' the old social categories of crowd types, and is about to switch them off for good.

Ethnic identity and prejudice

Social identity depends upon a person having a clear awareness of the boundaries between her/his social group or social category and those of others. Crowds based on ethnicity are common at high school, and may be a source of security as well as a liability in terms of peer status. Ullah

(1987) examined the social identification among English-born adolescents of Irish descent. He compared those who saw themselves as Irish with those who defined themselves as either English or half-Irish and half-English, using several indices of group behaviour: attraction to Irish people, participation in traditional Irish culture, intergroup differentiation between Irish and English, and negative reaction to being described as English. Social identification was reflected in all four sources of self-definition, with scores for those identifying as Irish being highest, and those identifying as English being lowest. The presence of a small proportion of adolescents who chose to identify as English and hide the fact that they were of Irish descent is also found among other minority-group adolescents. Hogg *et al.* (1987) report on the attempts of some adolescents of Indian descent to 'pass' as English. When Gaskell and Smith (1986) asked London young men of different ethnic groups and who had recently left school to state which social groups they belonged to, and how they ranked their group, they found that only a small proportion of the black respondents identified ethnicity as a membership group criterion. The majority chose to assign to themselves a different category, one which they ranked as having higher status than the social category 'black young people'. These findings are consistent with theory, namely that people strive for a positive social identity from their membership group as a means of enhancing their self-concept, and are thus more motivated to belong to higher-status groups than to lower-status ones, even if it means ignoring their ethnic background.

Verkuyten (1991, p. 284) examined the relationship between self-definition and ingroup formation in ethnic-minority youth from Turkey, Morocco, and Surinam, and found some evidence that youth with a strong positive ethnic identification had a greater sense of ingroup social preference, which suggests that investing in such a social category as personally meaningful is part of social identity development. Appearances, then, are not the determinants of social identification; identification and introjection of that identity are also needed. The Australian government recognises this in its policy for Australian indigenous groups; namely, a person is considered to be of Aboriginal descent if that person identifies with Aborigines.

Clearly, the issue of maintaining one's ethnic social identity versus acculturation in the majority culture is sharpened for adolescents from minority groups by the pressures thrust upon them by peer groups, and by schools themselves, to conform to the majority culture. These demands to assimilate may come into conflict with obligations to maintain traditional practices, which their family and community continue to impose. That adolescents are conscious of the way that different social identities may be switched on by the social context is clear from Rosenthal and Hrynevich's

Box 2.5 Social identities and context variations

Social identity	Context and situation
Greek/Italian	With family or relatives; with friends of same cultural group; at weddings or parties; eating traditional food; and when Australians tease or goad them.
Australian	At school; at recreational activities/events; when Australia is competing against another country; with Australian friends; and when eating Australian food.

(1985) study of ethnic identities among Greek and Italian adolescents in Melbourne. The context effects which differentiated minority-group identity from Australian identity were as shown in Box 2.5.

More than one-third of the migrant youth interviewed by Rosenthal and Hrynevich (1985) referred to situations where they were uncertain about how they should behave. Interestingly, the situations they described were ones containing both Australian and ethnic community social references, leading to possible conflict of social identities. For example, in situations where family members and Anglo-Australians were both present, the young people were uncertain whether to speak in the language of their community, which was Greek or Italian, or in English, the language of the host country. And in situations where migrant members of a peer group were teased or taunted by Anglo-Australians within the group, youth were unsure whether or not they should defend their fellow Greeks or Italians.

Ethnic group identity may be continually in an active state rather than 'switched on' by a polarising event. In situations which contain intergroup competition, sharpened by religious differences and differences in cultural practices, people are more conscious of their membership of a particular social category. A great deal of conflict between young people from different ethnic backgrounds is precipitated by name-calling intended to provoke a reaction. Press reports on racism in Australian sport during May 1995 highlight the difficulties which Aboriginal sportspeople continually face from spectator abuse as well as from the goading of fellow players, attempt- ing to put them 'off their game'.

FUNCTIONS OF PEER GROUPS

Having examined a variety of peer group structures and described the kinds of activity and relationship associated with them, we must now reflect on the purposes which peer groups appear to serve in the social development of young people. From what has been described of the social relations in these informally structured face-to-face groups, it can be seen that they serve as primary groups, as essential to the shaping of personality as the family is in childhood. They are emotionally supportive structures, affirming the individual members as somebodies with distinctive personalities. The central characteristic of these groups is an attachment relation. Cliques and crowds are not aggregates of individuals; they are distinct social units, because there exists an affective bond among the members. As Dunphy (1972, p. 63) explains, 'the most important motivational factor in the formation of peer groups is the desire for a personal, affective response from a few other individuals'. The need for these relations is similar whether the group referred to is a group of mates, a basketball team, a church youth group, a science prac. group, or a graffiti posse. These groups will continue to exist because they supply positive emotional experiences to their members, through acceptance and recognition of the individual as a contributor to what the group stands for, and by providing in return the sense of belonging and solidarity with the group which confirms the group identity for each individual member.

The peer crowd has been seen as a strategically important peer group for young people's social development, because it provides opportunities for establishing contact with members of the opposite sex, not in the casual, 'standing on the street corner' form of contact, but through joint participation in group activities not available to the single-sex clique. Its looser interactive network allows for a range of social relations to occur, while at the same time placing structural constraints on members who seek to pair off into exclusive relationships. Thus the crowd structure prolongs the period of general heterosexual social development, fostering such skills as making casual conversation, story-telling, attentive listening, turn-taking in conversation, giving emotional support, and group leadership. These may be practised by a number of young people in the group in the course of a year.

The crowd also frees the individual adolescent from the talons of her/his clique, and allows her/him to interact with members of other cliques within the crowd, in a way which does not sever the links to her/his own clique. After all, adults continue to socialise with their friends in single-sex cliques throughout their lives. Viewed as a social system, the crowd offers each adolescent member a very different network structure from that of the clique, one consisting of close ties with members of her/his own clique, and weak ties with some members of other cliques within the same crowd. In the course of crowd activities, these weak-tie contacts act as bridges for the individual into other cliques, and into contact with others of the opposite sex who would not be accessible without the vehicle of the crowd.

Friendships are embedded in other social ties within the person's social network. The skills needed to initiate new friendships have been honed from countless social interactions with companions and acquaintances. These people comprise the 'interactive network', people with whom we routinely interact in face-to-face situations, but whom we do not necessarily like or admire. From casual encounters with acquaintances, some relationships blossom into friendships, because of similarity and mutual attraction.

A second aspect worth emphasising is the role of these different peer groups in functions not easily supplied by exclusive friendship relations. These are broadly related to identity support. The way in which this support is given by the peer group will not be quite the same as friends' support for a particular identity; it is looser, in the sense that the peer environment provides a social identity to assist the individual to link effectively with the wider social system. Following Weiss (1974), there are two particular social provisions which peer groups are best fitted to supply: social integration into a network of young people of similar ages, and reassurance of one's worth through social validation by one's peers. Both these functions draw attention to the normative and conforming aspects of relationships with a social group. There is a tendency for these aspects to be devalued or even viewed with suspicion by those who promote individualistic values, as if peer group membership entails the submergence of individual identity, like enlistment in the Red Guards. We need to accept that peer groups provide young people with room to develop an identity of their own, using the vehicle of group identity.

CONCLUSION

The convoy model suggests that adolescents move through life as members of groups which are moving along with them. Attachments are established not only with individuals but also with the groups of which one is a member. It is easy to overlook the presence of enduring ties between an adolescent and the groups in her/his convoy, which 'run deep' like sibling relationships but may seldom be overtly expressed. In bonding with such groups the person experiences a sense of belonging and endorsement, a 'sense of place' in the group, and the secure feeling of being 'at home' with her/his mates or chums. The convoy model also implies that many individual life-events are experienced within this group context, with the group serving as a protective environment or 'psychological way station' which moderates the impact of growing sexual maturity, conflicts with parents and teachers, and the often pressing requirements from parents to arrive at a decision on one's future occupational path. At other times cliques as well

as crowds can serve as learning environments for inducting an adolescent
into the wider social world. By supplying interpretations of the events s/he
has encountered, together with models of coping behaviour, they help
develop the individual young person's self-confidence and social skills.
Similarly, youth gangs are a vehicle for breaking out of ethnic community
controls. A member of Melbourne's Lebanese community commented that
whereas for boys to associate with girls outside the community would be
forbidden by families, 'Being in a gang gave [Lebanese boys] the same
freedom as any other adolescent.'

Young people derive psychological benefits from belonging to a group
and identifying with the group, made possible through experiencing group
solidarity. For most groups, this is achieved by regular meetings in a
defined locality, and enhanced by activities which members share. These
may range from hiking, singing, eating out, and going to the cinema,
through to fighting others, stirring the police, tagging trains, and engaging
in other kinds of physical bravado or deviant behaviour. Group belonging
and solidarity are strengthened when acts are performed in the company of
a group of one's peers. Adolescents seek outlets for their energy; a fight or
'dustup' relieves the tedium, just as a prank or practical joke done 'for a bit
of a laugh' is a form of play which affirms group identity.

Membership of a group supplies status which strengthens attachment.
When a boy pulls on the jersey of the school First XV, or a girl walks onto
the athletic track to run the 200-metre sprint at the interschool meet, each is
aware of the honour which is conferred on her/him in representing her/his
school. The gang culture provides a means for youth to be distinctive and
attain status by an alternative route to the traditional success model. Status
may derive from the adolescent's awareness that other people recognise the
group as a gang and 'don't want to mess with you' (Campbell, 1984, p.
263). A member of Melbourne's Sandy Boys, asked to reflect on his
experience of group identity through the gang, made the comment that
'When you're in a gang, it makes you a bit more special. I reckon we've
earned our name. In some ways we're proud of it, in some ways we're not.
But we enjoy what we do' (Guilliatt, 1984a).

3 Friendship
The core relationship

Friends constitute the voluntary component of the social network; although you are stuck with your relatives, you can choose your friends. Examination of friendship interactions and the qualities expected of friends provides an appreciation of how attachment relations extend beyond the family into the peer world in the adolescent years. The developmental significance of friendship is captured in a sentence by Kon and Losenkov (1978, p. 154): 'As the first independently selected attachment, friendship prepares the individual for the more complicated forms of psychological intimacy.' This chapter is an invitation to think of friendship as attachment relations, not just with close friends, but extending beyond these to include other forms of friendship relations with mates and acquaintances. The chapter has two goals: first, to describe friendship structures and their formation within the social network, and second, to explore their significance, including the qualities valued in friendship, and the social provisions of close friendship.

FRIENDS, MATES AND ACQUAINTANCES

What do young people understand as distinctive about the term 'friend'? What are the special characteristics of friendship? 'Friend' is not a well-defined concept: there is a range of meanings attached to the term. These include the close friend described by C. S. Lewis (1960), who sees the same truths, accepts the same values, holds the same passions. This friend knows when help is needed and gives help without it being asked for. 'The mark of perfect friendship', writes C. S. Lewis (1960, p. 102), 'is not that help will be given when the pinch comes, but that having been given, it makes no difference at all.'

Other valid, less perfect kinds of friendship exist, which depend less on the personal qualities of a particular relationship and more on the enjoyment of the company of others. This broader kind of friendship is captured by the term 'mateship' or companionship, which G. Allan (1989) sees as an 'alternative form of sociability', but not an inferior form of friendship. Mates can be distinguished from the intimate circle of friends in that they are consistently referred to by a collective noun, such as 'some of my friends', or 'a few chums', and rarely by their separate names. They are welcome as companions to share in activities without making a lot of demands on you, and yet contribute to emotional well-being (Rook, 1987). Companionship serves different purposes from those served by close friendship; young people can enjoy the company and sociable qualities of mates without regarding them as close, or entrusting their worries and concerns to them. Some are more aptly described as acquaintances, average friends who are good to hang around with at times. They are on the periphery of the social circle, perhaps friends of friends, and belong more properly in other social networks than one's own.

In modern times, 'friend' appears to have become a residual label which is applied to any associate who is sociable, is similar in age, is not a relative, and has been known a fair length of time. Fischer (1982) found that adults commonly used the term 'friend' to define any member of their social network whom they were not related to. Friends comprised 83 per cent of the non-relatives in his respondents' social networks. Montemayor and van Komen (1985) conducted a study of natural groups of adolescents, and reported that the term 'friend' accounted for almost 92 per cent of the relations identified. These studies suggest that despite its shortcomings, 'friend' is 'too important a folk concept' to be ignored or replaced by something more precise. The meaning of friend is clearly not restricted to close relationships; a variety of friendship ties can be detected within the average adolescent's social network, and each holds some importance for understanding social relations.

The friendship network

If viewed as a set of concentric circles, the network of friends widens dramatically from close friends to those who are best called acquaintances. These separate sectors of the network, beginning at the centre, have been called the network of significant others (intimates or close friends), the exchange network (collectives of people who provide support), and the interactive network (comprising all those known with whom a person normally interacts). The networks are distinct from one another, and contain different people. There is a surprising consistency in the numbers of people located in intimate and exchange networks: approximately five and twenty respectively (see Milardo, 1992), and these figures are similar to those reported by Claes (1992, p. 44) in a survey of the friendship networks of

Canadian adolescents whose average age was almost 16 years. To overcome the problems in the meaning of friendship, Claes gave working definitions of intimate friends ('the small number of friends you meet regularly, share a lot of things with, and feel close to'), friends ('those you know well, talk to often, and enjoy meeting'), and acquaintances ('you know their names and exchange more than a simple hello when you see them'). The networks of these Montreal adolescents were made up of an average of thirty-six acquaintances, seventeen friends, and four close friends. Older youth reported fewer close friends (3.65) than youth in their early teens (5.24), and half the sample had kept the same best friend for over three years.

While Claes suggests that intimate friends are recruited from a more extended network of friends, the process could also work in reverse; that is, friends and acquaintances may be built from links to the friendship clique. However, the jury is still out on this question. Hirsch and Dubois (1989) traced the friend networks across the transition into junior high, and found that there was a clear tendency for close friendships to continue. Fifty-eight per cent remained close friends with their previously close friends, and among those who did not, over 40 per cent reported that their present best friend had been a friend at primary school. The remainder became close friends with someone who was previously not known to them, or who had gone to the same school but with whom they were not close at the time.

MAKING FRIENDS: ENVIRONMENTS FOR CONTACTING FRIENDS

Each young person occupies several separate but sometimes overlapping social worlds. These are potential environments for friendship formation. School is a major location for meeting and making friends, but out-of-school settings have become important venues for interaction when young people are seeking to develop the relationship into a closer friendship. The settings include milk bars, video arcades, cinemas or movie theatres, swimming pools, spectator sports, and especially shopping malls. The modern shopping mall has become an all-age social centre, as important for meeting up with friends as it is for shopping. Gill (1991) reports that teenagers who meet regularly in Melbourne's suburban Chadstone mall regard it as 'not only the civic space but their space', where adolescents from a range of different schools meet together in large numbers to socialise, particularly on Friday night. The same thronging pattern is repeated in many shopping malls in many cities.

The casual eating places in shopping malls, ranging from 'eating halls' surrounded by fast-food outlets to small coffee shops with their own confined space, offer situations with different meanings for young people. They contain what Canter (1986) calls 'place-rules' – social meanings about appropriate ways of behaving in the setting. A young person acquires knowledge of place-rules based on regular encounters with situations containing similar activity patterns, and learns to 'read' the characteristics of a place, in order to perform effectively in the situations it contains. S/he learns the variations in place-rules in these locations, so that meeting a group and hanging out is best achieved in a larger setting, whereas a more select environment is chosen for meetings with a few close friends.

Knowledge is also acquired concerning 'place-roles'. These norms about the appropriate roles to adopt are helps for interacting in a large group of peers, and safeguards against seeking privacy with one special friend at the expense of social interaction with the larger crowd. In the public arena of the shopping mall, adolescents continually struggle with the conflict between retaining group acceptance and being loyal to a particular friend. They desire simultaneously to belong to the larger group and be part of group excitement, and to pursue more intimate and exclusive relationships with chosen others. When adolescents are observed in these public settings, they can be seen working out the balance between these different forms of friendship, regulating the broader acquaintanceship demands from others in the crowd so as to retain the option of pursuing their own special friendship agenda. These interactions are subtle and complex.

Interactions in friendship cliques

Observations reveal several striking features about the behaviour of adolescent cliques in shopping malls. Their behaviour appears at first to be aimless, consisting of wandering past shops or into them, eating at take-away outlets, or standing about, often smoking, but doing nothing in particular. Our fieldnotes record, 'Although window-shopping was a major activity, none of the teenagers bought anything.' Similar findings are reported for American youth by Lewis (1989) and Anthony (1985), who hold the view that young people do not visit the shopping malls with commercial goals in mind. Instead, the present generation 'cruise the mall' in the same way that youth in the 1950s cruised suburbia in their Thunderbird convertibles. What is suggested is that malls provide a safe arena where youth can 'hang out' with their friends in a manner highly similar to that of the street-corner societies of previous times.

Evidence that these cliques served as primary groups was clear from the behaviour of the young people, remarked on so repeatedly in our fieldnotes that it denotes a striking feature of adolescent cliques. The two characteristics we continually detected in the interactions among clique members are *laughter* and *body contact*. The presence of laughter, joking, teasing, carrying on, and displays of general euphoria among teenagers was very widespread, at least among the Australian 12–18-year-olds seen in our numerous observations. Anyone who thinks that teenagers are sullen and taciturn will find that impression rapidly dispelled by a period of observation of young people in public leisure settings. Other observers of peer interactions have also been surprised at the extent to which joking and various kinds of humorous behaviour feature in adolescents' daily conversations with peers (e.g., Sanford and Eder, 1984). Our fieldnotes include descriptions like these: 'much noise and laughter', 'loud talking and laughing', 'talking and joking', 'fits of laughter', 'raucous laughter erupts from the entire group'.

In the company of their friends, these young people are very happy and relaxed, even when they do not appear to be absorbed in any specific activity. Where the level of excitement and emotional arousal was high, as observed at Brisbane's World Expo, the sense of joy and of feeling relaxed was almost universally reported by teenager interviewees (Cotterell, 1991). Only in the city amusement arcades, frequented almost exclusively by boys, was there a change in tone; the need for concentration on the video screens and games machines means boisterousness is incompatible with the skills demanded. A typical pattern was the silent grouping of three or four boys around another boy playing on a machine. In the daytime activity in seaside areas, where subjects were older adolescents, observers also reported lower levels of noisy laughter, indicating that the context, including time of day and general numbers of youth present, may affect these displays of euphoria.

A second feature of interaction in the friendship clique is touching. Whether the clique is male, female, or mixed, and whether it is mobile or stationary, there is an amazing amount of touching and jostling of bodies. It ranges from stroking, hugging, and back-patting among girls to more vigorous forms of body contact among the males, including pushing, wrestling, punching, and friendly karate chops or kicks. Others have noted the frequency of body contact among adolescents, but they report far more instances of cross-sex than same-sex contacts in the shopping malls, and restrict instances of robust physical contact or 'horsing around' to swimming pools (e.g., Silbereisen *et al.*, 1986). What I refer to seems different from the German report, both in the readiness of adolescents of all ages to touch one another, and in the fact that touching commonly occurs among peers of the same sex. A large number of these displays emerged when a new member joined the clique, and they appear to be a form of expressing group solidarity. Girls engage in emotion-laden hugs and embraces, accompanied by loud greetings. Partings are more emotional than meetings. An observer noted that the farewells when two girls in a clique of four were catching a bus in the city comprised 'much physical contact in the form of embracing, loud goodbyes and "ring me up tomorrow" . . . On the bus the talking changed to yelling through the bus window, and continued until the bus pulled out from the curb.' Boys were seen to greet a newcomer by such gentle displays of affection as a punch in the chest, several bangs on the upper arm or back, or a clip over the ear. Those 15 years of age or younger tended to be more vigorous; older boys were more subdued in their mode of physical contact with friends.

It is clear from what we have seen that physical contact is very important to adolescents. Whether expressed as a gentle and light brushing of the arm or body, or as a vigorous thump, touching is a highly important means of communication. Moreover, touching provides feedback; it seems that being able to touch someone else in the group gives adolescents a great feeling of acceptance among their friends.

Clique formation

Surprisingly few studies have traced the formation and disintegration of naturally occurring friendship cliques with any degree of precision. Among the few observations which have been reported is an account of the early stages of clique formation conducted by Eder (1985) in the school cafeteria of a middle school of about 750 students. Eder noted that girls entering the lunch area would reserve seats for their friends, and signal to any outsider seeking to join the group that 'these seats are taken'. She also detected status differences: the higher-status groups chose to sit on one side of the cafeteria, which was understood by students to be the classy side, where the 'good people' sat. Among younger adolescents, Eder found few stable cliques: girls sat in different groupings on different days, and there was no evidence of status differences between the cliques. By seventh grade the cliques had become more stable, and girls could be seen sitting with the same group for months at a time. The seating pattern became more obviously entrenched by the eighth grade, when clear social-class divisions could be detected, with popular students and those from middle-class backgrounds generally seated on the 'good' side, and less popular and lower-class students seated on the 'grits' side.

Adoption of these seating arrangements in what was a public area shared by all students was one means by which the status hierarchy in the peer groups was visible to all comers. It also made visible the status features of 'progress' of any girl who moved from one friendship clique to another. The control of seating as a process of inclusion and exclusion is simple and effective. For socially skilled youngsters, missing out on one location is no big deal: they join up with another group. But for those who are continually excluded by the cliques they aspire to join, the public nature of the exclusion has additional impact: it wins that person the label of 'tryhard'. The negative pattern was more clearly confirmed by the eighth-grade year, when clique boundaries were more distinct, and clique membership had become more strongly valued.

Cliques and social networks

Network ties act as bridges linking the outsider to the group. Box 3.1 shows the kinds of tie which may exist within a network structure containing two six-person cliques, ABCDEF and GHIJKL. The cliques A–F and G–L are linked by ties between C, a member of the first clique, and G and H in the second clique. There are more close-knit ties connecting the members in clique A–F than in clique G–L, and the cliques have different internal structures.

In Box 3.1, G is a more central figure in the second clique, whereas A's centrality in the first clique is balanced by E, with links to four members, and C, D, and F, who each have three ties into the clique. Thus clique G–L depends on member ties with G to maintain its cohesiveness, even though its structure is somewhat looser than that of clique A–F. Moreover, the pattern shows that boundaries between cliques are seldom clear cut. Is C a member of both cliques? In a sense, yes; C functions as a bridge linking clique members in A–F with those in G–L, and through these weak-tie links, A and D, for example, can make contact with G and H. However, for A to gain a ticket of entry to contact with persons I, J, and L requires not only mediation by C but the cooperation of person G. This illustration of course tells us nothing about the basis of these ties, and whether they are friendship choices or indicators of shared activities (as Freeman, 1992, has reported for eighteen women in the Old South database). Additional

Box 3.1 Social network showing ties between network members

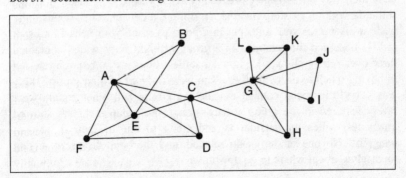

information may reveal other relations between the cliques, or the existence of weaker links between clique members and the somewhat isolated persons J and I (who are linked only to each other and to G). Such information would allow us to move beyond this structural analysis to examine the qualities within the clique relations.

Clique boundary maintenance

Boundary definition affects friend interaction. Salzinger (1982) reported that when members of densely knit cliques made new friends, it usually occurred through the agency of another friend or well-known acquaintance; in contrast, when members of loose-knit cliques made new friends, they were people not closely tied to their own clique. The differences in permeability of cliques were found by Zisman and Wilson (1992) to affect the extent to which cliques encouraged cross-race interaction in their observations in a school cafeteria. Cliques with loose boundaries functioned differently from those with tight-knit structures. The tight-knit cliques were smaller and racially homogeneous, while the loose-knit groups functioned like 'social waterholes' with much coming and going of members, so that the composition of these groups was more racially mixed and less constant from one lunch period to another. The openness of these cliques and crowds provided an opportunity for adolescents to 'table hop' into and out of a particular clique without the application of strict sanctions on them.

Friendship groups have their own boundaries, like surface tension on a soap bubble, which leaves the members of the clique often quite content to float along and leave things as they are. The internal dynamics of well-established groups are strong, often based on living in the same neighbourhood, years of schooling, and sharing activities and interests. Entry and acceptance into the clique is something to be worked for: adolescents do not usually find that a group simply opens up to include them. Joining a clique is like joining any club: it depends on aspiring members to push their way in; and entry is much easier if you have 'a ticket' through some tie with an existing member (a sibling, a cousin, a neighbour) who will 'speak up for you' and 'put in a good word on your behalf'. Cusick (1973) observed the relations in a group of eight boys which contained three overlapping cliques. He noted that these boys just were not interested in having much to do with others who were not part of their group. There was very little social contact outside the group, and other people were rarely featured in the group's discussions. The group members showed uneasiness when an outsider tagged along to one of their downtown hangouts. No one in the group relaxed, and the boys disagreed among themselves about where to go downtown.

Gender differences in clique patterns

Analysis of clique structures and boundaries by Eder and Hallinan (1978), using sociometric choices, documents changes in friendships across the year in five classrooms of pre-adolescents. On seven occasions in the year, children were asked to name their best friends (those whom they liked very much), as well as other friends, and no restrictions were placed on the number of friends named. The extent to which friendship choices were maintained as exclusive pairs, or developed into more open relationships, was assessed in terms of network ties to a third person. Of the nine triad patterns possible, three involve no recognition of the third person by the pair of friends (exclusive friendships), and the other six involve some form of inclusion, culminating in a pattern of reciprocal choice by all three persons. When the incidence of these triad types was calculated across the year, girls in all five classes were found to occupy more exclusive friendship structures than boys. This meant that when a girl outside the friendship pair expressed friendliness towards one of the pair, such an attempt was usually not encouraged, and the pair returned to its self-contained state.

Among the boys, the pattern of friendship formation was different. Pairs of friends were more likely to respond positively to overtures of friendship from a third party, so that the pairs tended to expand into trios of friends at a later occasion. Across the year, the percentage of threesomes where each chose the other as friend increased for boys, but remained stable and with a much lower incidence for girls. These relations between trios of boys are repeated, like a pattern in a frieze, so that boys are embedded in a larger crowd or 'gang' of friends and acquaintances.

Eder and Hallinan rejected the argument that both girls and boys were engaged in the same process of forming extended friendships, but at different rates. They instead proposed that there is a *different process* of friendship formation for girls and for boys. When contact is made with a pair of friends by a third girl, the circle of friends does not grow larger; instead girls return to their paired friendships, either by excluding the newcomer, or by one girl leaving her friend and pairing up with the new girl. It would appear that girls at this age understand friendship as an exclusive relationship, where there is a sense of being chosen by another person. Girls seem more ready to view their friends in terms of these mutually exclusive pairings, through expressions like 'Di is really Carol's friend.'

Boys, on the other hand, form expanded groups, where all three are mates together. Boys' friendships are more clearly group friendships in which particular dyadic ties co-occur; thus David and Andrew are good friends, just as David is a friend of Stephen, but the ties between Stephen and Andrew might not be as strong. This clustering process in male friendships attracted a comment from C. S. Lewis (1960, p. 92), who wrote: 'Two friends delight to be joined by a third, and three by a fourth, if only the newcomer is qualified to become a real friend.' In the dynamics of boys' group inclusiveness, the sum is greater than the parts, so that the relations of each member with another not only add to the overall quality of male group relations but enhance the quality of specific friendships as well. As Lewis put it, 'In each of my friends there is something that only some other friend can fully bring out.'

Acceptance and rejection by the clique

Clique membership is valued. A newcomer's attempt to join the clique may be viewed with suspicion, as likely to steal one of its current members away from the others. Eder's observations in a school cafeteria (Eder, 1985) deal with the problem of how girls handled their inclusion in the ingroup, or their exclusion from it, at the level of clique interaction. The most common feature of the social interactions between cliques of popular girls and cliques of less popular girls was ignoring or snubbing. Girls in the same class would pass each other without acknowledgment of the other's existence. Ignoring tended to be practised by girls in high-status cliques in response to friendly overtures made by those from lower-status cliques. Being ignored won the retort from the latter girls that 'She's stuck-up.' Thus a process of stereotyping becomes established, where the popular girl becomes less popular among a majority of her peers. The process (as viewed by girl A, who represents the majority) is shown in Box 3.2.

What is overlooked by girl A in this process is its inevitability: the obligations on girl B to show allegiance to her new clique prevent her from maintaining her old friendships. Some of the girls who were interviewed by Eder noticed that when some popular girls were not with their popular clique they were much more friendly to them, behaviour which they interpreted as 'two-faced'. This interpretation, though understandable, is unfortunate. It is not that the girl intentionally changes to suit the moment, but rather that the group context affects the girl's behaviour towards her old friends. The rules of group acceptance have an exclusive rights clause

Box 3.2 Popularity cycle in adolescent girls' cliques

Girl A is ignored by popular girl B	→	Girl A accuses girl B of being stuck-up	→	Girl A then avoids social contact with girl B	→	Confirms ingroup/ outgroup differences

concerning loyalty: as a new group member the girl has obligations to the group, and these obligations of loyalty preclude keeping up any lingering ties with former groups. But when she is away from the pressing reality of the new group's norms, she is free from any of these constraints and can be 'her old self'.

Popularity also has the effect of vastly expanding one's circle of acquaintances, so that even with the best intentions the popular adolescent is simply unable to maintain friendships with all those who would want this to happen. The finiteness of one's social network is an empirical fact. These limits on the network mean, as Wellman (1988, p. 42) points out, that 'as a person adds new ties and forms new dense clusters, other ties are given up'. Paradoxically, then, the cost of popularity is selective friendship. Eder sums up the paradox in this way: 'These girls are likely to ignore the affiliative attempts of many girls, leading to the impression that they are stuck-up. Thus, shortly after these girls reach their peak of popularity, they become increasingly disliked' (Eder, 1985, p. 163).

The principles of group acceptance and acknowledgement are portrayed in a highly realistic and amusing way in the 1994 award-winning movie *Muriel's Wedding*, which traces the adventures of a girl who has no friends, no job, and no confidence in herself. The clique of beautiful girls in her local town tell her to keep away from them and not to embarrass them. She sings along with Abba songs in her bedroom, fantasises about weddings, and tries on bridal gowns. Then she fools her mother into signing a blank cheque, flies to an island resort, and begins to have the time of her life. With her money and a new-found girlfriend, she gains the confidence to break the stereotype, do things for herself, and become a somebody.

A model of the stages of clique formation

Moreland and Levine (1982) proposed that a person's passage through a small group may be understood as a series of phases which reflect the changing status of the individual within the group as well as the changing nature of the relations between the individual and the group (see Box 3.3). These phases are highly pertinent to our understanding of clique membership. Within each of the phases, the authors suggest, a cycle of evaluation, commitment, and transition occurs. The investigation phase is the period when a person is viewed by the group as a prospective member; and as the group seeks to assess her/his suitability, the individual too evaluates the benefits of joining the group. If the commitment of both parties to the other increases, and both are satisfied that entry should proceed, there is a change in the relationship and the individual is accepted as a new member.

Box 3.3 Phases in group formation

Phase	Phase I Investigation	Phase II Socialisation	Phase III Maintenance	Phase IV Resocialisation	Phase V Remembrance
Target	Prospective member	New member	Full member	Marginal member	Ex-member

This new phase (socialisation) may see tests of loyalty and initiation rituals, as the group attempts to teach the newcomer the behaviour and attitudes which are appropriate for the group, and to mould the new member into the group's ways. Conflict is likely to occur as the newcomer responds, perhaps resisting some group customs and attempting to define her/his place within the group in ways that are of her/his own choosing. Later, during the maintenance phase, the person and the group are both engaged in specifying the individual member's role in the group so as to achieve maximum benefit to the relationship. When differences begin to emerge between the group and the individual, the phase of resocialisation is initiated, in order to bring the individual back into the fold. The most stressful phases of group relations are socialisation and resocialisation, because they highlight the tension between the goals of the group and those of the individual, and what must be done to satisfy the individual member's needs while maintaining group cohesion and solidarity. Thus in order to preserve group solidarity, groups exert coercive pressures to ensure that members remain in; any behaviour which is seen to be deviating from the group's practices is frowned upon. 'The groups to which a person belongs', said Cartwright (1951, p. 109), 'set standards for [his] behaviour, which [he] must accept if [he] is going to stay in the group.'

THE COMPOSITION OF FRIENDSHIPS

Whereas proximity is sufficient for childhood friendships to form, similarity in interests, attitudes, and beliefs becomes more important for forming adolescent friendships. In early adolescence, friends tend to hold similar views about the importance of schooling, and have similar educational and career aspirations. They also have similar music preferences and recreational interests (e.g., sport or movies), and similar views about smoking. Initial liking is based on general similarities salient in the context, for example, liking for basketball or rock music. The area of similarity in interests/values/tastes broadens as the friendship develops, for example, liking REM and U2 or Nigel Kennedy, and liking Mexican or Thai food, as each adopts some of the interests held by the other. Similarities between best friends' attitudes are, however, not as strong as similarities in observable attributes like gender, ethnicity, and behaviour, particularly smoking behaviour, misconduct, and peer involvement; and the similarities increase across adolescence (Kandel, 1978a; Tolson and Urberg, 1993).

Similarities between close friends are also found in the level of psychological development. Duck (1975) compared the constructs used by pairs of friends and pairs of acquaintances to explain different social relations. There was a significantly higher degree of similarity in the constructs employed by friends to define different relations, suggesting similarity in their personality development at each age level studied. Berndt (1982) suggests that similarity in attitudes and beliefs between friends may simply reflect the influence of geographic proximity and social prejudice on friendship formation. It may be easier, for instance, for people to develop close relationships where they already hold similar beliefs and endorse similar attitudes, in that there may be less work in building a relationship, compared with the risks of mixing with someone who is in outward appearance less similar to self, or whose attitudes are clearly at odds with the prevailing attitudes in the local community. Preference for others similar to oneself may also be actively fostered by particular communities and by families, so that the racial, ethnic, and class values and beliefs of one generation are maintained by the next.

Complementarity is an important psychological aspect of close friendship. Friends complement each other's personalities, perhaps varying in the degree of talkativeness and extroversion while all valuing a sense of humour. Werebe's (1987) interview study of French adolescents reports that close friends were predominantly of the same sex, age, and academic standing, but on other aspects there was less evidence of similarity. About 60 per cent of the friends had similar interests, the others reporting that they had few interests in common. When asked to estimate how much they resembled their friends in personality, the majority believed they were not much like their friends or only somewhat like them. Having complementary personalities seems more favoured among these French young people as a basis for forming friendships. We are not told whether the friendships were initially built around these complementary aspects, or whether (as seems more likely) the friends came to appreciate each other's individuality more as their friendship developed.

Same-sex and opposite-sex friendships

There is a 'sex cleavage' in friendship relations. The tendency for members of the same sex to associate with one another is traceable from the age of 3 years to mid and late adolescence, when it diminishes in strength. Montemayor and van Komen (1985) noted that the majority of male and female adolescents at high school were in same-sex rather than mixed-sex groups. The social worlds of children and adolescents are highly segregated along gender lines, and the persistence of the pattern into the 1990s is evidence that, for most of the time at least, adolescents prefer things that way.

The evidence from several studies (e.g., Buhrmester and Furman, 1987; Furman and Buhrmester, 1985; Kon and Losenkov, 1978; Youniss and Smollar, 1985) is that females attach more importance than do males to their same-sex friendships; for example, Lempers and Clark-Lempers (1992) report that females rated their same-sex friendships higher in affection, intimacy, companionship, and satisfaction than did their male counterparts. In a further study, Lempers and Clark-Lempers (1993) compared the importance of same-sex and opposite-sex friendships for each grade level of an adolescent population. Again they found higher ratings given by females to both kinds of friendship, with both males and females rating their same-sex friendships higher than their opposite-sex friendships, particularly in middle adolescence (grades nine to eleven). The key social provisions were reliable alliance, companionship, and intimacy. Conflict was also higher in mid-adolescence. The greater perceived importance of same-sex friendships suggests that adolescents experience greater affirmation and reassurance among friends of the same sex. It may also reflect the much greater proportion of time which is spent in the company of friends of the same sex.

Exchanges between close friends of the same sex may also have a greater degree of intimacy than those between dating partners. Werebe (1987) compared the level of intimacy of friendship relations with that of dating relations. The vast majority of adolescents who were interviewed stated that they had much better knowledge of their friends than of their dating partners. The tendency for attachments to same-sex friends to be stronger than attachments to opposite-sex friends was more marked among the boys than among the girls. Girls reported feeling about as close to their dating partners as they were to their friends on several aspects, although not for self-disclosure. It does not seem surprising to find that intimacy is greater with adolescents' friends than with their dating partners, when account is taken of the longer duration of friendships, and the greater stability of the environments where most contact with friends occurs, namely the school and local neighbourhood. In contrast, dating relationships are pursued through activities such as visiting discos and bars and other leisure venues, which are places for social excitement and diversion but not ideal for deep discussions.

Age similarity

It is assumed that adolescents have friends who are age peers, that is, who approximate to their own age rather than being of mixed ages. The age-graded organisation of schools, and the practice among researchers of peer relations and friendship of using class lists as prompts for nominating friends, may have given an exaggerated picture of the age similarities in adolescent friendship cliques. Whether cross-age friendships are desirable is an issue on which opinion is divided. Some authorities, particularly those with a custodial responsibility such as school administrators, take the view that associating with older peers is likely to lead adolescents astray and provide a career path into deviant behaviour by accelerating their exposure to adult lifestyles. There is some support for this viewpoint of friends and peers as convoys for deviant activity in the Jessors' work on risk behaviour (e.g., Jessor, 1992; Jessor and Jessor, 1977), Billy's research on sexual behaviour (e.g., Billy and Udry, 1985), work on drinking (Stattin *et al.*, 1989), and Oetting's peer cluster theory of drug use (e.g., Oetting and Beauvais, 1987a), as well as in studies of age mixing in schools (see Chapter 5).

Other viewpoints, derived from developmental psychology, take a more optimistic view of cross-age friendships, seeing interaction with older peers as beneficial to personality and social competence. Hansell (1981) proposed that individuals who are more ego-mature are more adept at, and prefer, social interaction with a wider age range of peers than simply those of their own age. These associations are likely to flourish outside the school. Observations of adolescents by Montemayor and van Komen (1980, 1985) in various locations such as parks, shopping malls, voluntary or-ganisations, and school grounds found them in more varied age groupings in the out-of-school settings than in the school grounds. Over half the adolescents studied by Csikszentmihalyi and Larson (1984), using electronic pagers to trace their social interactions, reported having at least one friend over the age of 20, indicating to the researchers that 'the potential for cross-age friendships does exist' (p. 74).

Siblings as friends

Sibling relations in adolescence have been neglected in the research on friendships. This is unfortunate, because the convoy model would lead us to expect that there are distinctive relationship provisions associated with sibling contacts. Studies of older adults document the benefits of close sibling relations for mental health and emotional adjustment (e.g., Cicirelli, 1989). So close is the sibling bond in some families that siblings are best friends who have no secrets from one another. Some adolescents as well as adults turn first to their sibling for support and companionship, particularly to an older sister, in preference to turning to their friends.

Although sibling relations have some of the characteristics of peer relations, they also contain features derived from the shared family environment, such as living under the same roof, being taught the same values, and being subject to the same parent discipline and expectations. A good friend may know you well, as a companion and confidant; but a sibling knows you in other ways, warts and all, within the relations of a family. Sibling relations, moreover, are almost always unequal, because age differences lend themselves to dominant–subordinate relations based on power or experience. These differences are of course more obvious in late childhood than in late adolescence, and become meaningless in old age. Unfortunately, little attention has been given to the way sibling relations function as a miniature social environment, where the relatively large age differences of childhood and early adolescence diminish over time, often with a corresponding diminution in the aspects of dominance and antagonism, and increased reciprocity in the relationship.

In several respects there is great developmental significance in the sibling relation. First, and most obviously, sibling relations have a longevity which is denied to most friendships, and this affords great socialisation and support potential. For many young people, the degree of intimate sharing with their sister or brother cannot be matched by that with any friend. Second, the sibling relation by being unequal affords all siblings an opportunity to learn how to relate to others who are more or less mature than themselves. In adult life, a great deal of everyday social contact occurs between people of different ages, whose attitudes and interests have a social history somewhat unlike one's own. Moreover, observing a sibling's struggles with identity or with deciding on a future career, whether at a different life-stage or at a different point on a similar developmental trajectory to oneself, affords great scope for vicarious learning. Merely witnessing a sister's turmoil in months of searching for a job, or agonising over a boyfriend who drinks too much, allows a younger sister to gain knowledge which may assist her to cope with future stressful situations; it may also enable her to understand and empathise when a friend is faced with similar difficulties. Third, siblings provide a testing site for trying out one's crazy ideas and practising one's social skills. The sharing in play activities in childhood becomes transformed in adolescence and adult life into 'trying out an idea', whether this is a new look or a career plan, safe in the knowledge that one's critic is one's sibling, who will tell it as s/he sees it. These sibling roles of model and source of vicarious learning, of practice partner, and of adviser and confidant have not been given sufficient attention in developmental research. Within larger families, the responsibility of caring for younger ones and teaching them the skills of doing household and outdoor chores is well established. Sibling influence on social development may have declined in recent decades, as families have become smaller. In families with two children, where the spacing between them is several years, these learning processes may be much curtailed, to the extent that siblings may now be isolated within their own age level within their family.

The social networks of siblings will of course contain the same kin members, but there may be minimal overlap in other sectors. Friends listed by each sibling will differ, even where twins are concerned. The uniqueness of each sibling's social network, both the strong ties with non-kin in the psychological network and the relations with acquaintances and others in the interactive network, means that each sibling provides a bridge to the other sibling of a set of distinct social relations and potential resources which, in some cases, will include potential friends and new acquaintances. Many a person has met her/his future spouse through the bridging tie provided by a sibling. The actions of older siblings in enlisting younger brothers into delinquent gangs are another example of the influence of bridging ties on gang membership.

Sibling conflict

Sibling relations should not be viewed through rose-coloured glasses; some siblings fight like cats and dogs. When asked to describe their relations, siblings admit to bouts of antagonism and quarrelling. In Furman and Buhrmester's (1985) study of 11–13-year-olds, the quality of relations between siblings was compared with those of friends and other family members. Siblings were rated more highly than friends on aspects of support such as affection and reliable alliance, but quarrels were also more frequent. Laursen (1995) reports that adolescents have about the same amount of conflict and disagreement with siblings as they do with their best friends, but the time adolescents reported spending in social interaction with close friends was four times as much as with siblings, indicating that sibling relations contain a higher rate of disagreement. Whereas the issues generating conflict with close friends were resolving differences of opinion and working out the friendship itself, conflicts with siblings were of a different nature, and particularly concerned with annoying behaviour and teasing.

Buhrmester and Furman (1990) examined developmental changes in sibling relations in four age groups, ranging from 8 years of age to over 17 years, and noted that on a number of aspects, there was a decrease in the emotional intensity of sibling relations as the respondents grew older: less power play and less conflict, but also less warmth and affection. However, the picture is complicated by age differences in siblings. Admiration and affection felt by a younger for an older sibling was greater where age spacing was wider; squabbling and antagonism were more acute where age spacing was narrow. Psychological closeness between siblings was greater where the siblings were similar in age and of the same sex. Girls felt greater affinity with their sisters than with their brothers, and enjoyed more companionship with them.

STABILITY AND CHANGE IN FRIENDSHIP NETWORKS

In the commerce of social relations, there are periods of consolidation, and periods of expansion. Much of early and middle adolescence is occupied with the task of making and keeping friends, and understanding how friendship relations work, rather than with building wider networks of relations. Friendships fade and die; they can wither through mistrust and jealousy, or be uprooted by the force of changing conditions. Girls are wary that their friend may leave them for a boy, whereas boys worry that their friends may not include them in what the group is planning to do. Some friends fall away because the foundations of friendship were never substantial, and the friends were better described as companions. Others are retained as acquaintances, but are destined to remain so, because of insufficient overlap of interests or incompatibility of temperament. Some friendships fade from lack of an opportunity to maintain them: as young people grow older, they attend different schools, or move to different towns; and although each for a while attempts to maintain the friendship by letters and phone calls, eventually, through lack of contact and opportunity for shared experiences, the friendship stalls. Denial of regular contact with a friend, or curtailment of contact, often weakens friendship bonds. Wellman (1992, p. 79) notes that 'friendships depend more on accessibility than do kinship networks', so that the maintenance of friendships is affected more than kinship relations by geography and circumstance, perhaps particularly so in adolescence.

Membership of friendship cliques changes from time to time. Young people often become concerned whether their friends are including them in activities or whether they are being left out. Considerable time and emotional energy can be directed into shoring up a friendship, repairing a damaged relationship, and maintaining one's position in the clique. Coleman (1974) reports that the topic of friendship in the small group became of greater importance from age 13 onwards, and aroused greater anxiety and tension among adolescent girls than among boys. Particularly threatening to a friendship is the arrival of a new friend. A feature of girls' concerns in Coleman's research was themes of rejection and exclusion from a friendship. Boys' concerns differed, and related to ways of including the new friend in the friendship circle.

Studies of friendship stability

Berndt (1982) claims that when researchers have assessed the friendship choices made at different times, either weeks or months apart, there is evidence of little change in the stability of friendship from fourth grade to eleventh grade, that is, across the greater part of the adolescent years. These findings would suggest that the rate of forming new friendships and preserving old ones remains roughly the same from about the age of 10 to the age of 17, at least in the stable conditions existing in the social environment of the average school and neighbourhood, which are the nurseries of early friendships. However, my reading of the source studies would suggest that it is a bit sweeping to conclude that friendships across these years are stable, merely on the basis that they are no more unstable at one age than at another. Are we talking of having the same close friends in September as we had in January? Or of still mixing with the same *wider* group of people over that period of time? Changes in the wider network of the crowd of friends and companions are likely to be more marked than changes in the composition of a friendship clique, so the degree to which friendships remain stable will be affected by who is included within the definition of friend.

According to Berndt *et al.* (1986) there was a relatively small amount of change in friendship during the school year for their eighth graders; two-thirds of girls' friendships identified as close in the autumn were still close in the spring. Boys reported lower stabilities, perhaps reflecting the broader friendship patterns pursued among boys. A different approach to estimating stability is to examine the length of the friendship. This looser notion yields information that the friends have often been friends for quite a long time. Kandel (1978b) reports that 73 per cent of her large sample had been friendly for more than three years; the friendships among French Canadians were of similar duration, according to Claes (1992); but Johnson and Aries (1983) report that the average length of friendship among college students was over seven years, and that a large proportion of those who were aged 18 and 19 years were members of the same circle of close friends as in their early adolescence.

QUALITIES VALUED IN FRIENDSHIP

To this point, we have been considering the friendship clique as a sociality structure built from social interaction. Now we turn to what adolescents expect from friendship and the qualities they value in friends, particularly close friends. Researchers over the years have adopted various approaches in order to discover what aspects of friendship are valued by adolescents. Some have simply asked young people to list the features which they value most in friends, and how these differ from those of acquaintances, as Bigelow and La Gaipa (1975) and Kon and Losenkov (1978) have done. Others have asked how important are various aspects of friendship, which is the approach taken by Bukowski *et al.* (1987). Another approach is to identify through interviews with young people those events which contain salient features of friendship. This latter approach is reflected in the pioneering work of Douvan and Adelson (1966) and Coleman (1974), but is not as widely used by developmental psychologists.

Friend loyalty

Conceptions of friendship change and the qualities of friendship become more differentiated as young people come to appreciate that their social world comprises different kinds of friend. Kon and Losenkov's (1978) investigation of friendship asked Russian young people to distinguish between the concepts of friend and companion. The qualities which were distinctive in friend relations were intimacy and confidentiality, loyalty and steadfastness. The requirement that friends are loyal and helpful declined in emphasis between 14 and 15 years, and declined further between 17 and 20 years, whereas the requirement for a friend to be understanding became more important from the age of 15 years upward. Berndt and Perry (1986) also noted that adolescents, in contrast to children, made a distinction between shared activity as the basis of friendship, and loyalty and the absence of conflict as friendship characteristics. Loyalty includes the notion of faithfulness and reliability. The concept alters from one based on reliable companionship (for instance not 'dropping' one friend for another) to one which contains more abstract psychological properties.

Others have commented that friends and associates are described in increasingly more sophisticated terms through adolescence (see Duck, 1975). Younger adolescents describe friendship in factual terms, but older age groups utilise constructs which are interactional and psychological. Duck argues that the changes in adolescents' conceptions of friendship do not evolve out of childhood roles and relations, but instead depend upon their exposure to experiences where the style of establishing relationships is similar to that among adults.

Direct knowledge of best friends shows similar development. Diaz and Berndt (1982) assembled pairs of friends in two age groups, 10 and 13 years, and compared their knowledge of 'external' information about the friend (birth date, home address, names of siblings) and 'internal' information (sports interests and TV preferences, and certain aspects of their personality, such as what worried them and how they reacted to being teased). The adolescents' internal knowledge was greater; they knew more than the 10-year-olds about their best friend's likes and dislikes, feelings and personality characteristics.

Friendship experiences contribute to these changes in understandings. Evidence is found in a study by Berndt *et al.* (1986) of the views of the same children and adolescents over a period of six months about what their best friend was like, and their likes and dislikes about the friendship. The adolescents in the study commented more about the intimacy aspects of their friendships, and girls referred more to intimacy aspects than did boys. Girls also expressed concern more often than boys did over the matter of friends' disloyalty. An interesting link was found between friendship stability and adolescents' views of friendship: those in more stable friendships made more reference to intimacy and responsiveness as desirable qualities of friends, whereas those whose friendships had not lasted the distance referred more often to the issue of loyalty. Adolescents who remained best friends commented on each friend's liking for the other, and on how often the friends spent time together. In contrast, those whose friendship had deteriorated across the six-month period reported at the second interview a decline in sharing, less closeness in the friendship, and greater evidence of disloyalty.

Friendship intimacy and expressiveness

A valued aspect of friendship is the opportunity for closeness and intimacy (see Box 3.4). Csikszentmihalyi and Larson (1984, p. 161) report from their detailed monitoring of teenagers' lives that 'time with friends is the best part of adolescents' daily lives'. A friend is someone you can confide in, and a distinguishing characteristic of a true friend is that s/he can be trusted with your private worries and concerns. Friendship should be experienced rather than evaluated; it has intrinsic benefits rather than extrinsic rewards. There is a *being* aspect of social interaction, which Rook (1987) reminds us is apt to be overlooked by those who argue that all social exchanges have extrinsic purposes, and who urge that the friendships one should cultivate are those which provide social advantage. Friends do not maintain a balance sheet of debts and credits; they function on the basis of simple enjoyment of one another's company, of sharing in common pursuits for their own sake, and effortlessly experiencing as a by-product a sense of acceptance and social affirmation, full realisation of which is sometimes only made following the loss or death of the friend.

Box 3.4 Qualities in friends valued by adolescent girls

Interviewer: What is the quality you most value in a friend?
Adolescent: Understanding. Being able to understand someone and share each other's feeling is the key to friendship.
Interviewer: What are the good things about having a group of friends?
Adolescent: Talking to a lot of people, getting more than one opinion, sharing your opinion and feelings with each other. It's nice to give and share.
Interviewer: What makes someone a close friend?
Adolescent: Being able to talk to them about your most inner feelings and thoughts. Just being able to express yourself is a big relief. You don't have to worry about saying the wrong thing.

Studies show that a consistent component of friendship at adolescence is the importance of self-disclosure. In lengthy sessions of sharing, adolescents discuss the nature of the problems confronting them and possible avenues for their resolution. A great deal of time is spent analysing the affective implications of interpersonal events and relationships. Self-disclosure involves honesty and confrontation, and the friendship itself comes to be reflected on, which is a means by which it is strengthened.

There is also talking or gossiping with a group of one's other friends: a form of sharing which is less intimate than with a single friend, but one which promotes group solidarity by allowing each friend to 'rave on' and talk shop, celebrating their common interests, and, through the exercise of mutual exploration, strengthening the friendship bond. In middle childhood this gossiping has the purpose of discovering the norms of same-sex peer groups. Adolescent gossiping has more to do with self-exploration, and clarifying the views of friends against one's own on important issues. Each adolescent gains confirmation that what s/he is worrying about is also the concern of others. Romantic relations are openly discussed with girlfriends in these forums as a way of learning how to cope with emotional states. Sharing of personal concerns with friends also occurs among males, according to the Sydney youths who talked to Walker, an example of which is given:

> You can love your father and your mother and stuff like that and when you get married you can love your wife, but, at least anyway until you get married the best thing is your mates, you gotta have your mates. There's things I'd say to Chopper or Murph – we've been together for years – but you couldn't tell nobody else that stuff.

(Walker, 1988, p. 44)

Gender differences in level of disclosure

In general, however, male friendships do not appear to achieve the same level of expressiveness (see Buhrmester and Furman, 1987; Claes, 1992). Findings from a range of studies indicate that females engage in greater disclosure of their innermost thoughts and feelings than males. By the time girls reach adolescence, they regard their relationships with girlfriends as providing considerably more intimate forms of sharing and companionship than their relationships with parents. Jones (1991) found that females reported greater levels of disclosure and more trust in their friendships than did males, although both sexes valued similar core provisions of friendship. Girls' greater use of telephones for the pursuit and maintenance of friendships through extended conversation is well known, but the telephone is not the preferred method of contact for boys, who are more likely to cultivate their friends through shared activities.

Sex differences are seen both in the topics which friends choose to discuss, and in the style of the conversation itself. The difference is highlighted in Johnson and Aries' (1983) study of 18- and 19-year-olds. Conversation topics between female friends were more 'personally-oriented' than those between male friends; for example, females were much more likely to talk about family problems, personal problems, and their doubts and fears. Discussions on these topics were also treated at greater depth by females, although there was some discussion of these personal areas by males. Male conversations, in comparison with those of females, are more concrete and event-based, which is consistent with the reliance of males on grounding their exploration of relationships and identity in the recounting of events and the analysis of activity. Topics mainly discussed between male friends were sports and reminiscences about things they had done together in the past. This study confirms the existence of different world views between the sexes, which may be adaptive to the different demands made upon males and females in our society. The apparent lack of depth in male sharing with their friends leads Johnson and Aries (1983, p. 235) to speculate whether males' friendly banter and story-telling 'may replace a deeper sharing between friends', with the consequence that males are less well equipped to resolve complex relationship problems.

Gender differences in style of communication in friends' talk

Observation of conversations between best friends seems to confirm that girls' friendship relations are more personal than those of boys, and that their talk with friends deals with the more intimate and emotional aspects of relationships. For example, Tanner (1990) noted that discussions by males were less personal and more abstract than those by their female counterparts. The latter were more interested in emotionally charged topics such as relationship difficulties with other people, including parents, whereas boys discussed their topics, even where relationships were at issue, in an emotionally neutral fashion. Girls' talk was more tightly focused on the topic, and engaged their listener in the feelings they experienced on the issue; boys' talk in contrast was more diffuse, and did not seem intent on involving the partner in the dialogue. There was a distinctive style about girls' conversation. A notable feature was the exaggerated intonation, which has the effect of injecting emotion and dramatic emphasis into what is otherwise a bland account. For example, the girls would say, 'I couldn't believe it', 'It was like, God, it was bad', and 'It hurts when you lose your best friend.' Accentuated speech patterns were absent from boys' talk.

These features illustrate what Tanner calls the 'cultural' differences between girls and boys. Having chosen an issue to talk about, girls elaborate on a common focus of concern, building joint understanding through mutual clarification of the issue, whereas boys take a different approach which leaves each partner more independent. Instead of each discussing the other's concerns, the boys seemed determined to maintain a focus on their individual preoccupation. Each would respond to the other's account by describing his own concern, as if engaged in a tacking duel in sailing, changing tack to match that of the other. When one boy is recounting the events associated with his concern, the other appears to give little input by way of feedback or reflection on the account; and when comments are given, these attempt to downplay the seriousness of the situation described by the friend. Tanner (1990) noted, however, that neither boy appeared unhappy or dissatisfied with his friend's responses.

The way that the partners arranged their chairs was an analogue of their mode of discussion. Girls sat opposite each other, in keeping with a joint focus on the concerns raised by one party. Boys faced out, made little eye contact, and each maintained a separate focus on his own concerns. The obvious differences in empathic communication invite value judgments about the lack of empathy in male relationships, in contrast to the greater level of engagement which appears characteristic of female interaction. Tanner cautions against hastening to such a conclusion. What appears at first to be a failure on the part of boys to listen actively to one another may be, Tanner suggests, *a difference in style*. Boys seek to downplay the seriousness of the friend's problem; they provide reassurance by affirming to the listener that 'you're OK; you'll be alright; it's not all that dreadful, so you needn't feel so bad about it'. If one accepts that the style of supportive communication between males and females is different, it may help to explain the frustrations experienced in communications between friends of the opposite sex.

An interpretation of sex differences in intimate sharing and disclosure in terms of differences in culture and style, and differences in world view, offers hopeful ways of breaking out of the stereotypes of female emotionality and male impassivity. Males and females do occupy different life-spaces, and these differences become established in the adolescent period. It would therefore seem not surprising for males and females to express intimacy and supportiveness in different ways.

CONFLICTED RELATIONS

Friendships are not all plain sailing, but instead contain tensions and contradictory feelings. Friends argue and disagree; friends can be jealous of one another, and the competition between friends can be fierce and anything but friendly. They may in a single day experience the sharing of intimate secrets, betrayal, stormy argument, exclusion from the group, and reconciliation and forgiveness. The conflicted aspects of friendship are infrequently discussed in the research literature. Studies tend to focus on the positive features and seem to assume that the presence of positive qualities is incompatible with conflict and disagreement. The methods of investigation may also have encouraged socially desirable 'my friends are great' responses from respondents instead of more frank and problematic ones (on this point, see Giordano *et al.*, 1986). Failure to consider the coexistence of supportive and conflictual relations within adolescent friendships risks idealising the relationship, when adolescents themselves know of the contradictions found in human relations.

There is evidence that at least by mid-adolescence an 'adult view' of friendship begins to emerge, which is able to entertain the presence of contradictory qualities simultaneously in a relationship. As they grow older, and reflect at more depth on their social experiences, adolescents come to realise that friendships are imperfect, and that even one's good friends can cause embarrassment and pain. In his study of French adolescents Werebe describes friendship as 'an equivocal relationship' (Werebe, 1987, p. 272) and provides interesting detail to show that some of his respondents were conscious of ambivalent feelings towards their friends, including aspects of rivalry and tension. They were aware of their friends' weaknesses and the points of irritation with them, while acknowledging at the same time their mutual closeness. Periods of sharing with a friend alternated with periods of distancing, and at times open hostility. Girls tended to voice these contradictions more than boys, in statements such as

'I like her a lot, but she's got everything I hate'; and 'Underneath it all, we really get along very well, but at times she makes comments that are a little aggressive.' Similarly, Berndt and Perry (1986, p. 646) comment that 'adolescents assume that friends who support each other may also argue or fight with each other'.

Close friends interact differently from those who are not close. Observations reveal that they display a broader tolerance towards one another, and a broader range of emotions, than is seen in social interactions between strangers or acquaintances. When observers of older youth compared the conversations of pairs of friends with those of acquaintances, a broad range of differences was found (Planalp and Benson, 1992). Compared with acquaintances, friends were more relaxed, more informal, more intimate, and more equal in sharing conversation, talked about a single topic more, and interrupted each other more. In addition, friends laughed more, talked faster, and showed more involvement and interest in each other. Friends were also more likely to express negative judgments, such as insults, sarcasm, and criticism.

Friendship patterns are a useful indicator of emotional health. Reduced friend networks, as well as conflicted relations with friends, have been found in emotionally distressed adolescents (Cotterell, 1994) and in those who are psychiatrically disturbed (Claes, 1994). Indeed, distortions in the structure of the social network may serve to indicate psychological difficulties. The Claes study points out that reduction in the social network of friends and acquaintances reflects a deterioration in friendship relations among adolescents referred for treatment: whereas the younger group of referrals differed little from normals in terms of their friendship characteristics, the older group's friendship relations 'were characterised by deficiencies at the level of communication, and the presence of doubt and suspicion' (Claes, 1994, p. 189). They had fewer friends and acquaintances and weaker attachments to them, and had suffered feelings of rejection and ridicule. Moreover, their relations with close friends were less intimate and more conflicted.

Friendships among delinquent youth have also been found to contain higher levels of disagreement, jealousy, and competition, with greater concerns about loyalty and more explicit pressures to conform to the group (see Giordano *et al.*, 1986). These aspects possibly reflect a more volatile friendship style as much as a more uncertain social world. Expectations of friends were high: delinquent young people were just as concerned as other youths with gaining the trust of friends, and having friends who really cared about them. But the social skills for expressing friendship needs or moderating the demands imposed by others were inadequate, so that conflicts quickly arose from the frustrations of poor communication. Thus in both delinquent and disturbed friendship networks, lower levels of trust and reduced communication skills have socially limiting effects.

CONCLUSION: THE SUPPORT OF FRIENDS

This chapter has explored adolescent friendship as a social experience of sharing, companionship, and affirmation, arising from the connectedness with others in the social network. Support has been implicit in the preceding pages, but viewed in a transactional sense, as a quality of relations rather than as a commodity which can be given and received. To draw a boundary around that which is support and that which is normal social interactions is futile, because, transactionally speaking, relations contain the seeds of support or non-support in the exchanges which occur.

A helpful way of understanding support, particularly in the context of friendship, is as a quality of relationships rather than a separate commodity. In this sense, support is not suddenly switched on in a relationship, but is there as an integral part of the interactions. Hobfoll and Stokes (1988) express this view when they describe social support as 'social interactions or relationships that provide individuals with actual assistance or with a feeling of attachment to a person or group that is perceived as caring or loving' (p. 499). In everyday interactions, support arises from the connectedness in social relations with friends, from the experience of reliable alliance and feelings of solidarity and belonging which are found in companionship itself (e.g., Rook, 1987). Support is channelled through the friendship network. Through the regular exchanges of friends, whose companionship creates a kind of psychological community containing support resources, help and advice from others are accessible when needed. A college student explained his experience of companionship support this way: 'You're living with these guys and there's always someone to talk to if you're in strife with your studies, your girlfriend has dumped you, your social life is a bit of a drag.'

Support from close friends differs considerably from support from acquaintances, because close friendships are based on commitment, whereas other friendships and acquaintanceships are what Fischer *et al.* (1977, p. 57) termed 'friendships of convenience'. Kahn and Antonucci (1980) suggest three types of support in their convoy model: (material) *aid*, (cognitive) *affirmation*, and (emotional) *affective support*. Affective support, the communication of understanding and sympathy, depends for its power on the closeness of the relationship; and affirmation derives its potency from the integrity of the personal tie in the relation. Those who are part of the intimate network of friends are best placed to reaffirm the fact that, despite any traumas which their friend has experienced, nothing has changed – either in their relationship or, more importantly, in the distressed friend. Despite grief or a deep sense of disappointment, or a feeling of being shattered, there is continuity of personality – and the comforting presence of one's friends makes this point known. In this respect, affirmation communicates stability and security, just as the presence of the caregiver is reassuring in itself to the distressed child.

When Tolkien gave the title of *The Fellowship of the Ring* to the first part of *The Lord of the Rings* trilogy, he affirmed the importance of friendship as a source of strength and motivation. The Ring trilogy is a masterpiece that may be appreciated at different levels, but at one level it deals with the theme that the collaboration of an ordinary group of friends can overcome the forces of evil. Friendships provide a sensation of strength; in the company of one's friends, one can feel powerful, confident, and free.

4 Loneliness and peer rejection

The objective of this chapter is to examine the costs of distressed and impaired relationships, through adolescents' experiences of loneliness. According to expert opinion, loneliness is particularly widespread in the adolescent years. We can speculate as to why this may be so: the heightened self-consciousness and introspection of youth; the consuming concern with being accepted by others of the same age; the acute sensitivity to hurt and disappointment when one seems to be ignored. Adolescents may be more vulnerable to loneliness because they hold 'unrealistically high expectations for their social life' (Peplau and Perlman, 1982, p. 253). Some forms of loneliness are the consequence of active social exclusion and ostracism; but adolescents also experience situational loneliness, arising from emotionally traumatic events such as separation, abandonment, and bereavement. These different kinds of loneliness are further related to the adolescent experience itself. For most young people, loneliness is intensely felt because it is intensely personal. Consequently it is an unpleasant experience to be avoided wherever possible.

Some authorities (e.g., Kimmel and Weiner, 1985) explain the growth in loneliness in adolescence in developmental terms, arising from attempts to establish a satisfactory personal identity. The process of becoming one's own person sees a psychological separation from parents, and a transformation of childhood forms of attachment relations. The changes in attachment may be accompanied by existential loneliness, an awareness that one is ultimately separate from everyone else. Along with developing an increased desire for meaningful relationships with others, adolescents realise that they are made vulnerable to hurt and rejection by choosing to enter into any relationship based on openness and trust. Thus the very intensity with which social relationships are pursued during adolescence increases the prospect of exposure to loneliness when the desired level of satisfaction from friendships is not achieved.

Is loneliness a serious matter? Does loneliness impair psychological development? It is because loneliness has serious long-term as well as immediate consequences for young people's mental health that it is discussed in this book. People who are lonely not only have greater difficulty in establishing friendships: their concern with gaining acceptance may affect their behaviour and impair their judgment. When loneliness is first experienced, it acts as a driving force which impels people to seek companionship and make social contact with others who are compatible. But if loneliness is prolonged, anxieties increase to a point where they inhibit action and reduce the motivation to make contact with others. In these circumstances, loneliness depresses a young person's motivation to participate effectively in community social activities and to be active in classroom life. It is the yearning for social belonging and the consequences if that yearning remains unfulfilled which make the topic of loneliness a matter to be considered from a motivational perspective as much as from the viewpoint of mental health.

THE EXTENT AND SIGNIFICANCE OF ADOLESCENT LONELINESS

Estimates as to the extent of loneliness among young people vary. Brennan and Auslander's survey of 10–18-year-olds in ten US cities (see Brennan, 1982) proposed that some 10–15 per cent were seriously lonely, and that over half those surveyed reported that they often felt lonely and left out. Ostrov and Offer's (1978) study of Australian and American young people in the 1960s found that 20–22 per cent of the 12–16-year-olds and 12–14 per cent of older youth agreed with the statement 'I feel so very lonely.' Recent surveys (e.g., Atkinson, 1988) have yielded similar incidence rates, with 13 per cent of Dutch adolescents reporting that they often felt lonely (see Meuss, 1994) and a study in southern Italy reporting rates of 25 per cent among girls (Ammaniti *et al.*, 1989).

Many definitions of loneliness exist, which Rook (1984) has attempted to summarise. She defines loneliness as 'an enduring condition of emotional distress that arises when a person feels estranged from, misunderstood, or rejected by others and/or lacks appropriate social partners for desired activities, particularly activities that provide a sense of social integration and opportunities for emotional intimacy' (Rook, 1984, p. 1391). This definition helps to limit the term 'loneliness' to experiences of distress through some persistent sense of separateness from others, rather than from a fleeting period of social withdrawal. It also reminds us that persons who limit their contacts with others or who prefer a solitary lifestyle are not necessarily lonely. The importance of the person's own perceptions and control over events also merits emphasis: de Jong-Giervald (1989, p. 205) defines loneliness as:

a situation experienced by the participant as one where there is an unpleasant or unacceptable lack of certain social relationships. The extent to which the situation is experienced as serious depends upon the participant's perception of his or her ability to recognise new relationships, or to improve existing ones.

Despite evidence that loneliness is widespread in the population at any one time, most people are reluctant to admit to being lonely. Perlman and Joshi (1989) suggest that people attempt to disguise their loneliness because it carries a stigma: feeling lonely suggests some kind of social failure. Among first-year university students living away from home, there is a high incidence of loneliness and homesickness; yet, paradoxically, a large proportion do not talk to anyone about their sense of loneliness or their need for help in order to overcome it.

The research also shows that adolescents do not handle aloneness well. Aloneness makes one vulnerable to feelings of anxiety and negative gloomy thoughts. In this respect, fear of loneliness may be a motivational force in adolescents seeking social contact. Coleman (1974) reported that young people took a negative view about being on their own, a feeling which was more acute among younger adolescents. A similar picture is reported by Csikszentmihalyi and Larson (1984). Using electronic pagers to capture adolescents' mood states, they found that adolescents reported their lowest feelings when they were alone, and these were the times when they were more prone to worrying thoughts. The younger adolescents coped less well with solitude than the older adolescents. The desire to avoid situations which trigger a sense of loneliness may explain the thronging phenomenon among adolescents – their urge to be in large groups and to prefer crowded, noisy settings to ones with less activity and fewer numbers. Loneliness is not a resigned state of distress among youth: it impels activity. Weiss (1973) wrote, 'The lonely are driven to find others, and if they find the right others, they change and are no longer lonely' (p. 15).

SOCIAL AND EMOTIONAL LONELINESS

The ideas of a small number of authors about the phenomenon of loneliness in adult experience have shaped thinking in the field. A central distinction is that between *emotional and social loneliness*. From clinical work with adults experiencing marital separation and bereavement, Weiss (1973) distinguished between the loneliness of emotional isolation, which appears in the absence of a close emotional attachment, and the loneliness of social isolation, which appears when a person lacks access to a social network and to socially integrative relationships.

Emotional loneliness is characterised by a sense of abandonment, emptiness, apprehension, anxiety, and fear. When people attempt to describe their sense of emotional loneliness, what is remarkable is the frequent reference to images of emptiness; the feeling is so tangible that it is experienced as a physical deficiency, often located as a hole in the chest or aching void in the stomach, an emptiness which needs to be filled. Following the loss of a friend or the dissolution of a close relationship, a person may expend a great deal of psychological energy in attempts to remedy the sense of abandonment and retrieve the conditions which produce assurance and emotional security.

Social loneliness is different; it refers to the sense of boredom, aimlessness, and marginality associated with a lack of affirmation by others. It often follows some kind of disruption to the social network caused by changed circumstances, for example moving to a new town, a new school, or a new job. It also is associated with the feeling of being rejected or ostracised, where the person feels misunderstood or alienated from the group. Adults experiencing social or emotional loneliness report overwhelming feelings of isolation and deep estrangement, and overpowering feelings of emptiness. These feelings may be associated with anxiety and diminished self-esteem.

Confirmation of the existence of distinct types of loneliness was produced by Rubenstein and Shaver (1982). They designed an eight-item loneliness scale from people's personal accounts of their experiences, and incorporated this into a broader questionnaire which was printed in the major newspapers of six American cities. Responses to the survey were factor analysed, yielding four interpretable factors, two of which described feeling states, which they labelled *desperation* and *impatient boredom*, and two of which described internal reactions to loneliness: *depression* and *self-deprecation*. The desperation factor was associated with feelings of being helpless, afraid, abandoned, vulnerable, and panicky – symptoms of emotional loneliness aroused by separation and loss of attachment to close others. In contrast, the factor of impatient boredom generated feelings of anger, restlessness, impatience, uneasiness, and an inability to concentrate – feelings associated with social alienation. Emotional and social loneliness appear then to have separate origins and arouse distinctive patterns of emotions, but both produce a sense of restlessness and unfocused dissatisfaction. Weiss (1973, p. 21) comments that 'the individual is forever appraising others for their potential as providers of the needed relationship, and forever appraising situations in terms of their potential for making the needed relationships available'.

SOCIAL LONELINESS

The loneliness of social isolation has received little attention by leading thinkers, but it may yield important insights into the situations faced by young people who lack the sense of personal community which is normally associated with being embedded in a social network. Social loneliness captures the notion of anomie, of not fitting in, of not belonging, of being on the margins and disconnected from those around you. So acute is this form of loneliness that in traditional Aboriginal society, social exclusion was sometimes imposed on a member of the tribe as a severe punishment for breaking tribal law, through the pointing of the bone, the consequences of which were often fatal. The practice of shunning by people in Amish communities towards a community member who has violated its norms is a modern form of social death.

However, it is not necessary to limit the debilitating effects of social isolation and marginalisation to these dramatic examples. Social loneliness may be particularly problematic in adolescence, when identity is closely bound up with group belonging, and when ostracism is employed as a weapon of social control by the peer group. It has been said that for an adolescent, Saturday night is the loneliest night in the week if you are not out with your friends. Feelings of social loneliness and estrangement may also be experienced in everyday circumstances: when you are not 'in on the joke' and others are talking away but not filling you in, when you feel out of step, do not fit in, have a hearing impairment, or look different from others. One teenager who was not included by the group expressed the feeling that 'I wish I could change myself.'

An aspect of importance for assisting the lonely is the time perspective of the person concerned (see Young, 1982). Coping is altered when a lonely person views her/his situation as endless and unable to be resolved, and is resigned to having no close relationships, compared with another who sees loneliness as a temporary state of affairs, attributable to unfortunate circumstances rather than to personal deficit. Whereas adults may have a history of chronic loneliness which has evolved over a period of some years, the typical experiences of loneliness among adolescents and college students are of short duration. Their loneliness is predominantly situational, generated by a stressful event, such as the break-up of a relationship, or through one party moving to another town or region.

Change in school as a source of social loneliness

Probably the greatest survival test imposed on friendships is that of environmental change associated with change in school, such as moving to high school or entry into college. Disruption to friendships associated with transfer to secondary school is a major source of stress on adolescents. Not only do some friendship cliques disintegrate, but the social environment itself becomes unstable (see Felner *et al.*, 1982). The network changes following a school transition have the effect of reducing the level of security in attachments to familiar others, and heightening anxiety. Younger adolescents when they move to secondary school experience powerful if temporary feelings of anxiety, separateness, and alienation contained in statements like those in Box 4.1, found in Power and Cotterell (1979). These accounts underline the social estrangement which is felt on entering a new school with a different organisation and peer structure from the previous school. Newcomers frequently referred to the greater size and complexity of their new school to explain their lack of confidence and problems in identification. School transition disrupts existing friendship ties, reduces levels of support from friends, and restricts opportunities to make new friends. Adaptation was lowest where the transition path taken by students involved the greatest change in school size (Cotterell, 1992).

In these circumstances, those who are able to maintain stable friendship ties appear to adjust better to school transition (see Berndt, 1989; Hirsch and Dubois, 1992). Berndt reports that those whose friendships remained stable were rated by classmates as more popular, more sociable, and less aggressive; whereas those who changed their friends were judged by their classmates to be more aggressive and less sociable, and rated by their teachers as engaging in more misconduct in class. The association between friendship stability and adjustment was also evident prior to the transition; thus a reciprocal process appears to be operating, where those who are

Box 4.1   Situational loneliness associated with school transition

---

The first day I arrived I felt lost and I even got lost once. I felt as if I had arrived in a new land.

(Girl, 12)

You had people there you did not know looking you up and down. I felt like a real small kid and being pushed around by older kids than I.

(Girl, 11)

The first few days I didn't no [*sic*] where anything was. I felt like I was going to do something wrong.

(Boy, 12)

I felt like I was just like a drop of water in a stream. There was nothing significant about you and you were a little grade eight.

(Boy, 12)

aware that their friends will be attending the same secondary school are better placed to face the uncertainties of their new environment.

Loneliness and transition to university

Loneliness is also an important factor in students' adjustment to university. In leaving home to attend university there is considerable disruption of the social network. Initial separation from old friends and from family generates feelings of loss and grieving, often accompanied by bouts of homesickness. Fisher and Hood (1987) found that English university students who moved away from home experienced homesickness some weeks after starting at university. For most new students the sense of loneliness is usually brief, as they meet new friends and become integrated into their new college. Where there are programmes for integrating students socially and academically into the new environment, student commitment to university is reported to be stronger (see Boyer, 1987).

Going away to college precipitates changes in friendships. Some friendships may have continued through the years of school only to founder when the move to college imposes the first extended period of separation on the relationship. For college students (age 18–19 years) the acid test for old friendships appears to occur at the end of the first term, when they return home for the Christmas holidays (northern hemisphere) or Easter holidays in Australia. They find that changes have taken place in themselves and in their friends; gone is the easy sharing, the identity of interests, the simple enjoyment of each other's company. They seem to be at the same station, but standing on different platforms. And without investing time and effort in bringing the friendship back onto the same track, the old relationship will in time inevitably diverge even farther. The shock of this alteration in friendship intimacy, sometimes mirrored in subtle changes in the relationship with parents as well, marks the starting point of serious adjustment to college for many students. They face the fact that friendships change without any party intending them to, and without malice or forethought. The realisation often galvanises the young person into facing the reality of her/his future, looking forward rather than back to the old ways, just as the parted streamers at the dockside force the emigrant to accept the fact that s/he has now embarked on a voyage to a new land.

Network change at college

Evidence that the social networks of college students undergo a major upheaval in the first semester comes from a study by Shaver *et al.* (1985) which monitored changes in social network relationships of new students at four time points: before starting college and at three points during their first year. They found that relations with old friends, particularly previous romances, were subjected to great strain following the transition to university. Many of the friendships established prior to college disintegrated: 46 per cent of old romances did not survive the first semester, while the ones which lasted to mid-year were rated as less satisfactory than they had been prior to entering college. Old friendships also were subjected to major disruption, with only one-third of the sample claiming that their closest friend from pre-college days was still their best friend, another third reporting a cooling of the friendship, and the remainder stating that the friendship had not survived.

Management of social relationships within the new college environment can be just as daunting. Our interviews with college students (Cotterell *et al.*, 1994) contain frequent comments about the distracting quality of social life in residential halls, and how there is always someone ready for a game of football, or a chat, or an outing to the cinema. A serious problem for many new students is how to regulate their social contacts so as to preserve sufficient privacy to achieve reasonable levels of academic performance. Vinsel *et al.* (1980) reported that students who remained in college differed from those who dropped out in their greater use of both contact-seeking and contact-avoidant strategies. Successful students employed techniques to discourage the attentions of others where the contact interfered with their studies; these included closing their door, telling others they were not going out socially for a week, or even relocating their studies to a quiet spot in a seminar room or the university library.

In the studies of adolescents in transition to a new school or college, loneliness appears to be related to network quality, not the number of network ties. Cutrona (1982) challenges the view that more (friends, dates, parties, phone calls) is better for a person's social well-being. Instead, she proposes that the degree of loneliness is more directly related to the level of satisfaction with relationships, rather than to the number of network members or frequency of contacts with them. Quality is a judgment which the individual makes about the adequacy of social provisions. In college situations these pertain to the quality of attachment relations, where newcomers are expected to develop relationships with strangers of their own age. Takahashi and Majima (1994) found that Japanese university students whose ties were 'family-dominant' (having close affective ties with their family) were more homesick and had more difficulty adjusting to college life than students whose ties were 'agemate-dominant' (having more attachments to age mates). The family-type students reported more loneliness, more anxiety about residential living, and more difficulties in establishing close peer relationships. This research illustrates that adjustment to new situations is moderated by a person's existing 'configuration of social relationships' (Takahashi and Majima, 1994, p. 370). While family relations affirm individual identity, openness to peer relationships is critical in alleviating loneliness in the new situation. The strongest moderators of loneliness in Cutrona's (1982) study of college transition were satisfying same-sex and opposite-sex friendships.

BEREAVEMENT AS A SOURCE OF EMOTIONAL LONELINESS

Bereavement from the death of a peer is a common occurrence in adolescence. Balk (1991) reports that almost one-third of the college students he contacted had lost a close friend within the previous twelve months; and over one-third of a high-school sample had experienced the death of a peer while at school. Friend or sibling bereavement is acutely felt as a sense of utter loneliness during adolescence, because of the centrality accorded peer relationships in these years, and the sense that death is incompatible with the youth world. The sudden death of a peer breaks into this world with a threat to identity; and loneliness is a response to the sense that something of one's own identity has been denied. Death of someone close alters one's perspective on the world.

According to Raphael (1983), it is only in adolescence that an adequate concept of death begins to emerge. She cites a study of 1500 Melbourne high-school students by Tobin and Treloar in 1979 which found that 38 per cent reported that their first encounter with death was through the death of a grandparent. This experience may have led them to think that death was associated with old age, as over 80 per cent saw the appropriate age to die as past 70 years. They also held the view that death should occur quietly, and most abhorred the thought of a violent sudden death. These notions of death as distant from youth may leave young people poorly equipped to cope with the sudden violent death of someone their own age.

Moreover, lack of attention to adolescents' needs to find ways of expressing grief may prolong the period of coming to terms with death. Raphael suggests that the process of mourning may be tangled up with the ongoing pressures of schoolwork, and perceptions adolescents hold that one should not show emotional distress in public. As a consequence, adolescent mourning may be unsatisfactorily resolved, and extend over a considerable period of time. A similar view is expressed by O'Brien *et al.* (1991, p. 431). They interviewed college students who had experienced the death of a friend in high school, and found that even after a few years had elapsed, some young people were still 'struggling through the grieving process'.

What is particularly distressing with the loss of a friend, especially a friend of the opposite sex, is that the young person may be a forgotten griever (see Balk, 1991). Her/his grief may be overlooked or not even acknowledged by the grieving adults in the bereaved family. The adolescent may feel shut out and unable to participate in the family's grief, as if her/his grieving as an outsider is of little importance, despite the fact that the mourning for a friend closely resembles that for a family member. Such experiences of silent unnoticed mourning, cut off from the grieving family, have been called 'disenfranchised grief'. Being denied a public outlet for grief is likely to generate a distinct form of isolation which is a mixture of both emotional and social forms of loneliness.

Sibling bereavement

Death of a sibling deserves special mention. It has been found that sibling death after a prolonged serious illness has traumatic consequences for surviving siblings. In situations where the sibling's death was the result of a terminal illness, adolescents are reported to experience anxiety, guilt, and depression: for example, blaming themselves for the way they handled the death, or experiencing a chronic sense of badness or guilt over outliving their sibling. Health concerns are also common. They worry over the possibility of getting a serious illness or of dying at an early age themselves, and experience mysterious physical complaints such as ulcers and severe headaches. Fanos and Nickerson (1991) agree with other authorities (Balk, 1990; Hogan and Greenfield, 1991; Raphael, 1983) that the nature of adolescence as a period of cognitive growth and transformation in social relationships makes the task of working through the grief of sibling loss particularly difficult. From a developmental perspective, the bond between siblings can be understood as an essential relationship for establishing one's personal identity, and thus loss of a sibling through death represents in one sense loss of part of the self. With the death of one's sister or brother, notes Raphael (1983, p. 146), the young person experiences the loss of 'a source of secure identifications on the pathway to adult life'. Bank and Kahn (1982) make a similar point, arguing that sibling loss 'can be crucial for the personality development of another sibling if the siblings' identities have been interwoven during their lifetimes' (p. 271). Their clinical studies point to the psychosomatic and emotional risks to which surviving siblings are vulnerable after their sibling's death, noting that these risks are seldom recognised by family members, teachers, or medical practitioners.

Separation and loss are highly personal, private experiences. Bereaved adolescents show ambivalence about close relationships with others. On the one hand, they are reluctant to become involved in new relationships at any level of intimacy, fearful that such emotional commitment to others will leave them vulnerable to devastating hurt from loss. On the other hand, they are overly anxious about the welfare of other family members, fearful that the strain of further loss would be intolerable. It has been suggested by Balk (1990) and Davies (1991) that in early to mid-adolescence the sense of feeling different as a consequence of sibling bereavement may impede adolescents' relationships with their peers, to the extent that some withdraw from the peer group or fail to become immersed in the concerns of others of their own age. Of course, the access to peers is likely to vary. One adolescent reported to Balk (1990, p. 117) that 'I couldn't reach anybody the first year because everybody seemed so shallow. They didn't understand.' But another reported, 'I found I really had a lot of friends that really did care, and that meant a lot to me.'

Consequences of bereavement for peer relations

The likelihood of withdrawing from friends appears to be greater for those who were very lonely and sad following the death of a sibling. One study by Davies (1991) analysed the coping patterns of 11–14-year-olds whose sibling had died from cancer within the previous three years. Selecting from the total sample the six adolescents who had the highest scores on internalising behaviour (i.e., sad and withdrawn response patterns) Davies compared them with the six having the lowest scores. She found that all those in the high group reported one or no friends, and/or 'shaky' relationships with their friends. Five of these young people had broken up with a friend since their sibling's death. In contrast, those with low internalising scores reported one or several good friends and/or good relationships with their friends.

An interview study of twelve adults who had lost a sibling during their adolescence by Davies (1991) recounts their feelings of 'shock, numbness, sadness, loneliness, anger and depression' (p. 89), emotions which they continued to experience for several years. All twelve interviewees reported an altered perspective on life which made them feel different from their peers: more serious, more mature, and remote from the adolescent antics and interests of their friends. One of Davies' respondents acknowledged how she changed from being 'quite an active, outgoing person at school . . . Afterwards, I never felt like doing much.' When her friends invited her out for a pizza, 'it all seemed so silly' (Davies, 1991, p. 91). Another respondent recalled how separate she felt from others: 'I always felt that nobody understood how I felt. How could they? Their sister hadn't died.'

This distancing from family and peers following the death of a sibling varies, depending upon the closeness of the sibling relationship, as well as upon characteristics of supportiveness in the family environment. Withdrawal from the family may be an attempt to limit the adolescents' personal anguish, because the sense of inadequacy in the face of the dying sibling's pain and wasting body was more than they could bear. Martinson and Campos (1991) report that observing the emotional pain of others in the family added to the adolescents' own pain at their sibling's suffering. Where the adolescents were given a role in caring for their ill sibling, however, the bond with their sibling was enriched, and at the same time the helper role enabled them to see and cope with the gradual deterioration of their brother or sister. Martinson and Campos point out that when the home is the setting for terminal care, it provides more opportunity for continuing contact with the dying sibling, and eases the adolescents' adjustment to sibling loss.

In summary, the developmental consequences of the grieving experience were to remove these adolescents from the normal peer world of fun and friendship, and catapult them into maturity. For some, the separateness from their peers was a matter of growing up overnight, having skipped the typically adolescent phase of joking and gossiping for hours, where life revolves around TV, clothes, and friends. They experienced rapid psychological growth, and sensed that they were made stronger but more serious by the knowledge that no one is immune to death and grief. The impact of feeling different also had long-term costs. Three of the twelve who were interviewed by Davies withdrew totally from their peer group, and experienced serious bouts of depression which required psychiatric treatment. Their withdrawal compounded the sense of isolation that accompanied the bereavement itself. Davies (1991, p. 91) commented that 'Instead of being able to turn to their peers for support and understanding, they withdrew from them because they found their interests and behaviour trivial.' Although the others interviewed by Davies had at least one friend to talk to, they admitted that they seldom shared thoughts about their sibling's death with their friends. Instead they restricted the sharing to more everyday activities: their private grief remained 'off limits'. Difficulties in communicating with peers about a sibling's death have also been reported in other studies (e.g., Balk, 1983; Martinson and Campos, 1991), and may arise from sensitivity to the loss, as well as from disturbed relations with the sibling. These difficulties were found to persist as long as nine years after the death, until as adults they found a deep trusting relationship which allowed them at last to deal with their feelings.

Implications for counselling

Bereavement has marked effects on study habits, concentration, and school achievement (Balk, 1990) as well as on peer relationships and personality.

The implications of adolescent bereavement for the work of counsellors and school administrators are several. Drawing on their clinical experience, Bank and Kahn (1982) stress the effects of sibling loss on personality development and emotional risk to surviving siblings, and recommend to counsellors that siblings 'be worked with individually, as well as with their parents and in support groups of brothers and sisters' (p. 295). Harvey *et al.* (1992) introduce the idea of 'account-making' as a way of finding meaning from a traumatic experience or loss. Noting that human beings have few resources to cope with the events which cause great grief, they focus on the ways in which people seek to adapt to loss though achieving changes in their understanding of self and the meaning of existence. 'Account-making' is the term they give to the process of resolving the dilemma and inter-preting the event through story-like construction. Some people keep a private journal or write poetry, as a means of gaining psychological control over the event, and detachment from the harrowing emotions. But it is not simply a mental reconstruction of events and memories of the deceased. Social interaction is also important, seen in confiding pieces of the account to friends and relatives. This confiding may resemble the private account, or selections from it, which are refined and reinterpreted through the experience of talking with another person. One young woman known to me wrote a eulogy which she read at her brother's funeral, in which she declared that 'he was more than my brother; he was my best friend'.

Given the school's importance as a context for friendship formation, it also has a role as a social system supporting adolescents who experience peer bereavement. It can play a part in creating group support and hosting opportunities for account-making to occur among the students and teachers affected. Many of those in the school experience awkwardness in ex-pressing support, and if left on their own are unsure what to say. McNeil *et al.* (1991) trace the grief reactions in a school following the death of a peer from a terminal illness. They noted that reactions to the boy's death were most acute among the boy's classmates, who were 'in a daze' for a week after his death. Teachers also reported feeling uncomfortable with their own feelings, and confused about what needed to be said to students. As a consequence, the grieving students perceived them as unapproachable. Fortunately, the school administration had initiated several activities to facilitate coping; these included a meeting to inform students on the day of the boy's death, a school assembly the next day, and class projects to prepare a memorial. These actions provided a structure for students to participate in the collective grief.

Attendance at the funeral is also an important aspect of peer memorial which school authorities would be wise to recognise. When a senior student attending a local Brisbane high school was killed in a motocross accident, so strong was the desire to express their collective grief that the whole senior year of eighty students petitioned the principal to be allowed to attend the funeral. Wisely, the principal agreed to their request.

SOCIAL REJECTION FROM PEERS

The desire for peer acceptance and group inclusion is a major motivating force in the everyday pursuit of social contact. From early in childhood, we develop a fine appreciation of the difference between being included in a group and being left out, and understand that the feelings of loneliness which arise from peer rejection are not the same as the feelings that accompany separation from a parent. From their observations of unpopular children in play situations Asher *et al.* (1990, p. 255) noted that the children 'often related loneliness to unfulfilled relationship provisions' such as companionship, belonging, inclusion, and reliable alliance. The examples which children gave were having no one to play with, feeling left out, and feeling that no one really knows you.

The concept of peer rejection in the developmental psychology literature is interpreted in terms of differences in peer status. Comparisons are made between the behaviour of those who are rejected and that of those who are popular or who have average status. This approach differs from that adopted in social psychology and clinical studies, where attention tends to be directed to the process of rejection itself. There may be excess meaning in the term 'rejected' where the procedure merely indicates which children are marginalised and not preferred (i.e., socially neglected), rather than actively rejected.

Observations of pre-adolescents in the classroom and the playground by Dodge *et al.* (1982) revealed that rejected-status children spent less time in class on appropriate kinds of independent seat-work activity, and more time in task-inappropriate activities, such as disrupting others, day-dreaming, and time wasting. They made more approaches to other pupils, distracting them from their schoolwork and prompting a hostile or unfriendly response. They required more teacher intervention or redirection. In the playground they changed groups frequently, and in negotiating group entry displayed more aggressive behaviour towards other children than did the majority of others in their age group. Dodge *et al.* (1982) interpret these patterns as suggesting that rejected-status children may be less competent at 'reading' the particular social script operating in the situation, and less skilful in knowing when to watch and listen and when to initiate social contact with those present. They may be more impetuous and pushy in group entry, whereas the popular children are more likely to ease themselves into the group, after they have taken time to understand its dynamics.

The barging-in strategy, on the other hand, attracts the tag of 'bully' or the disdainful label 'tryhard' rather than peer acceptance.

The distinction made by Dodge and Coie and their coworkers in the early 1980s between actively rejected children and those who were shy and ignored (who were labelled neglected) has proven useful in helping to differentiate the coping styles of socially isolated children. Earlier views which took aggression to be a defining characteristic of peer rejection and loneliness have been modified in the light of subsequent investigations (Cairns *et al.*, 1988; Coie *et al.*, 1990). One promising distinction is between rejected children who are aggressive and those who are unassertive or submissive.

Association of rejection with aggression

The significance of aggression as an attribute of rejected children has continued to challenge researchers. There is research evidence of an association between aggressive behaviour, low popularity, and social rejection: children who are disliked or unpopular are more aggressive than other children (e.g., Asher and Dodge, 1986; Coie and Dodge, 1983; Coie and Kupersmidt, 1983; Parkhurst and Asher, 1992). However, it cannot be concluded that children and adolescents who are aggressive are necessarily unpopular, and that their aggressive behaviour is reflected in, or a consequence of, a lack of friends. Aggression and popularity are not mutually exclusive characteristics, at least in adolescence. Some young people use aggression as a means of achieving group acceptance and exercising leadership. For example, Cairns *et al.* (1988) found that the highly aggressive 10–11-year-olds and 13–14-year-olds they studied had similar numbers of friends to those who were less aggressive, and, even though they were generally less liked by others of their own age, they rated themselves as being just as popular as their non-aggressive peers. Moreover, an analysis of the social networks of the aggressive group showed that they occupied very similar positions in these network structures to those of non-aggressive controls. On the basis of this evidence, Cairns *et al.* concluded that adolescents who are aggressive appear to have a reasonable degree of social competency, and could not be assumed to be socially inadequate. Although the younger age group had not yet developed a tendency for selective association on the basis of behaviour styles, the tendency was evident among the 13–14-year-olds, with aggressive 'birds of a feather' flocking together. Other investigators (e.g., Giordano *et al.*, 1986) also report this pattern, noting that teenage girls congregated with others who matched them in terms of socially deviant behaviour.

Rejection as a cause of antisocial behaviour

The consequences of peer rejection and peer unpopularity for the development of antisocial behaviour and educational problems are spelled out in several papers by Coie and his colleagues (Coie, 1990; Coie *et al.*, 1990; Kupersmidt *et al.*, 1990). They cite evidence from longitudinal studies that social deviancy in youth could be predicted from social rejection in childhood. Although it is easier to establish a link between aggression and later antisocial behaviour and delinquency than between peer rejection and delinquency, they suggest that rejection may be an early precursor to social deviancy. Across the years of childhood, the behavioural basis for social rejection gradually shifts from overt physical aggression to include indirect forms of aggressive behaviour as well. Thus a pattern of hostile coping with social relationships begins to develop, seen in the kid who cannot take a joke, or who is confrontationist and picks fights.

Peer rejection was also related to dropping out of school. When those who left school early were compared with those who stayed on at school, 46 per cent of the male early leavers were described by their teachers as socially rejected, compared with 7 per cent of those who stayed. Among the female students the pattern was less dramatic, 14 per cent of dropouts being defined as socially rejected, compared with 4 per cent of continuers.

Interaction styles and popularity

Dodge (1983) documented the unfolding differences in interaction style in 7- and 8-year-old boys who were previously unacquainted. Whereas the number of social approaches of the popular boys remained almost constant for each observational session, the approach patterns of the peer-rejected boys were quite different. They initially had a high rate of contact, moving about the group to obtain a play partner, but failing to find one. In later sessions they approached peers less often, engaged in less conversation, and showed growing isolation from other boys. One explanation for the negative reactions of the other boys towards them was their style of interaction, which was aggressive, intrusive, and physical. Dodge (1983, p. 1397) paints a profile of these rejected boys as showing 'antisocial behaviour and inept peer interaction'.

Parkhurst and Asher (1992) compared the behaviour and peer ratings of 13–15-year-olds with different peer status. The rejected-status adolescents were significantly more lonely than the popular students; but when the sub-groups of rejected adolescents were compared, the aggressives were similar to the average students, whereas the submissives were more lonely, and had greater levels of concern about being rejected or humiliated.

Parkhurst and Asher also looked for examples of adolescents who displayed aggressive or withdrawn coping styles but who were *not* classed as rejected, in order to explore the possibility that aggression and shyness are not in themselves sufficient for peer rejection. They found that most of the adolescents with aggressive and submissive characteristics were in fact not rejected, and were 'actually average in status' (p. 239), thus confirming what Cairns *et al.* (1988) have reported. Closer inspection of the peer ratings they had obtained on all their adolescent subjects showed that the rejected groups lacked 'positive interaction qualities' (Parker and Asher, 1993, p. 236). The aggressive sub-group of socially rejected adolescents was rated by peers as lacking in cooperativeness and trustworthiness, and the submissive sub-group was rated as unable to take a joke.

What can be concluded from the research on childhood rejection is that the sources of social rejection are to be found in children's social behaviour rather than in group labelling. Coie (1990, p. 367) argues that in acquiring status in the peer group, 'the behaviour of the child is primary and the behaviour of the peer group is secondary'. Children are active shapers of their own development, creating a niche in the peer group rather than having it assigned by others. The withdrawal of rejected children from the group, which Dodge and Coie have observed, is a response to their growing awareness of how others feel about them. As they recognise that they are unwanted they lose interest in participating in group activities. Acquisition of rejected status is therefore not simply a matter of group dynamics, but resides in a child's personality: 'there is something about the child that accounts for peer rejection' (Coie *et al.*, 1990, p. 45). The image of peer group determinism over social behaviour is overstated; groups are seldom so rigid or uncompromising that they demand conformity to set roles. There is typically a range of tolerance within a group for the way its members are to behave. An adolescent who may be marginal to the group may gain acceptance by acting as a fool and being the butt of jokes; if the jokes against her/him are tossed off in a light-hearted manner, the adolescent comes to be regarded as a bit mad but generally a good sport, whereas aggressive and defensive reactions to the jokes will alienate her/him from the group, as Parkhurst and Asher (1992) have shown. Unless the group itself has members with pathological problems which find expression through persistent scapegoating and victimising of those who are on the periphery, the socially marginal youth will win acceptance and gradually become integrated into the group, and the jokes made at her/his expense will decrease.

Peer group processes and rejection

There are signs of a gradual widening of the perspective on rejection and loneliness in the research field so as to take greater account of *the contexts of peer acceptance*, including the school and different sectors of the peer network, as several recent papers show (e.g., Claes, 1992; Parker and Asher, 1993; Renshaw and Brown, 1993). To mark this shift in perspective Parker and Asher (1993) have changed the name of the concept that has been the basis of the study of peer status from 'peer rejection' to 'peer acceptance'. This move allows them to focus on the role of different kinds of attachment relations in the experience of loneliness: close friendship as well as group acceptance. They provide evidence in support of the view that these two sources of social affirmation serve different functions in adjustment. A finding of particular interest is that children without a best friend reported being more lonely than those with a best friend, regardless of the extent of group acceptance they enjoyed, as measured by the number of sociometric choices they received. This study raises questions about the threshold of acceptance from peers in alleviating feelings of loneliness. Perhaps having just one good friend may compensate somewhat for the lack of a wider network of friends and acquaintances. Only more extensive research can determine whether the attachment relations provided by one friend are sufficient to ensure normal adjustment in childhood, and to ward off the uncertainties about being liked, being left out of peer activities, and consequently feeling lonely.

It is not clear from these studies of childhood contexts whether having a single friend would be sufficient in the more diverse social world of adolescence to prevent feelings of social loneliness. 'Friends' is overwhelmingly a group concept in adolescence, and the peer group value system emphasises the desirability of young people having 'lots' of friends and being part of a crowd. Adolescents who manifestly have few friends and do not feel that they fit into the larger crowd see a discrepancy between their experience and what is promoted as the norm, namely 'lots of friends', and feel deprived. They may attribute the perceived deficit of friends to personal inadequacy, in the belief that lacking a wide circle of friends means that there is something wrong with them.

Despite the valuable insights gained into the role of social skills in enabling children and adolescents to gain some standing within their group of peers, the group processes contributing to rejection and loneliness remain unclear. There is a difference between studying the behavioural patterns of those defined as rejected or lonely and examining the conditions whereby rejection and loneliness occur. If we are to avoid the tautological trap of trait psychology (expressed in the words of Polonius: 'to define true madness, what is it but to be mad?'), we must acknowledge the influence of context and situation in generating the experiences of rejection and loneliness. The adolescent period is characterised by a rich language of rejection, employed to differentiate those who are not 'in' the group from the group members, and as a means of social control within the peer group. Terms like *thick, dweeb, dork, dropkick, mental, loser, moron, spaz, deadhead, foetus,* and numerous others are part of an ever-changing litany of insult which rains down upon adolescents from their peers each day. Over one hundred insult terms were listed in the October 1990 Australian issue of *Dolly* magazine, and doubtless new terms have emerged since then.

Formal school structures such as pastoral care, camps, and extra-curricular activities are useful ways of integrating the lonely students into groups of their peers, but it is not sufficient for schools to create these structures and then assume that lonely students have been catered for. Attention has to be given to working on the process of inclusiveness as well. Teachers can model inclusiveness, and encourage their students to be open and accepting; and they can ensure that the group structures which the school puts in place contain levels of safety which allow the social risks of involvement of a lonely or rejected student to be of manageable proportions. When a graduate students' common room was set up in a department at Cornell University, the head of department regularly took lunch there so that the function of the room was established, and so that any student intending to go there in the lunch hour would not be discouraged from doing so by finding the room was empty.

SOCIAL SKILLS AND COPING PATTERNS

Are lonely people deficient in social skills? Is the problem of loneliness of their own making? If so, does it derive from a history of childhood problems which contribute to current social inadequacies, or is it a result of group processes which marginalise the lonely adolescent? Some answers have been provided in this chapter, drawn from research. The way practitioners answer these questions will determine their response to the problems of adolescent loneliness.

The argument that patterns of coping are established early in life and are embedded in the personality is prominent in many developmental theories of personality. Bowlby's thesis is that early experiences of rejection and loss contribute a working model of social relationships which is ill fitted for the development of appropriate later close attachments. In his book on separation, Bowlby (1974) reviews evidence in support of this thesis from a dozen longitudinal studies of personality development, and Shaver and Hazan (1989) supply evidence from studies of college students and newspaper respondents for a link between styles of attachment established in child-hood and patterns of relationship intimacy, including differences in the levels of loneliness.

Social skills of lonely people

Evidence has accumulated to show that lonely people have poor self-esteem and lack confidence in their own abilities, and that they hold negative and disparaging views of others (e.g., Jones *et al.*, 1981; Levin and Stokes, 1986; Wittenberg and Reis, 1986). A reading of Wildermuth's (1990) review suggests that individuals may contribute to their own lone-liness. For example, over-concern with gaining acceptance makes them extremely sensitive to any hint of peer rejection, and negatively distorts the social messages which others are sending. Second, pessimism over the outcomes of social interaction colours their expectations of others' be-haviour towards them, and contributes to lower rates of inclusion in social activities. Expectations and attitudes, both in respect of self (seen in out-going personality, social confidence) and in relation to others (non-judgmental attitudes to others, positive attitude to friendship), appear to contribute to peer acceptance and likeability.

In her study tracing the social experiences of beginning college students who remained lonely all year, compared with those who overcame their initial loneliness, Cutrona (1982) found that the differences in success appeared to be related to subtle variations in attitudes and expectations. The students who overcame their initial loneliness were found to hold higher expectations about finding friends than the students who continued to be lonely. The latter students lowered their goals, deciding that they did not need a lot of friends, or that they would focus on their work rather than on their social life. Others decided that the only way of alleviating their loneliness was to seek out an intense romantic alliance. They appeared to have given up hope of making friends and being accepted into a group; instead of working at improving their friendships they had decided to narrow their search for companionship to a single other.

Those who are lonely may have conversational difficulties. Among the deficits in social skills which have been listed are these: difficulty in initiating conversations; difficulty in engaging in intimate communica-tions; and difficulty in making appropriate kinds of self-disclosure. Observations report that lonely people are less talkative, ask fewer ques-tions, and recall less of the other person's conversation than non-lonely people. They are seen to be more self-focused and less able to refer to the other person. Peplau *et al.* (1982) also report that lonely people have a self-blaming style which is intolerant of their own faults. This makes them vulnerable to doubts and falling levels of confidence whenever they do make attempts to become socially active. Moreover, the strategies employed by lonely adolescents during periods of loneliness may follow a non-social pattern of coping: Roscoe and Skomski (1989) report a greater use of actions such as listening to music, reading, writing letters or a diary, forgetting it, sleeping, or taking a drive, thus thwarting efforts to alleviate loneliness, whereas non-lonely adolescents were more likely to talk with someone or find some activity to join in with others. The non-lonely also had greater involvement in professional groups, held more leadership positions, and belonged to other social groups more than did the lonely.

It is not easy for adolescents who are lonely or shy, or who have experienced rejection from peers, to overcome their hesitancy consciously in order to seek support from competent adults. To establish contact with a teacher, counsellor, or youth leader, then engage her/him in casual conversation, broach one's topic of concern, and request assistance or advice, requires the exercise of the very social skills and competencies that may be lacking. The direct approach to help seeking may be harder to implement than it looks, as some studies indicate. For example, East (1989) studied the perceptions of risks in seeking support among adolescents aged 12, and found those with low self-esteem were more sensitive to the risk of rejection than those with stronger self-worth. They expected to feel embarrassed, anticipated difficulties in social situations, and were poised to instigate self-protection strategies when these feelings were aroused. These lonely or less confident young people also perceived fewer benefits from others' social support.

Training social skills

If the social self is still under construction during adolescence, that same tentativeness about the self-concept may undermine confidence when things do not work out right. It is in these situations that specific social skills training may benefit the adolescent. The behavioural approach of Meichenbaum (1977) provides a useful practical method of working with the negative self-talk which interferes with the confident performance of a learned skill. Considerable value could be served by working with young people concerning their attributions for loneliness, their 'theories in use', and the relative weighting they give to personal traits over circumstances.

One of the most readable outlines of a social skills training programme is given by Lindsay (1987). His programme may be viewed as focusing on three skills areas: (1) recognising and interpreting communications, both verbal and non-verbal; (2) conversation skills, which addresses the strategies of initiating conversation, continuing a conversation, and breaking into a conversation group; and (3) situation management, which teaches adolescents how to be assertive, how to keep out of trouble with peers, and how to handle authority figures. Lindsay reserves the topic of interacting with the opposite sex to one of the final sessions, by which time 'a trusting atmosphere' has been established, and a set of social skills has already been acquired, both of which will assist the therapist in addressing a crucially important and anxiety-ridden topic. Lindsay warns that the programme's effectiveness may be undermined by difficulties which are attributable to differences in the social values and standards for social behaviour that may exist between therapist and teenage group. He suggests one way of increasing the social validity of the skills being taught is to incorporate knowledge of the composition of the adolescents' social network into the methods of maintaining the exercise of social skills.

The studies reviewed in this chapter also have implications for schools seeking to establish peer support networks for adolescents who are lonely, rejected, or depressed. Teachers need to understand a good deal about the conversational skills of the age group, and the extent of motivation among normal teenagers to befriend the friendless. La Gaipa and Wood (1981, p. 186) found that ease of communication is 'particularly important' for establishing healthy relationships between normal and disturbed adolescents. They point to the difficulties experienced by normally adjusted adolescents when relating to unhappy or depressed people of their own age, and note (p. 180) that interactions may be 'characterised by uncertainty, awkwardness, hesitancy and tension'. Referring to the issue of bereavement, Balk (1990) advocates educational programmes which train adolescents in attending behaviour, both attentive listening and empathic responding. These communication skills are of course valuable in all kinds of peer support network.

While it may be possible to devise programmes to support some lonely and depressed adolescents, what seems necessary is the involvement of skilled adults both in introducing a young person to a clique, and in teaching and modelling social behaviours which can assist the clique members to make that person feel accepted. A suggestion for the way adults could assist in developing supportive behaviour in school groups comes from the work of Gottlieb (1991); this is not only to train the lonely person in ways of communicating her/his need for support, but also to teach those who are in a position to provide support how to be more skilful in recognising when it is needed as well as in providing openings which allow support to be given. In short, an aspect of support which merits emphasis is that it requires reciprocal behaviour from the participants. This reciprocality is portrayed in Box 4.2.

Box 4.2 Reciprocality of supportive relationships

SUPPORT GIVER:	SUPPORT RECEIVER:
Available and accessible.	Able to signal an invitation to the
Recognises other's needs for	other to provide help.
support.	Perceives when help is being
Able to analyse what supportive	offered.
behaviour is appropriate.	Accepts the help of other.
Skilled in offering help in a way	
that the other will accept.	

CONCLUSION: IMPLICATIONS FOR BEFRIENDING LONELY ADOLESCENTS

What we have discussed in this chapter emphasises that the social processes contributing to loneliness and rejection, as well as supports to alleviate these negative states, involve exchanges between the person and social contexts over a period of time. The process whereby an adolescent's status is determined in the classroom group or within the group of her/his peers may be viewed as an accumulation of social exchanges which define her/his standing in the group. The interactions may not necessarily involve overt rejection or exclusion, because the subtlety of the group process does not require it. The sense of rejection, of feeling not wanted or not part of the group, may be inferred from the group interaction processes themselves: body posture, lack of eye contact, selective naming of people, deferring to the views of some members and ignoring those of others. In these ways, the group can effectively define the status and prestige of a particular member, curb that member's role in the group, and influence the member's self-definition. Cartwright and Zander (1960, p. 652) stated that 'A person's rank in an ordering of people according to prestige makes a great deal of difference to [his] behaviour, [his] interactions with others, [his] level of aspiration, and [his] self-evaluation.'

Settings as well as individuals contribute to social and emotional loneliness; shopping malls, playgrounds, school lunch hours, and sports centres can be socially alienating environments as well as sociable and friendly ones. The concerned adult will be interested in creating settings which are less alienating, both through contributing to the formal rule structures of the setting, and by attending to the informal group processes, with the goal of reducing feelings of social loneliness for the solitary teenager. Wellman (1981) reminds us that most adults have met their friends through institutional structures, not highly informal ones. The structured social settings which young people inhabit, such as classrooms, sports and hobby clubs, and church and voluntary organisations, are more important influences in the development of skills for social relations than the unstructured and informal leisure places where teenagers hang out – the shopping malls, takeaways, and amusement centres. Youth may practise and refine their social skills in these informal settings, but it is in the structured settings that these skills should be taught and learned.

Part II
Social influences

Introduction

Many of the themes addressed in the following chapters assume that some kind of social influence process is at work. Where adolescents are concerned, social influence is usually defined as peer influence or peer pressure, a theme which keeps reappearing in the subtext of newspaper stories and in snatches of conversation heard on buses and in the office, and a topic mulled over by friends at dinner parties. Peer influence is not only a concern of parents of teenagers; it is a factor in the work of educators, youth workers, and other professional groups who come into contact with young people. Although the influence of peers is beneficial to many aspects of social development, peer pressure is generally viewed as a powerful negative force in young people's lives, and one which adult society has difficulty in neutralising.

Social influence is exerted in face-to-face encounters between the adolescent and others, and is considered in terms of group conformity; but there are indirect forms of influence as well, including various kinds of social referencing, and influences derived from socialisation processes which span a considerable period of time to shape underlying values and attitudes. References to these various kinds of influence criss-cross each other in the research on adolescence, like the tracks of holiday makers on a summer beach. Detecting which of the theoretical trails lead to the water's edge, to yield some refreshing solace to the search, is no easy task. There is no general theory of social influence, apart from a paper by Parsons in 1963; nor is it likely there will be, because scholars see the relationships between the social environment and individual behaviour from different perspectives.

Discussions of social influence are linked to assumptions about friendship ties and group affiliation, and notions of group norms and social frames of reference. They imply that the individual is not entirely a free agent, but is a product of social relationships which exert influences on beliefs, attitudes, and behaviour; and take for granted that the person is only partly aware of the extent to which her/his behaviour, attitudes, and beliefs are shaped by social forces.

Peer pressure is not necessarily negative, although it tends to be discussed in this way in Part II of this book, where it is linked to the concept of group conformity (e.g., Berndt, 1979; Costanzo, 1970; Costanzo and Shaw, 1966; Sherif and Sherif, 1964). The concept was derived from Sherif's experiments where people were placed in a room with strangers and asked to make judgments about what were essentially ambiguous phenomena. Evidence of a person deferring to group opinion was interpreted as susceptibility to peer group pressure. Application of this research to adolescents suggests that conformity to peers increases from childhood to adolescence, and that adolescents are most susceptible to peer pressure at about the age of 13 or 14 years, although Brown *et al.* (1986a), using a different approach, found that for antisocial and for neutral behaviour, conformity peaked at a slightly older point, varying from 14 to 16 years of age. Brown *et al.* (1986a) distinguished between perceptions of peer normative pressure and actual conformity to these norms. Perceived pressures to engage in misbehaviour, as distinct from actual conformity to such pressures, were found to increase steadily with age, and were felt more strongly by males than by females. However, being aware of pressures from peers to misbehave at school does not mean that adolescents blindly follow. Indeed, Brown *et al.* show that the majority of adolescents are more susceptible to positive peer influences at school than to negative ones.

The greater conformity of younger adolescents to the opinions of others has been related to cognitive development and desire for acceptance, but a neglected explanation for the increased susceptibility to peer influences, and more so to antisocial influences in early adolescence, may relate to changes in the social field. Change in environment tends to introduce new members to the person's social network, and to reduce its density. Research on social networks (Barnes, 1954; Bott, 1957/1971) has pointed out that densely knit networks constrain behaviour. People who are embedded in their network by close and multiplex ties with others are bound by the obligations in these relationships to behave according to the expectations of network members.

In Chapter 5 the influences of peers are viewed in relation to the social environment of school and the peer groups which it contains. These peer groups widen the range of social identities available to young people, with consequences for undermining academic motivation as well as for induction into health risk behaviour and other forms of social deviancy. A consequence of moving into a larger junior high school is an increase in the pool of potential peer associates, who are unlikely to be known to many previous network members. Growth in loose-knit network ties will see a reduction in network density, and the normative constraints exercised over the actor's behaviour by established network members will also be weakened. Researchers have commented on the greater anonymity felt by students entering the high school (Cotterell, 1992; Jones and Thornburg, 1985), as well as on an associated increase in early adolescents' misconduct.

The same network changes may be invoked to explain the decline in crowd affiliation reported by Brown *et al.* (1986b) in late adolescence, where older adolescents became increasingly less willing to go along with the crowd. It would seem that as adolescents reach the senior years of high school, they are better able to manage their network relations so as to belong to a loose crowd membership but rely more for support and identity development on their relations with a more intimate group of friends. The crucial role of both the crowd and the circle of best friends is explored in Chapter 6 in terms of the power to influence adolescents in smoking and drinking, and is related to the leisure contexts of adolescents.

The broader public environment is the framework for youth behaviour in Chapter 7, which examines the social influence processes contained in street groups and in mass crowds, and the methods used to induce young people to engage in antisocial forms of public behaviour. Group processes are discussed both as intragroup forces which bind individuals into the group and in terms of intergroup activity, including hostility and bullying. These group influence processes are applied to the problems of football hooliganism and youth revelry, bearing in mind that adolescents are young people looking for a bit of fun rather than the media portrayals of them as vandals or yobbos.

5 The influence of the school on social relations

This chapter revisits the peer group structures of cliques, crowds, and gangs and looks at their operations when nested within the social system of the school. Secondary schools contain large numbers of young people who are separated from the wider society for sufficiently long periods of time each day for them to develop a social world of their own within the school. The extent to which there is a distinct peer society in high school seems to vary within Western societies, being stronger in the American high school than elsewhere (see Coleman, 1961; Brown, 1989), but in most parts of the world, the school and its classrooms are important arenas for peer group formation and friendship relations. Indeed, adolescent relationships are formed and refashioned to a great extent within the social environments which young people inhabit at school. But the school is more than just a backdrop for social interaction; its settings, organisational structures, and activities also exert influences in various ways on the nature of students' values, attitudes, and motivations.

In most Western countries, secondary schools are under strain. Their demography has been changing in recent decades, a consequence of increased participation from adolescents who previously left school as soon as they reached the school leaving age. As more and more of the youth of the nation remain in schools till their eighteenth and nineteenth birthdays, the school consumes an increasing amount of young people's waking lives, but not necessarily of their commitment. The school is the major social environment where peer networks are established, but it is also a major arena for clarifying future goals and determining a work-based identity. Through relationships with peers and with teachers, adolescent identity is shaped in ways which are critical to their future career and life-path.

The theme of this chapter is the school as a motivational environment, and the way personal motivations formulated in early adolescence contribute to the young person's development along the life-path. It is in the classroom and peer group settings of school that adolescent motivation is shaped, including attachment to school as well as alienation and classroom disaffection. There are two aspects of the young adolescent's experience in secondary school which are central to our concerns: the effects of immersion in the adolescent peer society, and the increased distancing from teachers and remoteness of teacher support. We consider the influences of these two major players, teachers and peers, in the settings of high school, guided by the following questions: how is peer influence manifest? Is it pro-school or anti-school? What role do teachers play in shaping student identities in the classroom? What effect does the school organisational structure itself have in shaping peer society? Mindful that schools are multi-level environments where classrooms and other social situations are nested within other settings, we begin with the broad school system and then focus in turn on classrooms and teacher–student relations.

EFFECTS OF CHANGES IN SCHOOL ORGANISATION

Young people experience considerable changes in the environments associated with their education: they change schools, sometimes several times in the course of their secondary education; and they change classes and teachers with grinding regularity. Some critics see the effect of these changes in school in terms of declines in academic achievement, particularly for youngsters with immature personality development (e.g., Nisbet and Entwistle, 1969); others draw attention to the vulnerability of young adolescents to a range of health risk behaviours as well as psychological risk, and attribute the onset of these risks to the growth of peer influences and the increased distancing from adult society which occur with secondary schooling. The alienating effects of the high-school environment on young adolescents' attitudes, motivation, self-concepts, and school achievement have been a topic of concern for over fifty years in commissioned reports and research studies. Many of the reports have acknowledged the contributing influences of the social ecological characteristics of the secondary school, particularly population size and social climate, as in the recent report of the Carnegie Council on Adolescent Development (1989) in the United States and Australian reports by the National Board of Employment, Education and Training (1993).

One of the most obvious mistakes made in American education, notes Entwistle (1990), was the decision in the 1960s to enlarge the high school and consolidate smaller local schools into mammoth institutions housing thousands of students. The presumed efficiencies of resource use have been elusive, and accompanied by lower levels of student participation in school activities, increased apathy, misbehaviour, and violence, and the loss of capability on the part of the school system to be responsive to student needs. Although it is known that smaller schools are associated with warmer and more cohesive climates, more chances for each student to participate in key roles, and greater student commitment to pro-social values (see Barker and Gump, 1964; Lindsay, 1984), governments have viewed schools as subject to the same management principles of efficiency through economies of scale as are found in other production units.

Schools for young adolescents

Because of the proven inadequacy of these high-school environments to cater for the needs of younger adolescents, the problems of transition to secondary education have re-emerged in recent years, in the United States and in other countries. Evidence of a decline in school achievement and of reduced participation in extra-curricular activities following the move into secondary school is widely reported (e.g., Blyth *et al.*, 1978; Eccles and Midgley, 1989; Felner *et al.*, 1982; Power and Cotterell, 1981). The effects of transition may also be manifest in greater levels of apathy and disaffection among young adolescents, and classroom misconduct. The problems for students have always been there; they may be summed up as environmental discontinuity. The high schools are a world apart from the primary school environment which youngsters have known: their organisation is larger and more complex, their curriculum more diverse, their administration more distant, and teaching dispersed so that students may encounter six or seven different teachers within the course of a single day.

Moreover, the high schools are less person-oriented, and thus deny young adolescents the opportunity to build attachments with teachers in the way that they had been able to do in primary school. The discontinuities in size, curriculum, and social organisation affect the sense of belongingness. They are reflected in student difficulties in making an initial adjustment to the new environment, as well as in difficulties in mastering the academic demands of secondary school. Students report a sense of uneasiness and disconnection when they move into secondary school; and the demeaning terms which these adolescents use to describe themselves – 'ants', 'worms', 'grubs', 'babies', 'nothings' – underline their sense of insignificance (Cotterell, 1992). They find the new school unsympathetic and unsupportive. One diarist wrote, 'As soon as I got here I thought it was terrible. I was lost completely and I didn't know anybody. After a while I found out that nobody cared about you so I had to make friends by myself and do everything by myself' (Power and Cotterell, 1979, p. 109).

In the United States, where high schools had emerged in the latter part of last century, a separate junior-high-school structure began to appear early this century, expressly to cater for the distinctive mental, social, emotional, and vocational concerns of younger adolescents, which authorities of the time acknowledged were in danger of being neglected. Regrettably, Cuban (1992) suggests, the plan has failed. The junior high school that emerged soon imitated the senior high school. In urban areas it has now become a large school, with populations of over a thousand students in one grade, remote administrations, separate academic departments, teachers who teach separate subjects, and students grouped by ability rather than in heterogeneous classes. Similar disappointment has been expressed with middle schools (e.g., Jackson and Hornbeck, 1989), introduced in the 1960s as a solution to the junior-high problem; they too have increasingly come to resemble the structures they sought to replace. They have grown in size and become departmentalised, and their teaching staff have become distanced from young people at the very age when accessibility to adults is an important factor in identity development. In the opinion of Hirsch and Dubois (1989, p. 261) the American junior-high structure 'appears to set up obstacles to developing and maintaining friends'. No provision is made for students to belong to an intact class group; instead, students follow their own independent timetable of classes, with the consequence that a student can be with a different set of classmates during each of the lessons s/he takes during the day. The institutional climate seems productive of alienation in boys and girls at the very point of their school careers where they have the opportunity for new beginnings. One boy remarked to Power and Cotterell (1979, p. 115): 'I felt very left out. It felt very impersonal.' Once routine has become established, the school does not seem to rouse itself to open out its treasures to the students. Structures of support and encouragement to the newcomers seem lacking. Thus, instead of creating environments sympathetic to the needs of younger adolescents, these structures replicate the impersonality of the senior high school, and inherit its problems.

Despite the introduction of junior highs and middle schools ostensibly to create a better community, there continues to be a developmental mismatch between the secondary-school environments and those of the elementary schools, which has marked the transition to secondary education as a period of vulnerability for young adolescents, in terms of lower academic achievement, psychological maladjustment, and initiation into risk behaviour. As social systems, the large and impersonal high schools and junior highs have failed to create the kinds of attachment and belonging which theory would suggest is desirable for young people. The concerns of adolescents have gone unheeded in the approach taken by governments to the provision of mass secondary education, as major reports make clear. In her review of services for younger adolescents, commissioned in the late 1970s by the Ford Foundation, Lipsitz (1980, pp. 86–87) remarked that:

We have no societal sensitivity to the developmental importance of early adolescence. We lack even the pragmatic, if less sensitive, vision to see this age group as at least pivotal in the schooling process. It is our 'missing link'!

In its report on schooling for early adolescents, the Carnegie Council urged that 'the situation must change drastically', and singled out the need for teaching staff 'to invest their efforts in the young adolescent . . . and understand and want to teach [them]' (1989, p. 58). The issues raised by the North American research are not isolated to that part of the world, although they may be more acute there. In Australia, teacher groups have urged that more attention in secondary education be directed 'upstream' to the early adolescent years, rather than downstream to the exit point. Recognising that alienation and disaffection must take root before they flower, they have canvassed ways of rewarding teachers for specialising in early adolescence and of overcoming the negative image which is associated with teaching this age group.

EFFECTS OF AGE MIXING ON YOUNG ADOLESCENTS

The demography of secondary schools – their population size and age mix – constitutes the school's social environment, with consequences for motivation and antisocial behaviour. Concern is often expressed that the presence of older adolescents is likely to have negative effects on the attitudes and behaviour of younger adolescents. The creation of middle schools and junior highs in the United States was in part an attempt to insulate younger adolescents from the negative influences of older peers on their behaviour. Both social and educational benefits were seen in locating younger adolescents in separate school structures, physically apart from older students. Restriction of one's social world to that which is predominantly populated by others of the same age seems likely to decrease individual susceptibility to negative influences associated with the behaviour of older peers, but while such arrangements may limit risk to their client population, what opportunities are provided by schools for meaningful social contact and growth in social competence? In other words, are the organisational structures created for younger adolescents merely protective or truly developmental? Two longitudinal studies which explored these questions are reviewed; each examined the effects of organisational changes within the same schools on aspects of social relations, where the same students experienced different school structures in successive years of schooling.

Case studies of changes in age mixing

Allen (1989) took advantage of an alteration within a junior high school containing seventh, eighth, and ninth graders to examine the effects of the different organisational arrangements on friendship choices and competence. Students were grouped in three 'houses' which were highly similar in all respects, except that one house had adopted a mixed-age organisation of its classes in contrast with the age-segregated pattern found in the other houses. The curriculum of the mixed-age house was less locked to age cohorts and more topic-oriented than that found in the other two houses, since it was accommodating different ages in the same class. Classes in the other houses were composed of grade seven, or grade eight, or grade nine students.

When the friendship choices of students in the two structures were compared, it was found that for adolescents in the age-mixed structure, proportionately more regular friends and more best friends were drawn from different age groups than was true for adolescent students in age-segregated structures. However, the total number of friends listed was similar in each house, and there were no differences in competence levels. In further analyses, Allen examined the relations between individuals' social competence and the proportion of older or younger friendships they reported. These analyses suggested that the most socially adept adolescents associated primarily with peers of the same age, and that the young people who had formed friendships with peers who were younger or older than themselves tended to have lower estimates of their own competence and popularity.

Allen interprets his findings as confirming the strong normative preference for same-age friendships among these upper-middle-class American teenagers; he sees the adolescents with friendships which do not fit the norm as expressing less confidence in themselves. This explanation may be appropriate for the ninth graders who mixed with younger ages, but it sits less well with the seventh graders who had older friends. Access to older friends in the mixed-age settings may have created greater dissonance in the minds of these seventh graders about their social maturity than would have been the case in age-segregated settings. These younger adolescents may therefore have devalued their competence because their access to an older, presumably more competent group of peers provided a frame of reference which led them to be more critical of themselves. In developmental terms, such dissonance could be expected to generate greater developmental change over time.

Blyth *et al.* (1981) focused on the effects of changes in the age mix of schools on peer group contexts. Their general concern was to assess whether there were negative effects of the presence of older students on

participation in activities, on experiences of being victimised, dating behaviour, and substance abuse, and on students' perceptions of school
climate (such as feelings of anonymity). The schools which were investigated consisted in the first year of two junior highs with seventh to ninth
graders, and a senior high with tenth to twelfth graders. The schools were
reorganised the following year to form two new junior highs for seventh
and eighth graders, an intermediate high containing ninth and tenth graders,
and a senior high for eleventh and twelfth graders. Thus younger
adolescents were housed with ninth graders in the first year, and separated
from them in the second year; on the other hand, the ninth graders were in
a school with younger age groups in the first year, and with tenth graders in
the second year. Blyth *et al.* were interested in comparing the experiences
of the grade seven and eight students across the two years (when they lost
an older age group) with those of the ninth graders (who lost a younger age
group and gained an older one in the same period).

The analyses showed that removal of the older students improved the
social opportunities of the younger adolescents (the seventh and eighth
graders), while inclusion of the ninth graders in a school with students older
than themselves had generally negative effects. For the seventh and eighth
graders, the most consistent effects of being separated from the older
students were seen in their positive perceptions of the school environment,
which they felt had less anonymity and a greater sense of teacher control.
Boys reported less victimisation such as physical threats and drug offers, as
well as less actual cigarette and marijuana use. The decline in substance use
appeared to reflect changes in the peer norms following the transfer of the
ninth graders to the intermediate high school.

Effects of changes in the age mix were also found among the ninth grade
group who were placed with tenth graders in the second year of the study.
Here the social experiences of the ninth graders following the organisational
change were less favourable: they reported lower levels of participation in
school activities and in school leadership roles than in the previous year,
higher levels of substance abuse, more victimisation (for the boys), and a
sense of greater anonymity in the new school. For these adolescent
youngsters, the presence of older students appeared to increase the number
of models of antisocial behaviour, while at the same time it restricted their
opportunity to participate in healthy forms of school activity.

ALIENATION AND COMMITMENT

The school context is distinctive in that engagement in present activities is
linked to outcomes in the future, including outcomes in contexts distant
from those of the school. When discrepancies are sensed between school

tracks and the pathways to adult success, commitment to school may diminish. The routines of school generate disaffection and apathy. Students get a sense of 'serving their time' at school without perceiving that they have grown and developed socially and intellectually, in ways valued by society. The weakening link between school curriculum and the economy prompted Musgrave (1985, p. 298) to ask, 'How can teachers . . . prepare adolescents to be successful in life . . . whilst at the same time preparing them for the unemployment that they will increasingly have to endure?' In her research on school leavers, Poole (1983, p. 110) asked, 'What turns adolescents away from future planning and from sociable contacts with others? What makes them defensive and anxious in existing school structures?'

Central to an understanding of youth alienation is the extent to which identity is problematic. The emerging identity is shaped in part by the social environment of the school: the role possibilities it offers, the coping processes it fosters, the resources for identity exploration it provides. Foote (1951) linked identity to motivation, asserting that 'when doubt of identity creeps in, action is paralysed' (p. 18) because of the loss of meaning. Others refer to the way youth have become 'redundant' in modern society (Andersson, 1992) and 'roleless', so that they are 'insulated from the real business of life', and from the opportunity to give service and have significance (Nightingale and Wolverton, 1993, p. 481). Part of the difficulty for youth lies in our individualistic approach to success and failure. The ideology of individual striving and responsibility is a contributing factor in the production of alienation in school when young people have difficulty in seeing the link between present behaviour and future outcomes.

In an essay where he reflects on the shortcomings of schooling from a developmental perspective, Andersson (1992) reports Swedish research that finds a decrease in competency from elementary grades to those of junior high. He notes that school leavers interviewed by Dahlgren in 1985 described school as 'a complete waste of time'; the activities were meaningless, they could not understand the lessons, and 'the only thing they learned was that they were totally worthless'. A study in Swedish by Hammarstrom in 1986 is cited, which examined whether there were psychological costs for youth who continued at school when they preferred to leave. Greater psychological disturbance was found among the group of 'conscripted' returnees than among other stayers. A similar conclusion was made about the schooling experiences of Scottish youth from analyses of several recent surveys, leading Furlong (1989, p. 51) to state that the psychological health of those who continued with their schooling was 'worse than those on Youth Training Schemes or in jobs'. Many students who continue at school may not regard experiences of further schooling as a buffer against the risk of later unemployment.

Emergence of a new alienation

The concept of alienation was originally employed by Marx to capture the sense of social separation between the worker and her/his work, which left the work devoid of meaning and purpose. Later writers, especially those writing during and after the Second World War, linked alienation with notions of marginalisation and estrangement from social institutions, producing a pervading loneliness and distrust of others, and a loss of value and purpose in their lives. Seeman (1959) traced the theme of alienation through the classical works of Marx, Weber, and Durkheim to the writings of Merton, Mannheim, and others during the 1940s, and identified five basic meanings of alienation. These are *powerlessness*: the sense of being unable to influence events which affect oneself; *meaninglessness*: the sense of being unclear as to what one ought to believe in order to be able to act intelligently; *normlessness*: being located in situations where the social norms have broken down and are no longer able to regulate behaviour; *social isolation*: the sense of being apart from the goals and beliefs held by society in general; and *self-estrangement*: the loss of intrinsic meaning in one's work and the absence of pride and contentment in one's daily activity.

In the current societal context, where youth access to the workforce is increasingly delayed, and replaced by extended forms of education and training, a new kind of alienation appears to be emerging. According to Conger and Petersen (1984, p. 607), this new alienation is 'more subtle, elusive and private' than the dissent of youth in the 1960s and closer to the anomie described in Seeman's (1959) review of earlier understandings. In older youth it is characterised by a lack of purpose and direction, difficulties in forming a career identity, and reluctance to make commitments to future plans; in younger adolescents it presents as carelessness and lack of persistence with respect to classroom activities. Furlong (1991) describes such students as disaffected. Musgrave (1985, p. 293) suggests that such signs of disaffection, though not permanent, denote a mood state wherein one crosses a 'threshold' of alienation on the basis of declining attachments to features of the school, including relations with teachers and the meaning of classroom tasks.

If we look upstream for sources of student alienation, the ability of the high school to answer the social as well as academic concerns of adolescents may be questioned. Upon entering secondary school, the friendship network from primary school may for a time provide a supportive micro-environment which reduces the symptoms of adjustment difficulties for students, but there are no long-term beneficial effects (see Hirsch and Dubois, 1992). The types of stress experienced in junior high school differ from those encountered in the transition phase, and pertain more broadly to academic adjustment and establishing a niche in the adolescent world of high school. The creeping sense of disaffection with school is captured in the blunt comments of a year-eight boy: 'It was good the first couple of weeks, to change classrooms every half hour. It was easy to get lost, but now it's just the same. We do everything the same every day' (Power and Cotterell, 1979, p. 115).

Classroom life

Classroom life comprises large numbers of discrete tasks, the meaning of which becomes obscured under a mountain of routine activities. Students come to view their classwork as lacking in meaning, in that many of the tasks given them in school seem designed just to keep them busy. What I wish to suggest is that resistance and disaffection in classrooms at secondary school may be a logical response by some students, frustrated by the overwhelming concern with work tasks at the expense of fostering social meaning in classroom relationships. The significance of a distant goal like becoming a dress designer or journalist or marine biologist is subsumed under more present meanings like 'We have to do this, even though it is boring, because it's included in our assessment', and these latter meanings prompt avoidance behaviour. A cautionary note is expressed by Doyle (1986, p. 374), who says, 'In many hours of classroom observation, I have seldom seen students accomplish tasks in which they are required to struggle for meaning.'

Shifting one's focus to the class rather than the individual members allows us to see the meaning of classroom tasks as constructed by classroom members as they share in the common experience of being, for example, in the year-ten geography class with Mrs Sloan. Just as factory workers create a culture, so the students create one, based on shared understandings of their roles as students as well as on the knowledge base of geography. From this viewpoint, devising their own social and interpersonal goals is a way of making meaning out of classroom experiences when the tasks are boring and bereft of significance, and are thus unable of themselves to sustain student attention. In these circumstances, adolescent students seek out their peers in order to alter the classroom goals in ways which are intended to make the task more palatable.

Dropping out of school as a failure of attachment

Some students find difficulty in finding meaning in school tasks and connecting to the school; and lacking a sense of attachment they drop out altogether. Circumstances such as the experience of failure, and exclusion from a desired group, can contribute to the weakening of attachment to school. Holden and Dwyer make the point that early school leaving does not necessarily indicate a rejection of education as such, 'but rather the structures that exist within the school system' (1992, p. 22). Attachment and commitment are related to social integration in various educational writings, both at the college level and at the school level. For example, Finn (1989) follows Hirschi's (1969) theory of social bonds, and locates the school dropout syndrome within a participation–identification model, where identification is an internal state, concerned with belonging and valuing, and participation is the outward sign of a sense of identification. Indicators of participation include verbal responses and on-task behaviour in class, the allocation of time and energy to learning and study out of class, and active participation in sport, school government, and social activities.

The perspective of the dropout and school-leaver studies is on the relation between the individual and the school system, and the conclusions drawn tend to be based upon the motives and attitudes of individual adolescents. Thus one can easily overlook the contribution of the school environment itself to student disaffection. Wehlage and Rutter (1986) draw attention to the role of schools themselves in contributing to the dropout problem, and single out three key social processes: the extent of the teacher's interest in the students, the fairness of school discipline, and the effectiveness of discipline. Where these are found wanting, they argue, students display lower commitment to school. The school system also contributes indirectly to the depersonalisation of classroom processes, through limiting the teacher's material resources and time, and restricting the provision of emotional support which should be available to students in need.

The role of social psychological and environmental factors in contributing to 'fit' (that is, fitting into the institution) and to the student's commitment to the institution's programme is detailed in Bean's (1985) model of student dropout at the college level. Noteworthy is its motivational focus: it emphasises that students are selected for or socialised into certain behaviours and attitudes by the social system itself, and these contribute to dropout, or protect the student from dropping out. Bean argues that because of the size and impersonality of large universities, actual contact between students and staff members is of little importance in the process of socialisation or selection; more important is interaction with peers and support from them in becoming connected to the institution, developing goals and plans, and investing energy in their attainment. A similar argument may be made for large high schools.

At the classroom level, Kagan (1990) also alludes to 'the match' between the environment and the student, reminding us that classroom environments are selective of particular student behaviour and attitudes, and not necessarily supportive of alternative behaviour. She argues that qualitatively different 'cultures' exist in the one classroom, and that dropping out of school is a response to a particular classroom 'culture' or social climate. Student engagement and cognitive involvement in activities are affected by the students' reading of the classroom interaction processes associated with these climates, which indicate the niche in which they are placed. Students' interpretations of their place in the classroom relational system may accentuate their despair and frustration. The longitudinal study of alienation and involvement of boys in Detroit by Kulka *et al.* (1982) focused on two key aspects of interest: their attitudes towards school and their involvement and participation in school activities. Kulka *et al.* concluded that general attitudes to school were the predominant factors in determining students' attitudes towards teachers and involvement in school life; that is, attachment to the school shaped their participation in school activities. The association between student reactions to school authority and control, participation in school activities, and aggression and deviance is portrayed in Box 5.1.

In summary, the central concerns of youth remain those of finding a place in society and a sense of a future, through establishing a viable identity for oneself. Alienation occurs when there is a discrepancy between a person's current identities and those sought or desired as identities in the future. In school, these identities find expression in a student's participation in everyday tasks and social relations. They have much to do with the sense of connectedness and belonging to the school community and the social groups which it contains. Successful identification depends upon whether the conventional classroom group, with the concurrence of the teacher, allows the adolescent enough breathing space for exploring identity so that commitment to the goals of the school becomes possible.

Box 5.1 Pathways to school commitment or to alienation

Feelings of acceptance	→ Identification with school activities and groups
Feelings of self-worth	→ Positive perceptions of teachers and other students
Engagement in school misbehaviour	→ Resentment towards teachers and school staff
	→ Lower involvement in school activities
	→ Increase in deviant and rebellious behaviour

Identity, self-direction, and goals

The psychological dimensions of the new alienation have particular poignancy when we focus on the difficulties individual young people encounter in resolving uncertainty about the future. At a global level, there are concerns about nuclear war, destruction of the ozone layer, and the greenhouse effect; at the level of interpersonal relationships there is the risk of AIDS, and increasingly the sense of lost possibilities occasioned by the denial of employment opportunities. Foote (1951, p. 15) noted that 'motivated behaviour is distinguished by its prospective reference to ends in view'. Trommsdorff (1986) and others (e.g., Nurmi, 1991) point out that future orientation consists of cognitive aspects whereby the person projects the self into the future, together with motivational and affective aspects associated with goal setting and feelings of optimism and pessimism. Thus, without a perspective on the future, and a way of making the future imminent through some kind of recurring goal-seeking procedure that reflects the individual's personality, motivational processes are stalled.

Markus and Nurius (1986) offer a theoretical frame which links beliefs about the future to individual affective and motivational states, via the notion of 'possible selves'. Possible selves are beliefs which individuals hold about what is possible *for them*, and include the notion of sense making, where selves are the 'carriers of general aspirations, motives, identities' (p. 955). Thus possible selves are susceptible to change in response to environmental change; they are like architects' drafts, projections as to how the (self-)structure will look in the future, and guides in its construction, yet open to modification when information is provided which is inconsistent with these projections. The better the person is at visualising these possible selves in specific terms, the more closely s/he is able to bridge from current to desired states (Markus and Ruvolo, 1989). An aspect of the possible self is the *feared self*. The anxiety aroused by invoking a feared self may reduce organisation, make the person vulnerable to self-defeating strategies, and inhibit responding by directing attention to personal incapacities, previous lack of success, or anticipation of failure. It is this aspect of self-conflict and its manifestation in youth depression and anxiety which is symptomatic of the apathy and pessimism associated with the new alienation.

Although the theory of possible selves is argued at the individual level, possible selves can be appreciated in terms of embeddedness in the group, self-categorisation, and social identity. Each of us inhabits multiple social worlds, each of which may be congruent with the others in terms of values, or incompatible with them to various degrees. Value congruence between the motivational systems of family and school may not extend to the peer society, for example; and it is the peer group, at clique level or at the level of the crowd, which has the capacity to shape the possible selves during the years of high school.

CROWD INFLUENCES IN HIGH SCHOOL

The secondary school brings together a broad mix of students in sufficient numbers for the conditions to be ripe for crowd structures to emerge as a determinant of status differences among the student body, and for individuality to be easily submerged in the mass. The significance of peer crowds was given particular force by Coleman's (1961) study of ten high schools in Illinois, which argued that the high school operated as a social system where student status is related to membership of a particular 'crowd' within the school. Those with the highest status have the greatest influence on their peers, because they determine the peer value system which pervades school life. Coleman's report gave prominence to the overt symbols among youth of social status: friendliness, good looks, popularity, personality, and sporting ability. The top sportspeople and the social elites had more ways of gaining recognition in the peer society than was true for the best scholars; thus, because of their high visibility among students, the values which the leading crowd represented were assumed to be the values endorsed by adolescents in general. An adolescent subculture based on such values was assumed to be capable of 'nipping in the bud' any early signs of support for adult-endorsed intellectual achievement values among youth in high school.

Coleman's discovery of an adolescent subculture in high school with a powerful anti-education influence on adolescents ensured his report a place in a generation of texts on education. Despite the vagueness of the term 'leading crowd', the peer group became a convenient folk devil for concerns among parents and educators about the lack of commitment among adolescents to academic values and achievement motivation. But was Coleman right in his assertion that an anti-intellectual adolescent subculture dominates student life in high school? Is the peer group to blame for declines in motivation during adolescence? What is the role in youth alienation of the loss of emotional attachment to the school?

Influence of the leading crowd on academic motivation

Other large-scale studies of the time, such as that by Friesen (1968), concluded that Coleman's assertions about the power of the peer subculture were too sweeping, and that he overestimated the influence of elite students on the attitudes and plans of other adolescent students. Friesen surveyed over 10,000 Canadian students in grades ten to twelve. Like Coleman, he found that they ranked friendliness and good looks as the most important values in the leading crowd. Academic achievement was ranked as less important than personality and friendliness, which were held to be the most important characteristics for success in life. However, athletic and sporting ability also ranked low. Rather than blaming the peer group for the lower value assigned to academic achievement, Friesen considered how the high school operates as a social system allocating social recognition and defining identities, and suggested that the way in which schools are organised may restrict the range of opportunities for adolescent students to satisfy the need for recognition among their peers, except through achieving status on the sports field. Achievements in sport are more public and regular, and often given more recognition in the school context, than are cultural and academic achievements. He noticed that school authorities themselves, through their promotion of sport and rewarding of cheerleaders, give strong endorsement to student popularity, personality, and friendliness, which are prime values in the present-oriented adolescent society.

Crowd identification as a means of adaptation

The significance of peer crowd types and affiliation with various crowds has been discussed by Brown and his colleagues (see Chapter 2) in terms of identity development rather than in terms of academic motivation. While peer crowds may not exert direct pressures on adolescents concerning academic goals in the way which Coleman's work suggested, crowd stereotypes may nevertheless offer a lifestyle which inhibits adolescents from focusing on long-term goals. The crowd may also restrict them from being themselves, particularly in early adolescence, when youth appear to be more categorical in their thinking, more active in group boundary maintenance, and more sensitive to the viewpoints of others in determining their self-concepts. For example, being one of the brainy kids may have been acceptable to peers as well as parents at primary school, but may be viewed as a liability in the peer system at high school.

Our study of adolescents in transition from primary to secondary school (Power and Cotterell, 1979, 1981) noted that the social categories of brains and toughs, which had existed in the primary school, became more prominent in secondary school, forming the basis of adolescents' identities as student, stirrer, or potential dropout. The smart ones struggled with maintaining their status without being seen to work too hard at it. Any strategy which becomes obvious to one's peers suggests insecurity about one's reputation. Thus the bright student who assiduously seeks the teacher's approval by seeing the teacher out of class, cooperating fully in classwork, and completing all assignments on time runs the risk of peer disapproval for being 'a crawler' or 'the teacher's pet', and of becoming the target for the peer contempt and rejection that faces all posers and tryhards. The students categorised as average were the majority. They tended to get on reasonably well with their teachers and classmates most of the time, but included some who would follow along with the toughs and 'stirrers' and 'fool around a bit' in class when the occasion arose. It is the adolescent who drifts from group to group who is a candidate for deteriorating motivation early in secondary school.

The account given by Kinney (1993) of the peer society of a middle school underlines the importance of crowd affiliation for social identity in early adolescence. It appeared to Kinney that the peer culture of the middle school he investigated was primarily shaped by the concerns of the sports-people, the cheerleaders, and their friends. The visibility and prestige of these 'trendies' and 'jock-populars' within the school allowed them to define who were the ingroup and who were the outgroup, which included making fun of the latter, calling them nerds, and shunning them. Kinney's interviews with older adolescents who had been regarded as nerds in seventh and eighth grades draw attention to the oppressive peer culture which operated when the respondents were in the middle school. So rigidly defined were the social categories that the peer society gave little room for alternative routes to popularity; one interviewee stated, 'You had one route [to becoming popular] and then there was the other. And we were the other' (Kinney, 1993, p. 27). The dominance of the trendy crowd had an effect on the self-image of these so-called unpopular students, who felt 'outsiders' and 'social outcasts'. They judged themselves by the values of the trendies: they believed that there was something wrong with them, and were continually afraid of offending someone. One reported, 'I was just a loser. I didn't have many friends' (Kinney, 1993, p. 28). Things improved for the nerds when they moved from middle school into the more open environment of high school, where they were free of the rigid group boundaries and reference group system which existed in middle school. Instead of one powerful and exclusive trendy group dominating the value system of the peer society, there was a greater variety of groups in the high school, and more routes to visibility. The nerds reported that they felt 'relieved they were in high school'; they became more confident, were able to shrug off the negative social identity they had acquired, and became 'normals'.

CLIQUES AND LIFESTYLES IN SECONDARY-SCHOOL CLASSROOMS

It is in the everyday world of the classroom that peer influence on motivation is likely to be most direct, and processes of group acceptance and rejection most powerful. To the extent that teachers maintain an awareness of the group dimension of classroom life, they will consider how an individual's motivation and task orientation is mediated by social processes generated in the clique and at intergroup levels. However, teacher awareness of clique structures within the classroom is often limited to those aspects of classroom life salient to the *teacher's* definition of the world. Consequently, knowledge of clique structures as a source of friction among students is at times very meagre.

The existence and activities of classroom cliques have been reported in several ethnographic studies. For example, Cusick (1973) observed adolescents at a senior high school in class, and found the seating arrangements reflected the pattern of clique relations. The sportspeople, the drama group, and Ed and Bill's friends all occupied different sectors of the classroom and engaged in very little contact with one another. Nash (1973) studied three cliques in a classroom of Scottish adolescent boys, and reports how conscious each clique was of its distinctiveness from the others. Boys had names for the other cliques (for example, the 'hard' group called another clique 'mentals'). Underlying school-related attitudes, such as work attitudes and the tendency to fool around in class, shaped their group identity, confirmed by teacher reactions to them. Nash's pessimistic prognosis was that these clique labels would become a lifestyle, and that when students were later 'banded' into streams or tracks, the destinations would parallel the clique divisions. In similar style is the report of Walker (1988), who examined four friendship groups of year-ten boys in a boys' school in Sydney. These groups had adopted the labels of the 'Footballers', the 'Greeks', the 'Handballers', and the 'Three Friends' (derogatorily called the 'poofs' by the Footballers). The Footballers identified with the values of macho assertiveness, but they did not entirely resist schooling since they could see the benefits of getting a school certificate. They maintained an uneasy relationship with the teacher in which clowning and horseplay in the classroom affirmed their sense of group identity. The Greeks liked to have a good time, and had a classroom style that was a mixture of assertiveness and compliance. They valued what school offered, because they had clear plans of being successful and making money. Teachers described the Greeks as louts and nuisances, and also as good kids, mature, and responsible (p. 51). The other groups were not noticed in the classroom. For example, the Three Friends were marginal in terms of the dominant peer culture: they disliked sport and preferred drama and artistic pursuits. They saw friendship as sharing interests, not joking at another's expense or trying to impress each other with false bravado.

These small observation studies portray classroom cliques as different social types carving out different lifestyles for themselves in school. The types are constructed by the groups themselves and endorsed by the manner in which other groups, and teachers as well, respond to them. Walker and Cusick both treat these 'cultures' as formed in part as a response to the activities and attitudes of other groups in the school; that is, the cliques provided a means of solving social relations with others through devising a protective and even assertive group identity. In this sense they mirror the social identification processes reported on peer crowd types. But the ethnographies are limited in that the significance of these group cultures as lifestyles or pathways for shaping *an educational career* is sidetracked or not considered relevant. The social benefits of group identity for academic motivation are ignored in what is essentially a tribal account of peer culture. There is no entry point for the educator.

Motivational patterns in cliques

Others have attempted to understand the relations between classroom cliques and school by giving somewhat more attention to academic concerns. Angus (1981, 1984) undertook a study of the coping processes of a group of boys who called themselves the 'Sweathogs' after the name of their class football team. They were reputed to be 'hard to handle', and, while conscious that they had 'a bit of a reputation' for having fun at school, believed that they were pushed around by the system and that their needs were not considered. Their manner of coping with what they saw as a hostile and rejecting environment was to develop a negative labelling of themselves which protected them from being defined as failures by the school, and insulated them from its definitions of their capabilities. They volunteered the information that 'We're the rejects'; 'We're the dumb ones' and rationalised their lack of effort as follows: 'We don't work as much because we're put down too much. Teachers put us down . . . It's a waste of time so everyone mucks around.'

The 'swots', 'rems', and 'ordinary kids' who feature in Brown's (1987) account of schooling in Britain also developed distinctive coping strategies which reflected their own frames of reference and social identification. The rems were eager to escape school and limited their involvement in class because they saw real work as occurring outside. The swots accepted the chance which school offers for developing an alternative identity based not on family circumstances but on personal effort and ability. They worked at school not so much because they valued learning as because they were determined to avoid the negative consequences of their present lives. The majority, the ordinary kids, accepted the achievement values of the school, in moderation, and expended enough effort to 'get by', pulling their weight rather than competing for rewards at the expense of their classmates.

RESISTANCE IN STUDENT–TEACHER RELATIONS

Teacher–student relations are not always harmonious. Classrooms are places where teacher power is exercised over, and often resisted by, adolescent students. The importance of peer support is particularly appreciated when a student is feeling humiliated or harassed by a teacher. One of the features which distinguish secondary school life from that of primary school, according to Meighan (1977), is teacher actions which appear intended to humiliate, and to remind students of 'their insignificance as individuals' (p. 126). Teachers who are disliked are those who undermine the basis of the personality system – who 'put you down', intimidate students, and appear to be motivated by revenge to 'pin something on you' rather than concerned with helping the student cope with classroom life in a more positive manner. Davies (1978) cites instances of the indignation of female adolescents at being 'shown up' by a teacher 'in front of everybody in the corridor' (p. 104). The girls did not like teachers who hit them, or teachers who insulted them by attacking their female identity. Accusations of 'tart' or 'slut' were keenly resented. Adolescents are very sensitive to such disparaging treatment, and one often finds that the 'bad attitude' displayed by a particular student can be traced back to the actions of an insensitive and bullying teacher. The arbitrary and inconsistent application of rules by teachers, and their unwillingness to help students having difficulties with schoolwork, were listed by Samuel (1984) as the major complaints of girls in a working-class Australian school; she concluded that student resistance arose from the feeling that teachers treated them unfairly, not from resentment against teacher authority itself. Students believed that they were not entirely to blame for stirring up trouble in class and 'sending up' the teacher; they saw the teachers who were targets of resistance as deserving it.

Samuel (1984) notes that the coercive cycle of student resistance and teacher retaliatory punishment forms 'a vicious circle', and that, in her view, 'a critical sector of this circle is provided by the way teachers categorise pupils' into good girls and bad girls (p. 23). Once you are labelled a bad girl, teacher attention is directed at you only in a negative way; support from the teacher for coping with difficulties of understanding and of goal setting in relation to the classroom tasks is withdrawn. If you are seen to be cheeky or ungrateful, in effect you are cut out of the favoured circle of good students. A similar difficulty in relationships with teachers was found by Philippi (1994) to be a critical factor in the dropping-out syndrome which she investigated in her work with at-risk students. A common theme noted in these studies is that students valued being treated by their teachers as intelligent, responsive, individual human beings. Davies found this value endorsed by students who were frequently on report for misbehaviour in school, as well as by those who could be described as well behaved. Because of the power differential between teachers and students, young people crave tolerance and understanding from their teachers; as one girl put it, 'they should get to know you as a person' (Davies, 1978, p. 105).

Peer support for resistance

In the expression of resistance, peer support is important: just banding together at school and having common experiences as students, including 'stirring' and 'mucking up', may relieve the boredom and routine, as well as providing the necessary basis of identification for an adolescent to 'get by' at school 'with a little help from my friends'. What Everhart (1982) called 'goofing off' is an adaptive response by adolescents to being treated at school as if they were just a class of students rather than individuals. It is an indication of the disaffection felt among generally cooperative students about the grinding sameness of their classroom life. Like 'mucking up', 'goofing off' is a general term which covers a wide range of behaviour, from making noises, throwing or shooting things, teasing others, and talking, to acting in an unusual way, the overall effect being that it annoys or 'bugs' the teacher. The actions may be classed by school authorities as misbehaviour, yet few would be listed as offences in most published school rules. They are not intended to overthrow the teacher's authority as instructional leader, but they are nevertheless acts which undermine teacher authority. Their meaning can only be understood within the context of daily life as a member of an aggegrate of adolescents in a school classroom. The underlying reason for goofing off, Everhart says, is for adolescents to create their own place in the classroom and impose their stamp on events by varying the style of their response to the routine work tasks which comprise classroom life.

As a form of release and harmless fun, this resembles the expression of adolescent high spirits seen in public places, and does not occur randomly in school. Everhart (1982) noticed that goofing off required an appropriate peer group climate, and the presence of sympathetic friends in the class. It arose from a collective awareness among one's peers of a common state of mind. It did not occur in maths, where the work was highly individualised and thus a group climate was absent. In short, goofing off or mucking up is chiefly a group expression, where the peers provide an audience as well as the necessary group solidarity to trigger the action.

Resistance by social loafing

Resistance is regularly expressed when students are assigned to group work. Many a teacher has introduced group work into her/his secondary school classes as a motivational strategy, in the belief that students will enjoy their schoolwork more, and that they will learn more effectively, only to become frustrated by the time wasting of some students. As a consequence, many retreat from the use of group work in their teaching. Group processes may be appreciated from the perspective of ingroup–outgroup relations, where the teacher is a member of the outgroup, and the task of the ingroup is to alter the work agenda to more favourable activities. Cusick (1973) described with a sense of amazement the amount of time which senior students spent in class on non-academic activities; one of these was planning a fishing trip. In interactions in class with friends, adolescents are likely to be more talkative, more energetic, and more prone to get off-task.

There are two principles, *social facilitation* and *social loafing*, which are relevant to the application of group work to the classroom. They yield opposing findings on the effects of grouping on learning, and represent the poles of any debate on the application of group approaches to teaching adolescents, as well as offering insights into the way peers can support or undermine the work goals of the classroom. The principle of social facilitation asserts that the presence of others increases the work rates of people above what they achieve when working alone. In contrast, 'social loafing' describes the process where persons working in a group perform at work rates reduced from their normal individual rate. However, rather than being contradictory, the principles provide complementary explanations for complex group motivational processes, as Harkins and Szymanski (1989) recently pointed out. A crucial underlying factor is the presence or absence of evaluation in facilitating or inhibiting the effort expended by the target individual in task performance. The mere presence of another person engaged in similar activity at the same time appears to heighten the actor's attention and direct it more to the activity, and create demands to behave as if some norm existed for the behaviour. However, these enhancing effects of social facilitation are generally restricted to the performance of relatively simple or automatic skills. If the task is more complex, the presence of an onlooker or other actor may inhibit task performance.

For teachers and youth workers, greater interest lies in understanding the group process of social loafing, and learning how to avoid its disadvantages when using group work. Social loafing is a minimising strategy, where people work only as hard as necessary 'to keep the teacher off your back'. Under the cloak of a group effort, the individuals' contribution is masked, so they rely on the others to do some of their work. Loafing, not surprisingly, is related to anonymity. At the class level, where several groups may exist, social loafing will occur between groups, with some relying on other groups to satisfy the teacher. Situations of working together where individual outputs are pooled, rather than individually owned, lead to loafing.

By itself, working together does not necessarily lead to group members putting in less effort than they would as individuals. For example, Williams *et al.* (1981) found that as soon as the potential is created in the group structure for individual evaluation of the participants' efforts, social loafing disappears. What can be concluded is that social loafing will occur where there is no standard for performance (either because the goal is not defined in that way, or because the task is vague) or where some contributions are difficult to measure and compare with the contributions of others. Loafing is also likely to occur where the task is perceived as easy, or where the group is larger than it needs to be to perform satisfactorily (which is common in classrooms). However, when the task is sufficiently demanding to require 'all hands on deck', even if the 'hands' are anonymous, loafing is not an issue.

Resistance and teacher–class mismatch

Most young people tend not to muck up at school, or to stick their necks out as individuals who are overtly critical or rebellious; they are reluctant and unwilling parties rather than rebels. Their resistance takes the form of emotional disengagement and evasion or avoidance. Students may use defensive strategies which 'negate or distort the task' (Hansen, 1989, p. 186). Hansen concluded that defending strategies were more subtle and complex than mere rejection of classroom demands. For example, some students ignored the instructions on a task which was complex and spent their time doing the bits of it they liked, and left it to others to answer the teacher's questions. Hansen called this form of defending 'evading', and noticed that among some students it had been developed into an art form. More frequently, defending was expressed as overt compliance, where the student would appear to make an effort and pretend to understand, in order to convey an impression to the teacher of trying and participating and, through this 'dissembling' mode, to avoid teacher intervention. These strategies are attempts to maintain the sense of self when students are not openly rejecting the culture of achievement, but struggling to find meaning in the curriculum.

In secondary school, adolescents are more aware that the lack of meaning in classroom tasks indicates a mismatch between the teacher's approach and their mode of learning. If they perceive a lack of opportunity to be heard, and inability to connect with their teachers as adults, disaffection may boil over into frustration and resentment. Alpert (1991) reports on the experiences of middle-class adolescents who expressed their dissatisfaction with the teacher and the academic programme by limiting their participation in class, and by arguing with the teacher about the content of the lesson and the evaluation procedures. The classrooms of three teachers were observed, all of whom were teaching English literature to seniors (twelfth graders). The two teachers who encountered resistance from their students displayed a more 'academic' teaching approach than the teacher who experienced no such resistance. Their style of interaction was more formal; for example, they asked 'What's the tone of the poem? How are symbols used?' The other teacher incorporated the students' personal knowledge into the classroom discussion, and engaged the adolescent students' own feelings and attitudes through questions like these: 'Do you feel sorry for any of the characters? Do you want Eliza to marry Freddy?'

In the resistant classes, students' resentment arose from their feeling of estrangement from the teachers as well as from the subject matter they were transmitting. Alpert portrays this process as one which is within the teachers' powers to remedy, because 'by being too much of a teacher, the teachers alienate themselves, the knowledge they represent, and the school from the adolescent students' (Alpert, 1991, p. 361). This study, viewed largely from the teacher's perspective, describes the gap which often exists in teacher–student relations, and the ways that academically capable students signal their frustration when such a gap is not being bridged. Interestingly, the teachers who encountered resistance were aware of their students' reactions, but they were unaware that it was *their style of teaching* which communicated the message that students' views were not being heard and valued. They tolerated the displays of resistance, and did not act to discipline the students, although Alpert thought that they felt strain in teaching these classes. Alpert's observations suggest that resistance is more subtle than questions of curriculum relevance, and has to do with the mismatch between the teacher's style and the preferred interaction style of adolescent students, who may be viewed as clients whose voice is to be heard.

Differences and conflicts between teachers and adolescent students arise because there is an ingroup–outgroup structure in classrooms, where opposing groups hold different values, compounded by the striving of adolescent students for a more equal partnership where inhabitants can relate to one another on more or less the same level. Students resent being treated as kids and reminded of the gulf between teacher and student. The teachers who create conflict situations are those who allow no room for negotiation, and no space for a young person to make mistakes without being criticised or bawled out. Those who are effective in relating to the same students are often described as having a sense of humour, 'being able to joke with you'; that is, being able to see things in proportion. They have the ability to fill out their role, monogrammed with their own personality and style of relating to students. As a consequence they are described as 'real people' who are 'tuned in' to where the students are coming from, who can tell the difference between mischief and malice, ratbags and rebels, and who see everybody in the class as 'basically good kids'.

Classrooms as sources of meaningful goals

What can be seen in these accounts is the way teachers and students continually define and negotiate the social meanings of the events and actions occurring around them. Classrooms are social systems which differ from other small-group systems in that social interaction between class-room participants is structured by the roles assigned to them by the school. Within the classroom, motivation has a social dimension, as the product of interaction between the individual and her/his environment, and is not merely a characteristic of the individual. The high-school classroom en-vironment provides students with many opportunities to pursue non-academic goals as well as academic task goals.

The secondary-school teacher's task is doubly difficult. Not only are there several kinds of social goal present in the typical classroom, which are either in conflict with or tangential to the achievement goals that are central to the academic concerns of schooling, but these achievement-related goals do not appear to be connected to the adolescent's broader life-goals of workplace entry and career fulfilment. Instead these goals are buried under large mounds of 'schoolwork' – collating information, describing, organ-ising, writing reports, answering written questions, reciting and memor-ising formulas, practising procedures, and sitting for tests. Intrinsically interesting material is in short supply in the high-school classroom; the concept of achievement becomes corrupted into performing well on tests, and achievement motivation becomes defined as competing with one's classmates for marks and ratings. The factory model of education, with its emphasis on the worker's single-minded persistence and avoidance of distraction, where achievement is measured in terms of completion of piecemeal tasks at defined standards of accuracy and speed, is not too far off the mark as a description of how students often perceive life in secondary-school classrooms.

CONCLUSION

What we have been discussing in this chapter is the school context of motivation, and the way activities have meaning when they are situated in a meaningful context. Motivation is not simply an individual attribute; it is a product of social interaction. Involvement, engagement, and commitment are motivational words which also imply a connection between the person and an activity or group. To focus on academic tasks on their own in a study of motivation leaves unanswered the question of the relation of the tasks to broader meaning contexts. We need to ask these questions: what is the frame of meaning for adolescent students? Is it within the classroom, or beyond it? How do lessons, or phases within the lesson, relate to the social and personal concerns of adolescent students? And if they do not do so at present, how can the environment be altered so that they do?

Good teachers know that the goal structures of classrooms extend beyond the design of lesson activities to include concerns about social processes, and that their work requires them to consider how to structure the relations between them and the class, as well as the relations among the students within the class, in ways which match broadly with the concerns, interests, and personal histories of the students, and even to the history of the class as a collectivity or group. Their everyday relationships with students are patterned in a complex rhythm: some lessons and parts of lessons meander along, while others race forward, fuelled by high-level work pressures. The rhythm may be dictated by the curriculum and the stage the class has reached in a work cycle of, say, two weeks, but it is also affected by the time of year and the term pattern; for example, whether there are mid-term or mid-semester examinations. Motivation flows according to this rhythm, being more urgent at some times than at others, in keeping with the broader cycle in which the present work rate is located, so that a good teacher knows when s/he has to urge the class along and 'cover a lot of work this week'. Motivation also reflects the variations in moods and energy that are characteristic of the social climate of any group of people who meet regularly together. Some days everyone is bustling with energy, seeking challenge; on other days everyone wants the chance for quiet and not much to do. Classrooms may be generally busy places, but that does not mean they are on high alert for long periods of time. Teachers who understand this rhythm, and give a breathing space to their students so that there is time for real learning to occur, are less likely to have to contend with student resistance.

6 Peer pressures on health risk behaviour

It is during the pre-teen and adolescent years that nearly all alcohol and drug use begins, although the health consequences of practices such as smoking and the use of marijuana may not be apparent for some years afterwards. The peer group is now widely regarded as an important social environment capable of influencing both the initiation of substance use and the maintenance of the patterns involved. Peer influence is frequently invoked to explain adolescent risk behaviour, even when there has been little or no attempt made to measure such influences in any serious way. Investigators have often inferred that peer influence is present from similarities noted in the behaviour of groups of friends. Having friends who smoke, however, does not constitute peer pressure to smoke, although it is true that such friends are likely to provide models of smoking and direct access to cigarettes. The presence of smokers in one's network of friends may be as much a matter of social selection on other criteria than smoking as it may be a matter of social influence.

Kandel (Kandel, 1978a; Kandel *et al.*, 1978) may be credited with clarifying the notion of peer influence. She distinguished three kinds of interpersonal influence: direct influence, where parents and friends set an example and reinforce certain behaviour; indirect influence, established through interpersonal ties which create commonality of interests and values; and conditional influence, where one source of influence modifies a person's susceptibility to some other influence. Most discussions of peer influence focus on direct influence, sometimes called peer pressure. Peers may approve or disapprove of smoking, drinking, or other health risk behaviour, and express these attitudes in the form of direct pressure, such as urging and teasing, or overt disapproval. Direct forms of persuasion occur in concert with association with others, where socialisation is indirect and normative (see Chassin *et al.*, 1981) and the adolescent is motivated to behave according to her/his perceptions of how others behave and of what others expect her/him to do.

In this chapter, peer pressure is distinguished from the broader concept of peer influence, and is reserved for direct forms of social persuasion, including adolescents' perceptions of such influences. A useful working definition is provided by Brown *et al.* (1986a, p. 523): peer pressure is seen to occur 'when people your own age encourage you or urge you to do something or to keep from doing something else, no matter if you personally want to or not'. What adolescents understand peer pressure to mean can be seen in the responses given by 13-year-olds at a local school (see Box 6.1). These comments underline the actor's role in maintaining relations with friends by conforming to what s/he thinks these friends expect.

SOCIAL INFLUENCES ON CONFORMITY

The issues of alcohol and drug use occur in social situations where there are conflicting values and social messages: for example, 'Be sensible and avoid risks with your health', but 'Be cool and with it just the same.' When young people find themselves in situations containing uncertainty as to how they are to behave, they typically rely on social comparison processes, checking whether their behaviour is similar to that of others, and adjusting their actions according to the information obtained in order to achieve this. There are two broad kinds of social influence on behaviour, which Deutsch and Gerard (1955) called *informational influence* (the use of information from others who are perceived to be reliable sources in order to steer one's own behaviour) and *normative influence* (the use of such information to behave in ways that are seen as desirable by others, and which meet with their approval). Informational influence deals with supplying details about

Box 6.1 Peer pressure experienced by young adolescents

Interviewer   Have you ever done something you didn't want to do, just so people liked you more?

Adolescent 1   I broke a window because I wanted to be more popular, and I just got into trouble.

Adolescent 2   I tried to jump a jump on my bike, to be cool in my bike club.

Adolescent 3   When Steven and the rest of his friends were going round acting tough – and they were popular, so I would go around being like them. Soon after I learnt that they were being stupid for a bit of attention and I fell for it.

Interviewer   Is it easy to stay popular in a group?

Adolescent 4   No, because if you do something wrong they tell you you're dumb.

Adolescent 5   No, you have to play along with the group.

objective reality. Normative influence is based on pressure to comply, in situations where the group has some form of power to exact conformity.

In the conformity experiments of Sherif and others (referred to on p. 102), the participants were unknown to one another. This is in sharp contrast to Parsons' transactional view of the nature of social influence, which linked social influence to information dependency. Parsons (1963) reasoned that where the person needing the information turns to another person for advice, that person is put in the position of influence. What is central to his concept of social influence is the issue of trust: a person's willingness to accept information from an outside source depends on the person's trust in the source as being genuine and reliable. Clearly, such reliance on another involves a degree of risk; the information obtained from the source may be inaccurate, but since the actor has no way of verifying the information, or does not want to take the trouble, reliance is placed on the trustworthiness of the relationship. Parsons explores the conditions for inspiring trust, and suggests that the most favourable condition is 'a mutual relation of fundamental diffuse solidarity' and common belongingness, where people 'belong together in a collectivity on such a basis that . . . A could not have an interest in trying to deceive B' (Parsons, 1963, p. 49). The security base which Parsons is describing is found in close friendship ties and in family relationships.

Using the analogy of the monetary system and the market, Parsons (1963) also takes into account other relationships, where the notion of trust is based not upon primary group relationships but on the norms and obliga-tions of contracts and statements of intention, which he calls 'the normative system'. In these sectors of the social network, which Milardo (1992) calls the 'exchange network', and which include the school administration and voluntary organisations, the trustworthiness of the personal source of the information is less at issue, and the information is viewed as being reliable because of trust in the 'market' performance of the system.

Influences based on social identity

A more sophisticated version of these social influence processes is offered by social identity theory, which includes in the influence process both direct social pressures to conform and the motivational role of individual perceptions and self-categorisation as a group member. A test of the power of social identity theory to explain group pressure was mounted by Abrams *et al.* (1990), who revisited the pioneering conformity experiments of Sherif and Asch. They manipulated the subjects' awareness of the judg-ments made by other subjects to create two sets of conditions: one where they were categorised into sub-groups, and one where they were not, thus imposing a social category frame onto the original experiment. The category condition was further varied by creating three levels of group salience: one where groups were given labels, one where attention was drawn to the labels by conducting a group pre-test, and one where the group differences were implicit. In contrast to general social influence theory, which would predict that norm formation is the product of interindividual informational referencing, they predicted that the members of the different categories would differ in their judgments, with the differences reflecting the salience of the social categories to which they were assigned. The results demonstrated that the creation of situational ambiguity led to subjects seeking information mostly from those who had been categorised as similar to them rather than from other subjects in general; that is, subjects conformed to the norms of the group to which they saw themselves belonging.

A second experiment replicated the Asch paradigm of estimating the length of lines displayed for a brief time, and examined normative influence in relation to subjects' membership of the group (ingroup) or non-membership (outgroup). In addition, visibility of responding was heightened by having a public and a private mode of reporting one's judgments. They found that informational ambiguity was heightened when disagreement was with those categorised as the same (ingroup), and that normative pressure to comply was greatest in these circumstances. Behavioural conformity was greatest under conditions of publicly responding in the presence of ingroup members, and least under conditions of being required to respond publicly in the presence of an outgroup. Thus, when group membership is salient, 'in-group members are seen as more correct while out-group members are seen as less likely to be correct' (Abrams *et al.*, 1990, p. 109).

This study has been reported in detail because of its implications for understanding the processes of peer group pressure which educational programmes on health risk behaviour need to take into account. What Abrams *et al.* (1990) demonstrate in these experiments is that the vehicle of social influence is not group pressure or social comparison in the broad sense, but what Turner calls 'referent informational influence' derived from social identification with a particular social category, and 'awareness of one's social identity as an ingroup member' (Abrams *et al.*, 1990, p. 99). It is the people who are regarded by the individual as belonging to the same group or social category as s/he does who are the relevant social reference sources; and it is from seeming to disagree with those with whom one expects to agree that uncertainty arises. Abrams *et al.* suggest that normative influence only arises when people are subject to interpersonal pressure. That is, in a situation where a person is consciously aware of her/his group membership, only ingroup pressure has any effect on her/his attitudes or behaviour. Pressure exerted by an outgroup, including parents, teachers, or health educators, is resisted or ignored. People do not change their behaviour just because they are noticed by other people, because these others may not be salient influences on social identity. When, however, those watching are members of one's ingroup, and are thus significant others, they are recognised as possessing information concerning the ingroup's norms, and one is likely to change her/his behaviour in line with these norms.

SMOKING AND DRINKING: ISSUES IN ADOLESCENT HEALTH

Smoking and drinking are of central importance in the adolescent period as markers of the social transition to adult lifestyles. Both are also regarded as deviant behaviours, of significance in relation to adolescent health. The seriousness of the health risks from smoking has resulted in increased government legislation in many countries. Smoking is now prohibited in Australia in all government buildings, airports, public transport, and domestic aircraft, and tobacco advertising is prohibited. The social influences on alcohol use are different from those of smoking, just as the health consequences are. Drinking is less clearly designated as a health problem for the individual young person, despite the dangers from excess alcohol intake and binge drinking, and acknowledgment that alcohol is the major drug of abuse in society. Of course alcohol consumption can have traumatic social consequences for others, particularly in its association with violent assault, domestic violence, and road fatalities.

Prevalence of teenage smoking and drinking

The problem of teenage smoking is of major importance: health reports in Australia estimate that each year over 200,000 children and adolescents begin experimenting with cigarettes, and of these 70,000 will become regular smokers. It is estimated that there are currently 211,000 under-age smokers in Australia. The prevalence of teenage smoking fluctuates across the age groups, peaking at around 32 per cent at the age of 16 years. Following a decline in the rate of smoking since 1986, there are now signs in the mid-1990s that the incidence rates for teenage smoking are on the rise again in Australia, and that they have eroded the apparent gains that had been made in reducing the rates of smoking among young Australians in the previous decade. Whereas the rates of boys' smoking have been decreasing in Australia, the rate of smoking among older teenage girls now exceeds that of boys of the same age. It is disturbing to note that the uptake of smoking from age 11 and 12 is more rapid for girls than for boys, so that there are now as many girls smoking at 17 years of age as there are boys. In one national survey conducted in 1984 the percentage of male non-smokers declined from 41 per cent at age 12 to 19 per cent at age 17, whereas the percentage of non-smokers among females shrank from 53 per cent to 21 per cent across the same year bands.

Adolescent alcohol consumption is also of major concern in most countries. Public and parental concern is often focused on adolescent use of illegal drugs, but the major drug of abuse is alcohol. The social acceptability of alcohol in many Western countries, where drinking alcoholic beverages is normative among adults, creates a press among youth to prove their adult status by drinking, often in immoderate amounts. The amount of liquor consumed at youthful drinking sessions can hardly be viewed as adolescent experimentation, and constitutes binge drinking. A survey of New South Wales high-school students (Homel and Flaherty, 1986) found that 14 per cent of boys and 12 per cent of girls at age 16 were drinking on a daily basis. Moreover, about half the boys in the age group and one-third of the girls consumed five or more drinks on a single occasion. Some surveys (see Raphael, 1988) have assessed the intake per drinking occasion of males aged 17 years at 70 grams, which is well above safe daily levels of alcohol consumption.

A framework for understanding health risk behaviour

Earlier work on youth substance use and risk behaviour arose from a public health concern, and was theoretically limited, particularly in its lack of understanding of adolescents and of their relation to the wider society, and this may lead to behaviour being interpreted as deviant. Social psychological theories of problem behaviour and deviancy in adolescence view these behaviours as indicators of autonomy strivings and resistance to adult control, thus emphasising the constructive aspects of deviance (Chassin *et al.*, 1989; Galambos and Silbereisen, 1987). The emphasis on peer relationships and peer pressures, which is the focus of the present chapter, is only part of the total picture on risk behaviours. It is best appreciated within the frame of problem-behaviour theory (Jessor and Jessor, 1977), which acknowledges the influence on smoking and drinking of other social environments apart from peers, such as the family and the community, as well as the influence of the personality system. The value of problem-behaviour theory is in offering a comprehensive social psychological theory of the varied factors affecting the onset of smoking, drinking, drug use, and sexual activity during adolescence, thus helping us to avoid falling into the trap of oversimplifying the complex influences on deviant adolescent behaviour. The Jessors' argument is that adolescent risk behaviours are goal-directed and reflect lifestyles which are valued by particular groups of young people. These risk behaviours incur disapproval and adult sanction because of age-graded notions of when it is appropriate to adopt certain behaviours, such as drinking alcohol and smoking. Early adoption of these activities is interpreted as unconventional and rebellious, but may reflect a striving for independence rather than destructive anti-conformity. The social environment is conceptualised in terms of a system, in interaction with the personality system and the behaviour system, to exert influences over current behaviour. Bearing in mind the complexity of environmental influences on health risk behaviour, the discussions in the present chapter address influences arising from the proximal environment (e.g., Harford and Grant, 1987; Hirschi, 1969; Jessor and Jessor, 1977; Mosbach and Leventhal, 1988), where the actions of peers are likely to be critical in the adoption of new behaviour.

Mechanisms of proximal peer influence

Several useful theory-based reviews of youth smoking, alcohol, and drug use have appeared over the past decade or so (e.g., Glynn, 1981; Hundleby and Mercer, 1987; Marcos *et al.*, 1986; Oetting and Beauvais, 1987a; Simons *et al.*, 1988), which help to point the discussion of social influences beyond an examination of particular variables in explaining risk behaviour to an appreciation of how the peer group and family operate as social environments. These reviews move the debate beyond the so-called 'hydraulics' model of competing pulls on youth from parents and peers, and into an appreciation that social influences operate as a complex web of obligations and patterns of identification based upon affiliations between young people and significant others, which are usually maintained by some kind of continuing social contact.

Oetting and Beauvais' psycho-social theory of peer clusters emphasises the importance of peer influence on risk behaviour, which they assert is 'the single dominating psychosocial factor in drug use' (Oetting and Beauvais, 1987a, p. 138). Peer clusters are small subsets of peer groups which act as social environments for the pursuit and learning of risk behaviour. In contrast to the notion of peer pressure, which they see as implying 'a passive acceptance of a barely resistible power' (Oetting and Beauvais, 1987b, p. 206), these writers point out that the process of influence in a peer cluster is reciprocal. The mediating role of the peer cluster is emphasised in the following passage from Oetting and Beauvais (1987a, p. 137):

> When drugs are actually used, it is almost always in a peer context. Peers initiate the youth into drugs. Peers help provide drugs. Peers talk with

each other about drugs and model drug-using behaviours for each other and in doing so shape attitudes about drugs and drug-using behaviours.

The notion of the peer cluster is similar to the convoy model. It describes a miniature social environment with common values, beliefs, and lifestyle, which provides a supportive structure for the maintenance of a group identity, in this case based upon the acquisition and refinement of antisocial behaviour. In their conceptualisation of the social environment of peers, Hundleby and Mercer (1987), for example, take into account the friends' warmth and trust, the friends' level of conformity to rules and conventions, the nature and extent of joint activities, together with friends' attitudes and beliefs. Their empirical analysis of the influences of family and friends on drug use found that these social environments exerted separate although overlapping influences on drug taking; they found little support for the argument that young people who received little affection from their parents were compensated by greater trust and affection from their friends. Rather, the social environments of parents and peers operate differently.

PEER PRESSURES ON SMOKING

Despite the frequent reference to peer influences to explain adolescent smoking, few studies have actually measured and traced peer pressures on smoking. One problem is that notions of who comprise 'peers' vary considerably in the literature. These range from 'other pupils in your school' to 'your five closest friends' to 'your best friend'. In an attempt to unravel the notion of peer group influence, Morgan and Grube (1991) compared adolescents' susceptibility to influence from different sectors of the peer social network. They proposed that social influence is related to the closeness of relationships, and distinguished the peer network on that basis, so as to separate peer acquaintances, other friends, and best friends. They found that the strength of influence on smoking, alcohol use, and the use of illicit drugs was consistent with the level of closeness of these three relationships. Initiation into smoking was predicted best by the smoking behaviour of the best friend, as well as by that friend's approval or disapproval of smoking. Maintenance of smoking was explained by the best friend's smoking as well as other friends' smoking. The research highlights the significant influence of the best friend rather than some group of peers in general in initiating and maintaining health risk behaviour.

Urberg's (1992) longitudinal study of smoking among 17-year-olds investigated the role of the wider peer group in exerting normative pressures on adolescents to become smokers. It contrasted the influence of best friends with the influence of the peer crowd with which they identified. She obtained measures of peers' actual smoking behaviour according to their crowd affiliation (e.g., burnouts, jocks, etc.) rather than relying on estimates of smoking from the respondents. The mean levels of smoking of the peer crowds ranged from over two packs of twenty cigarettes a week for the burnouts to a half-pack for the averages and a quarter-pack for the jocks/ preppies. The value of a longitudinal design for teasing out the influence process is seen when Urberg examined changes in the level of smoking one year later. The influence of the peer crowd was found to be negligible, whereas the influence of the best friend was significant. The strength of peer influence was most evident on those who were the most conforming. From what has been noted about best-friend influence, it is important that smoking interventions focus more on friendship choice and the causes of friendship selection as a source of peer pressure (see Eiser *et al.*, 1991; Marcos *et al.*, 1986).

Best-friend influence

The central influence of best friends on smoking is confirmed in several large studies, including the British study by Eiser *et al.* (1991), the Waterloo Smoking Prevention Project, Study II (see van Roosmalen and McDaniel, 1989), and a survey by the Nebraska Prevention Center (Gerber and Newman, 1989). On the basis of careful analyses of the smoking behaviour of adolescents who could be accurately identified as friends in their survey data, Eiser *et al.* and Gerber and Newman (1989) concluded that the friends of smokers tend to be smokers as well. Van Roosmalen and McDaniel (1989) report too that when the best friend was a smoker, there was a strong likelihood that the respondent, whether male or female, was also a smoker; further, adolescents were more likely to stop smoking if their best friend was not a regular smoker than if the friend smoked regularly. This latter study also found that those who were smokers were more likely to have many friends who had tried smoking than was the case among non-smokers. They interpreted these patterns as suggesting that the social environment of peers contains 'a degree of indirect pressure . . . upon the nonsmoking adolescent to smoke' (p. 807).

An investigation by Urberg *et al.* (1990) compared pressures from friends not to smoke as well as pressures to engage in smoking. The adolescents studied were either regular smokers, experimental smokers, or non-smokers. Direct as well as normative pressures on their smoking were obtained, with information about the actual smoking pattern of the subject's best friend, and the subject's estimate of the number of friends who were smokers. Only one measure of peer pressure was found to be consistently related to adolescent smoking: normative pressure to smoke. Direct pressure not to smoke was also related to smoking, but statistical support for the pathway was not entirely clear, perhaps because these pressures could be directed only at the sub-groups of smokers and not at all sub-groups. It is the normative peer climate, including perceptions of their friends' smoking, which provides the motivation to experiment with cigarette smoking. But Urberg and her colleagues found very few adolescents willing to admit that their friends directly encouraged them to smoke, even among those who were already smoking. Urberg *et al.* (1990) comment that 'it may be the absence of perceived disapproval from friends rather than the presence of perceived encouragement' (p. 254) which results in normative pressure to smoke. The lack of friends' disapproval may thus be interpreted as tacit approval, and pressure by default. Youths may feel hesitant about telling their friends how they ought to behave, which is not surprising in a society where smoking is widely promoted to youth as part of a glamorous lifestyle. So immense is the investment of tobacco companies in Australian sports advertising and sponsorship that it prompted a councillor from the Australian Council on Smoking and Health to remark to the media that telling young people not to smoke when the tobacco industry spends $70 million each year in promoting cigarettes 'often seems as effective as spitting into the wind'.

Smoking initiation

Models of the role of social bonding to peers as influences on smoking have not stressed strongly enough the critical ages for susceptibility to initiation into smoking. Smoking is so addictive that once smokers have had a few cigarettes, they are hooked: the social influences on smoking then become less important for maintaining the practice than is the case for other substances like alcohol and marijuana. This means that research and intervention which are concerned with peer influences on smoking must necessarily focus on the initial experimentation phase, which occurs from age 10 to 14 years. In stressing the increased potential for risk behaviour in early adolescence, Jackson and Hornbeck (1989) cite evidence in the US that over half the graduating seniors in high school had begun cigarette smoking prior to the tenth grade.

Several studies report that peer pressure does not operate in the same manner on those who have already begun smoking as it may be expected to do when influencing young people to try their first smoke. Three motivational processes were examined by Covington and Omelich (1988) in relation to smoking scenarios presented to adolescents aged 11, 13, and 15–16: perceived pressure, temptation to smoke, and expectation of smoking. The 13-year-olds were the most vulnerable group in terms of higher temptations and expectations to smoke; they also affirmed the values of smoking for achieving maturity and autonomy more strongly than the older and younger groups. The temptation to smoke was primarily linked in this study to the belief that smoking enhanced one's maturity. Sensitivity to peer pressure varied with the individual's smoking history: regular smokers were unaffected by peer influence, whereas non-smokers and those defined as experimental smokers felt more tempted to smoke as peer influences increased.

It would be interesting to explore the links between temptations to smoke and patterns of experimental smoking, given that these views were endorsed more by younger than by older respondents, and in the light of responses to a 1985 survey of Victorian adolescents (Australian Government, 1990). This study contrasted the beliefs of 11-year-olds, 13-year-olds, and 16-year-olds about the health risks and social benefits of smoking. Respondents were classified according to whether they had ever smoked or never smoked cigarettes. In this study, the proportions of regular smokers were 6 per cent (age 11), 21 per cent (age 13), and 26 per cent (age 16). General health-related beliefs such as 'smoking can harm your health' and 'smoking affects your sporting ability' showed increasingly strong endorsement with age (health 88–94 per cent, sport 69–81 per cent). Beliefs about the social benefits of smoking were supported more by younger age groups, and were endorsed much more by smokers than by non-smokers. For example, 31.5 per cent of 11-year-old smokers and 31 per cent of 13-year-olds agreed that 'smokers are usually more popular than non-smokers' compared with 18.5 per cent and 21.4 per cent of non-smokers in these age groups, and 15.7 per cent of smokers and 12.7 per cent of non-smokers aged 16 years. More smokers also agreed that 'kids who smoke seem more grown-up'. Again the responses in agreement declined with age, percentages dropping from 17.5 to 12.3 and to 4.1 for smokers, and from 10.7 to 8.0 and 4.4 for non-smokers.

These statistics suggest that young people in Australia are aware of the health risks from smoking, but do not necessarily integrate this knowledge with what they perceive as social benefits from smoking, particularly during the period of peak experimentation, namely in the pre-adolescent and early adolescent years. Survey research in Britain by Eiser *et al.* (1987) suggests that the motives which smokers agreed with, and endorsed more with age, such as 'smoking is enjoyable', 'smoking calms your nerves', 'smoking is hard to give up once you start', may be socially learned accounts and rationalisations about smoking, which young smokers come to accept as true and which assist them in maintaining their habit.

PEERS AND DRINKING ALCOHOL

The importance of peers, particularly friends, in reinforcing drinking behaviour has been widely noted (e.g., Wilks, 1987). A study by Smith *et al.*
(1989) tested a model derived from problem-behaviour theory and employed
Jessor and Jessor's (1977) distinction between distal and proximal social
environments. They found few distal influences (e.g., family socialisation
and perceived parent and peer encouragement of drinking) on adolescents'
drinking patterns; but there was a strong association between drinking and
proximal peer influences. The major influence was friends' level of drinking and attitude to drinking; this interacted with the extent of cohesion and
communication in the adolescent's family, and also with the level of the
adolescent's social skills.

In discussing initiation into drinking behaviour, let us consider some of
the conditions which may increase susceptibility to influence at a particular
age, and, in particular, the impact of peer influence from the perspective of
conditions of influenceability. This directs us to ask, 'Under what conditions is a person more likely to behave in a way which is similar to that of
her/his peers?' By adopting this perspective, we are able to acknowledge
that influences on behaviour are complex and multiple, and that they are not
constant. A major condition of susceptibility to health risk behaviour is the
absence of adult controls. This may occur because the venue chosen for
leisure activities is one where adults are seldom seen, and where adult
prohibitions on drinking or smoking, for example, are less likely to be
enforced, as is the case for amusement centres and local street hangouts
(Selnow and Crano, 1986). An interesting aspect of the Bauman and Fisher
(1986) study on drinking and smoking relates to the link between type of
social setting and social pressure to engage in risk behaviour. They found
that the subject's own behaviour was more strongly related to her/his
perceptions of the friend's behaviour than to the friend's actual behaviour,
with the differences for drinking being much larger than for smoking,
which highlights the different impact of social context for these activities.
Drinking occurs in peer crowd situations where the behaviour of some of
the peer group is likely to affect the individual's estimates of the amount of
drinking of her/his friends. An emergent norm situation occurs, so that
participants' estimates of the drinking norms become inflated.

The alcohol studies highlight the cultural importance given to drinking
and drinking contexts in Western society as a means of acquiring adult
status, particularly where this need is accentuated by poor family relationships. Like smoking, drinking is seen by youth as a marker of social
sophistication, with the additional (if dubious) benefit of helping the youth
adapt to social situations. The social contexts of drinking deserve mention,

because adolescent drinking, and much adult drinking as well (e.g., Simpura, 1985), occurs at parties and special occasions not in the normal context of living, and in narrowly defined time zones within the weekly round of activities. Indeed, for most young people, their first encounter with alcohol, and with drinking to excess, occurs in private homes (see Box 6.2), but peer influence may still be the major influence on binge drinking. In addition to the special events mentioned, an Australian social custom which Wilks (1987) points out as contributing to excessive drinking is the 'shout' of a round of drinks at a pub, which institutionalises peer pressure over the rate of drinking as well as the quantity of liquor consumed. These contexts of pubs and parties induce young people to behave in an unconstrained manner, including drinking more than is wise, and thus expose them to various kinds of social and health risk. Adolescents who regularly attend parties and other peer outings such as discos, dances, and driving around in cars adopt drinking patterns at an earlier age than the majority of their peers (Margulies *et al.*, 1977).

The problem of teenage binge drinking

In terms of problem-behaviour theory, youth drinking is a problem when it is non-normative for the society. Concern arises at conditions which accelerate the induction of young people into drinking; for many youth, settings dominated by peers slightly older than themselves accelerate their entry into adult styles of behaviour, including alcohol use. The aspect of youthful drinking which causes special concern is binge drinking or 'getting wasted'. The New South Wales Alcohol and Drug Service estimates that about 40 per cent of boys aged between 12 and 18 years, and about 30 per cent of girls, regularly engage in binge drinking, which is defined as five standard drinks in a session. Studies link alcohol use with peer contexts

Box 6.2 Teen parties and the demon drink

> The dilemma facing the parent of any child who has not been forcibly restrained from approaching the drinks cabinet and the bottle shop can best be appreciated when one observes an event only those with an iron constitution will have anything to do with – the teenage party.
>
> We had one once. We will have another one when hell freezes over.
>
> It went basically like this. The teenage persons all arrived and drank our grog in five minutes, then found all the bottles they had hidden and drank those, then they were all sick.
>
> (from Crawford on Sunday, *Saturday Mercury*, Hobart, 6 November 1993)

where cliques gather in leisure settings, rather than in organised groups or cultural activities (Engel *et al.*, 1987; Pulkkinen and Narusk, 1987; Wilks, 1987). Peers in these settings promote motives for drinking which increase their exposure to risk; for example, arguing that drinking helps you to make friends with the opposite sex, and that it is good to get drunk sometimes. Perhaps most tellingly, the normalising effect of these social leisure settings is seen in Broadbent's recent report that youth in Melbourne 'did not see the issue of alcohol use or abuse as an important one' (Broadbent, 1994, p. 33).

The significance of drinking as an end in itself, and therefore a potential risk factor, is dramatically seen in the 'O-Week' (Orientation-Week) activities at Australian universities. Large numbers of 18-year-old students new to university life are encouraged to attend these events, where kegs of beer are provided, and they are expected to finish up 'legless'. The attraction of 'free kegs' is intended to generate heavier than usual drinking in the participants, whatever their normal level of drinking, and put pressure on others who may be non-drinkers to 'have a couple' and not to be 'wowsers'. Harford and Grant (1987) have remarked on the greater 'wetness' and prevalence of student binge drinking at 'time-out' events located at the beginning and end of the academic year. These equate locally with Orientation Week at university and Schoolies' Week (an end-of-school celebration, discussed in detail in Chapter 7) among school leavers. For many young people, these special occasions and the events which they spawn, like the Toga Party at the University of Queensland each mid-February in O-Week and the Faculty Balls later on, are thinly disguised modern orgies, and are understood as such by students.

In these peer-dominated out-of-school social settings, older youth play a crucial role in inducting younger ones into drinking. Evidence of their influence is documented in a study of Swedish youth by Stattin *et al.* (1989). Taking the view that drinking is an instance of a social transition, they proposed that students associating with peers who were older or who were working are exposed to experiences outside the normal age range of schoolmates, and would be more likely to engage in adult behaviours like drinking at an earlier time. They reasoned that adolescents whose networks contained these 'non-conventional' peer groups would be experiencing different social environments. The peer socialisation processes would be different, and would influence the timing of when regular drinking habits were acquired. The longitudinal nature of the Stattin study gives special point to its findings, which show that associating with older peers or working peers was related to more reports of respondents being drunk, and drunk often. The pattern was consistent for both sexes. In contrast, those whose peers were all schoolmates reported stronger sanctions against drunkenness and less permissiveness from their peers. Another interesting finding was that classmates were much less important as a reference group for those whose network included older pals, suggesting a shift in the reference group towards older peers. The pattern was stronger for males; it was less marked for females because of the greater role of the best friend as a reference point.

Use of alcohol for social coping

The significance of the social setting for drinking activity is highlighted in Harford and Grant's (1987) study, which shows that across a variety of social contexts, the frequency of drinking was best explained by normative support from peers ('my friends drink') and from parents ('both my parents have a glass'). It is worth noting the important role of parents in modelling drinking behaviour in adult contexts, including adult parties where heavier than usual drinking may occur. The second strongest explanation for drinking was the positive social functions attributed to drinking, including helping to overcome shyness and being a sign that one is grown up; these were related to teenage drinking contexts, such as parties and social outings, and not to adult settings.

Smith *et al.* (1989) emphasise the vulnerability of the socially inadequate or insecure adolescent who strives to gain acceptance from peers via the use of alcohol as 'a replacement social skill' (p. 139). Adolescents in fragmented family situations appeared more likely to have poorer social skills, which may have led to attempts to seek approval and acceptance from drinking companions, and to model their behaviour. The patterns are consistent with those reported in other studies, which have argued that adolescents seek to compensate for poor social skills by drinking, in the belief that a few drinks will help them relax and become more outgoing, or will confer an adult status which is difficult for them to attain in other social settings (e.g., Engel *et al.*, 1987; Galambos and Silbereisen, 1987). Among a group of peers where drinking is an approved activity, such young people may view alcohol consumption as a badge of entry and a means of becoming 'one of the lads' or 'one of the girls', as well as achieving an altered (intoxicated = happy) emotional state. Indeed Pulkkinen (1983) traces a path of socially inept behaviour, including aggression, in youth who were heavy drinkers, which reaches back into their childhood.

Healthy attachments as protective factors

Focus on the interactive relations with peers should not blind us to the continuing influence of parental controls and bonds of attachment to parents. Evidence from various studies reminds us that adolescents differ in their susceptibility to risk behaviours such as smoking, alcohol abuse, and the use of illicit drugs, and that this variation is largely related to the quality of attachments with parents and with peers. Young people who have healthy relationships with parents are less susceptible to influence from antisocial peers. Status among one's peers also affects influenceability: those with marginal or rejected status are more influencible than higher-status group members.

Chassin *et al.* (1989) report that adolescents whose attitudes to 'constructive deviance' were strong (that is, they described themselves as creative, independent, assertive, and unconventional) were less susceptible to peer opinion than were other adolescents. For these young people, their cigarette smoking was less related to peer influence, and was an expression of their own wish to assert themselves. These results suggest that young people who have weaker ties to prevailing peer group norms are less vulnerable to peer pressure to adopt them.

Differences in the quality of attachment relations to parents were found to be associated with the attitudes to drinking of Dutch adolescents by Kwakman *et al.* (1988). Adolescents who were anxiously attached particularly mentioned drinking as a means of helping them socialise with others. Attachment relations also featured in Foshee and Bauman's (1994) research into the influence of parents on adolescents' initiation into smoking, where data were obtained from adolescents tested in two waves two years apart. At the time of the first testing, these adolescents had not smoked at all. Attachment to parents (i.e., closeness) was found to delay smoking initiation: the stronger the degree of adolescent attachment to parents, the less likely were adolescents to smoke cigarettes at the measurement point two years later. Attachment also influenced adolescents' beliefs in, and endorsement of, conventional rules. Thus the effect of binding adolescents to parental expectations and to the norms of the wider society was to deter them from smoking cigarettes.

Some similar kind of process occurs in parent influence over levels of drinking, as Mitic's findings on different drinking contexts point out. Mitic (1990) compared the levels of drinking among Canadian adolescents who drink in the company of their parents with those who drink only with their friends. He found that adolescents consumed between three and six times as many drinks in the company of peers as did those who drank in their parents' company, clearly indicating that peers encourage the consumption of greater quantities of alcohol. He noted, however, that these peer context influences also increased the consumption levels of youth who drank at home, when they were out with their friends. Thus attempts by parents to assist their teenagers to be responsible drinkers by introducing them to alcohol at home showed no evidence of reduced consumption when they were out with their friends.

IMPLICATIONS FOR HEALTH EDUCATION PROGRAMMES

Various education programmes (of an informational kind) focusing on the long-term health consequences of smoking, as well as behavioural interventions utilising principles of modelling and skills training, have now been in place for over a decade in most countries; and they have proven about equally ineffective in reducing the incidence of smoking among young people, beyond delaying the entry of youngsters into experimental smoking (see Flay *et al.*, 1989; Leventhal *et al.* 1991). Similar information-based approaches to curbing teenage alcohol abuse have been ineffective. On this aspect, Dielman (1994, p. 272) observes: 'The underlying premise was incorrect; changes in attitudes or knowledge were not correlated with subsequent behavioural changes.' Education aimed at avoiding alcohol abuse among youth has found little acceptance where young people themselves do not perceive that they have a problem. We may doubt the effectiveness of school health education campaigns directed against teenage smoking, when the numbers of children taking up smoking each year show so few signs of diminishing. One may question the commitment of governments to health education, when research funded by the New South Wales Cancer Council states that Australian federal and state governments obtain $60 tax revenue yearly from each under-age smoker in this country, but fund anti-smoking programmes at the cost of 11 cents per under-age smoker (*Bulletin*, 7 May 1995).

Motivational factors

One of the benefits to emerge from the vigorous smoking interventions developed in the 1980s is the increased attention being given to motivation: to what adolescents want to do, rather than to what they should do. Discussions of peer influences and socialisation are found on closer inspection to be concerned with motivational processes (see Box 6.3).

Box 6.3 Young people's views of drinking

It's easier to talk to people if you have a few drinks.

Drinking makes you popular and you get to go to more parties.

If you don't drink you're not in the group.

Everyone drinks at parties.

If you drive carefully you can get home even if you're drunk.

Moreover, when intervention programmes in risk behaviour are considered from a motivational and educational standpoint, rather than merely from a prevention-via-information standpoint, questions of primary group values and attitudes, of individual needs for acceptance and recognition, of the role of previous experiences, of situational cues and reinforcements, and of the relevance of timing in interventions all come into consideration. Dielman (1994) pinpoints the transition from primary to secondary school as a very important ecological transition in relation to initiation into drinking, which he sees as independent of the age at which the transition occurs. Given the significance of peer pressure noted in this chapter and in the work of Dielman and others, a significance which increases through access to larger numbers of peers at secondary school, there is logic in ensuring that programmes are introduced before this transition occurs.

There has been insufficient recognition given to the meaning of the experience of smoking, drinking, and so on as seen from the adolescent's own perspective. Health educators have assumed that the values of youth and adults are broadly compatible: for example, that we all agree that smoking is harmful to our health, and that the side effects of heavy drinking are undesirable. Such a view blithely assumes that 'the target audience [of adolescents] already has an intrinsic motive to avoid use', Leventhal *et al.* (1991, p. 584) note; it ignores the possibility that adolescents see things differently, and even ascribe positive meanings to smoking. After all, the positive meanings are vigorously promoted by advertisers, with images of smoking as sexy, successful, sophisticated, and associated with fine clothes, classy hotels, and expensive cars, and drinking being associated with parties, celebrations, happiness, and friends. And none of the models ever coughs, or has stained teeth, or begins retching violently, or develops liver failure, bronchial diseases, or throat cancer.

Recent research points out that even where the evidence is clear that social forces are operating to influence individual behaviour, it does not necessarily follow that educational programmes based on the social inoculation model, which alerts participants to this fact, will be effective. Few of us find it easy to accept that our behaviour is influenced by conformity to group pressures. We prefer to explain our actions in terms of intrinsic motives and personal reasons rather than as evidence of group conformity. Indeed, Smith (1985) reports that a large majority of British youth denied that they copied their friends, or did things just because their friends did them. Programmes which alert us to the external influences on our behaviour are likely to meet resistance; more so when the participants are adolescents, for whom group acceptance is especially valued.

There are several possible reasons why a focus on resisting group pressures will have limited success with youth. First, drawing young people's attention to the ways in which they are influenced by others could imply that trusting one's peers and friends is questionable, if not misplaced. Second, there is an inference that adolescents are weak and 'easily led', and fall victim to peer pressure because they lack nous, moral backbone, or social competence. Third, by failing to appreciate the leisure context in which smoking and alcohol use occur, these programmes diminish the social meanings which have become associated with smoking and drinking in the company of one's friends. Eiser *et al.* (1987, p. 383) state that if smoking education programmes are to be effective, they must be prepared to take the experience of the smoker seriously. They warn that young smokers are likely to reject any approach which is unwilling to accept that smoking may be an enjoyable and valid accompaniment to social activity, and which instead portrays smoking as group conformity, even if there is evidence to support this view (e.g., Covington and Omelich, 1988; Stacy *et al.*, 1992; Urberg, 1992).

Peers as allies not foes

The notion of peer pressure has proven to be a bogeyman whose shadow continues to diminish in size as we shine the torchlight further into the alleyways where it is thought to hold sway. There is now sufficient evidence from the empirical studies of smoking to suggest that the influence of peers has been exaggerated. The conclusions of these studies cast doubt on the effectiveness of anti-smoking programmes which attribute the adoption of smoking primarily to peer influence, and which focus on teaching youth to resist peer pressure. It is unproductive to search for one single process or entity named 'peer pressure'; social influences vary with the situation and circumstance, and with individuals. Moreover, the strength of a particular source of influence depends on the relationship others have with the actor, as well as the acuteness of the situation.

Rather than adopting a hostile view of the role of peers in socialisation in smoking, it is preferable to note the value of peer relationships for healthy development, and recognise the folly of attempting to alienate adolescents from their friends in the misguided belief that youth are 'easily led' and socially naive. For young people, just as for adults, friends are chosen on the basis of similarities of interests and attitudes, of which smoking may be one. Smoking may be important as a defining characteristic of a group of friends, just as clothing and hairstyle may be important, as Mosbach and Leventhal (1988), Denholm *et al.* (1992), and Urberg (1992) suggest; but it may be more appropriate to see smoking as an aspect of a group lifestyle than to assume it to be a necessary badge of group membership. Evidence of the significant influence of best friends on smoking initiation and maintenance suggests that programmes which focus on teaching young people how to resist peer pressure in some abstract form may have limited success. Morgan and Grube (1991, p. 168) are among those who recommend that social skills programmes 'should not be concerned with remote anonymous peers, but rather with friends'. Eiser *et al.* (1991) also emphasise the point that young people are not passive victims of peer pressures, but belong to groups because they choose to do so. They suggest that intervention programmes could be designed so as 'to help young people achieve greater self-awareness about their choice of friends, and about the mutual influence processes which such friendships supply' (p. 346). A similar theme is expressed by Ennett and Bauman 1991), who urge educators to consider the peer group as 'an ally rather than an enemy' in preventing smoking. They recommend more attention be given to social skills training for healthy functioning with peers and improving communication skills, rather than emphasising how to resist peer influence. Stacy *et al.* (1992) identified a significant moderator of the effect of friends' influence on smoking as self-efficacy, the belief held by the individual about her/his ability to cope with a given situation. The practical significance of self-efficacy is that it is a characteristic of the person which is able to buffer the external social influences of the peer group. In the context of smoking, self-efficacy refers to the individual's belief in her/his ability to resist the social influence of peers, both by having the knowledge to identify the harmful effects of smoking, and by having the social skills to negotiate the attempts by friends to cajole, badger, or tease her/him into smoking, without losing them as friends.

CONCLUSION: EDUCATING FOR RESPONSIBLE BEHAVIOUR

The message from several large studies of smoking which have been cited is that if we are to reach an understanding of why young people take up smoking, we must look beyond the notion of susceptibility to peer pressure as the principal influence on smoking, and give more emphasis to the beliefs held by the young people themselves, recognising of course that some of these beliefs are fostered through peer association. Eiser *et al.* (1987) found that teenage smokers were quick to reject suggestions that they smoked in order to look more grown up, tough, or important. But while they may reject these motives, it is clear from the body of research that initiation into smoking is affected by such concerns about the symbolic value of smoking and drinking in the quest for adult status. The implications for educational programmes are clear, if not easy to implement: design programmes which promote social skills and knowledge about the consequences of behaviour so that self-efficacy is enhanced. The approach which Leventhal *et al.* (1991) advocate is to intervene at the point of initiation into smoking, when the experience is unpleasant, and where the adolescent can draw on her/his own experience to validate the claims made by health educators. At this early point of smoking initiation, where peers challenge the youngster to have a smoke, the educator attempts to strengthen the meaning of the experience of the coughing, the burning throat, and the dizzy feeling as the body's warning system before the meaning is stifled by addiction.

A similar set of principles is advocated in alcohol education through the principle of harm minimisation being implemented at the time of writing in the Cheers Drink Safe Project and trialling in eighteen schools in Victoria and New South Wales (Harris and Sheehan, 1995). The approach taken is to recognise that young people have a right to make up their own minds about alcohol use, and that the majority do want to learn how to avoid the harms of alcohol use, such as losing control, being sick, having accidents, encountering violence, and getting into trouble with parents or police. Included in the programme are activities encouraging young people to identify for themselves the situations they know which constitute the greatest potential harm and are therefore best avoided.

Education in health risk behaviour has to address wider aspects than individual behaviour. It has to be linked with challenges to the prevailing social norms. In Australia, television has been an important tool in changing public awareness. A smoking programme promoted the image to young people that smoking was socially undesirable, with the slogan 'Kiss a non-smoker; taste the difference.' The Australian Medical Association is currently launching a smoking education programme aimed at young women, raising their awareness of the cost of smoking on the environment, in bushfires, the detritus of litter, and billboards. There is also a television campaign concerned with drink-driving which currently features the theme, 'If you drink and drive, you're a bloody idiot.' What is commendable about these ads is the recognition that people easily forget responsible social behaviour in free-flowing leisure contexts, where the ambience of the setting is about having a good time, and where emergent norms about relaxing and going with the crowd hold sway. The drink ads feature a series of party scenarios which end with the punchline 'bloody idiot' branded on the forehead of the miscreant. They focus on the actions of friends, watching out for the person with the problem and speaking to them about their drinking, in order to help them avoid becoming branded.

In seeking to inform adolescents of the consequences of risk behaviour, educational approaches run the risk of being too informative, too rational, and too parental, and of emphasising albeit with good intentions the limited knowledge and experience of their audience. Broadbent (1994) found that young people she worked with became 'ferocious' at the thought of discussing the issue of drinking with their parents. Our knowledge of young people should make us wary of programmes which advise them to wait until they know more and can handle situations better, to wait until they are more grown up, to wait till they learn about the negative consequences before trying something, while the wider world is beckoning them to explore and find out now what it is like for themselves. The motives for risk behaviour change considerably across the period of adolescence, and are linked to other changes in social and psychological development, particularly those which touch on autonomy and identity. Rather than seeking to instil self-control and resistance skills, programmes could take more account of adolescents' social awareness and existing social skills. By recognising that young people are capable of adopting a responsible course of action in relation to health risk behaviours, and of building their own harm minimisation strategy, programmes could seek ways of establishing the appropriate basis of trust and respect which will encourage them to want to do so.

7 Antisocial behaviour in groups and crowds

Since the 1970s, the term 'hooliganism' has reappeared as a label for group forms of antisocial behaviour. In Europe it has come to be synonymous with football, the implication being that hooligan behaviour is peculiar to the nature of football and that football crowds are particularly unruly and undisciplined. An additional concern among teachers and psychologists is that violence and aggression among children and adolescents have increased. Schools are reporting an increase in recent years of bullying, 'stand-over' tactics (discussed later in this chapter), robbery, and assault with a weapon. Antisocial behaviour, in the form of physical threat, aggression, and property damage, is now found across a wide range of social settings, and has become a topic of great public concern. Explanations of hooliganism often invoke family histories of poor parenting on the one hand, and the weakening of law enforcement controls on the other. Seldom is the group environment itself seen as a credible influence source.

The subject of this chapter is the group and the mass crowd as social vehicles for committing hostile acts, particularly aggression and property damage. The chapter focuses on the experiences of young people as members of groups in public places, where territory is often contested. The tendency for youth to seek leisure experiences in groups and attend mass entertainments (rock concerts, street festivals, and sports matches, for example) underlines the importance of these public assemblies in young people's lives. The broad question which directs our enquiries is, 'How important is the group context for encouraging individual members to engage in hostile or antisocial behaviour?'

HOOLIGANS, CROWDS, AND DISORDER

The importance of the group or crowd as an extra-individual context capable of altering the normal behaviour of its members has been a topic of long-standing interest (e.g., LeBon, 1896/1908). Among the more recent commentators, Sherif and Sherif (1964, p. 65) drew attention to 'the dramatic significance of group membership in performing seriously unacceptable acts', and Milgram and Toch (1969, p. 507) remarked that 'Many actions which seem beyond the range of human capability, both from the standpoint of heroism and of destruction, come to light in collective episodes.' Group influence appears such an overwhelming force on people when they are part of a group or crowd that some are willing to behave in socially unacceptable and even violent ways. The extra-individual characteristics of crowds are not imaginary phenomena. J. Allan's (1989) account of travelling by bus to football games with the Aberdeen Casuals provides explicit details of the way that a hooligan group can 'egg on' individuals to perform acts which are destructive, loutish, and in very poor taste. The group context of antisocial behaviour prompts a series of questions. Are antisocial groups composed of antisocial individuals, or does the group context induce deviant behaviour? If peer groups instigate law-abiding youths to engage in vandalism and violence, how are the group and crowd norms transmitted, and why do they gain acceptance by the membership? How does the group context provide opportunities for things to 'get out of hand'? Does it provide mutual reinforcing conditions, or a cloak of anonymity where troublesome youth can behave in outrageous ways? These questions of group influence on antisocial behaviour are very broad in scope. Different kinds of group influence are implied as affecting behaviour, both direct and indirect, and ranging from small-group influences to mass crowd phenomena.

The public context: media, moral panics, and 'folk devils'

While the phenomena of crowd disorder and intergroup hostility are not new, theoretical analysis has been difficult, and often unsatisfactory. The running has often been made by the media, who are 'not neutral observers of the social scene [but] active elements in . . . the defining of social problems' (Murphy *et al.*, 1990, p. 123). They create the public context for discussions of hooliganism. The tabloid press finds it convenient to explain problems of mass crowd unruliness by headlines about 'riot', 'rampage', 'day of shame', and 'mindless mob'. In the search for interpretations of crowd behaviour, the more reactionary groups enclose it in a discourse of *moral panic* (Cohen, 1973), which condemns all populist activities from rock concerts to football as signs of tribalism and mass hysteria. The antisocial types of toughs, skinheads, yobbos, and football hooligans are constructed by the popular media from an inventory of 'deviant' features of young people's clothing, appearance, and collective behaviour; they fill the role in modern society of what Cohen (1973) called 'folk devils – visible reminders of what we should not be' (p. 10). An expectation is generated that the presence of youth possessing these features symbolises the decline of community and the imminent outbreak of violence and destructive behaviour.

Cohen stressed that deviance is not a property of the act which a person commits, but rather is the consequence of a labelling process applied to an 'offender' by certain groups of people. Society creates deviance by valuing and upholding certain rules of order, so that people who do not fit neatly into the rules are labelled as outsiders (see also Marsh *et al.*, 1978). The media are active in shaping the issue of deviance through the use of exaggeration and distortion. Headlines construct negative images and symbols, regardless of any basis in actual events. Once a set of negative symbols is assembled which relates, for example, to youth and trouble making, the reader's own selective perception will strengthen the categorisation.

When the mods and rockers youth types were emerging in Britain in the 1960s, Cohen analysed the reports of several British newspapers about a clash between mods and rockers in August 1964, heralded as 'the Battle of Hastings'. Under banner headlines of 'Riot police fly to seaside', 'Break it up now!', and 'Battle of the Wild Ones', and garnished with photographs of crowds of young men, the reports spoke of 'trouble' and skirmishes between groups of youths, of police being 'bustled' and in one instance 'knocked down and kicked'. Cohen produced a different set of photographs of the same scenes which showed families relaxing on the beach, apparently oblivious of the 'riot' which surrounded them.

Reporting of crowd behaviour at football matches has also been subject to distortion by the press. Moorhouse (1991) compared newspaper reports of two invasions of the pitch at Wembley (in 1967 and 1977) by Scottish football supporters, and showed how differently the same kind of event was treated. Whereas the 1967 event was *not even mentioned* in the *Times* report of the match, and only mentioned in a minor way in the *Daily Mirror* and the *Sunday Express*, the apparently similar acts were given very different treatment by the press a decade later. The pitch invasion now received front-page coverage, and was given an entirely different interpretation from that of ten years previously. Whereas in 1967 the behaviour of the Scottish fans in removing pieces of the Wembley turf was seen as an act of reverence by fans seeking a memento, in 1977 the same action was strongly condemned in highly emotional language.

Historians show that expressions of moral outrage about degenerate youth are found in press reports throughout the twentieth century, and match fairly well with periods of rapid urban or demographic change (e.g., Gilbert, 1986; Pearson, 1983). It is a myth that there is greater lawlessness and hooliganism among the present generation; the truth is that these are not new phenomena but continuous with the past. Pearson shows that moral panics have long been a feature of public debates, and that the reach of personal memory back to a calmer age is usually about twenty years, that is, one generation. He argues that when these moral panics and respectable fears are recognised as excursions into nostalgia, ineffectual for addressing the real divisions in society which stigmatise and disadvantage a large proportion of young people, the focus of analysis can shift from a study of prevailing myths to the structures and social influences actually affecting youth behaviour. It is to these studies of youth in crowds that we now turn.

HOOLIGANS AND LARRIKINS

The term 'hooligan' emerged in Britain in the late 1890s. Some sources (such as Rook, 1899; *Webster's Third International Dictionary*, 1966) link the term to Patrick Houlihan, an Irishman in Southwark, London, who, according to Rook (1899), 'walked to and fro among his fellow men, robbing them and occasionally bashing them'. However, Pearson (1983) is sceptical of Rook's claims, and discusses in detail the origin of the term (pp. 253–256). Instead, Pearson suggests that 'its abrupt entrance into common English usage . . . during the hot summer of 1898' (p. 74) characterised a style of youth behaviour not dissimilar from that later associated with such youth styles as that of the Teddy Boys. Hooligans were similar to the larrikins who had existed earlier in Britain in their style of flashy dressing and rowdy street behaviour, but in 1898 the term hooligan 'established itself', Pearson (1983, p. 98) notes, whereas Australians preferred to speak of larrikins. The similarity in origin of these terms to describe a 'young urban rough . . . one who acts with apparently careless disregard for social or political conventions', according to Hughes (1989, p. 303), is important. It may assist in retrieving the sense of mischief in the behaviour of street gangs, loutish as they may appear from first-hand accounts (such as J. Allan, 1989; Ward, 1989), and highlight the different public perceptions of larrikinism in Australia (where the term 'hooligan' has far less currency) compared with what are generally similar kinds of behaviour in Europe. Larrikins dressed in distinctive styles, and were rough in their behaviour, coarse and irreverent in language, and inconsiderate of other people's rights or sensibilities. The word 'larrikin' may have derived from 'larking about' or from the Cornish word 'larican', meaning to make mischief.

'Larrikinism' and 'hooliganism' both refer to the spirit of defiance of authority and collective irreverence which characterises the public behaviour of Australians and Britons, particularly young males. Larrikinism should be understood as a group phenomenon, because an audience is necessary for its expression. Thus larrikin displays are fostered where there is a large group, and an opportunity to show off and play to the crowd. The most accessible public forums for giving fullest expression to larrikinism are those where crowds assemble in leisure settings at pubs and sports events like cricket and football. The link between hooligan behaviour and sport first appeared in Australia in press descriptions of a riot at the Sydney cricket ground in 1879.

Time-out behaviour

There is a temporal rhythm to crowd disorder and hooligan behaviour. In noting this rhythm, Smith (1983, p. 152) commented that 'much of what is called soccer hooliganism smacks strongly of time-out behaviour'. The time-out is a period of the year when the conditions are right for producing deviant behaviour. It has a long tradition, derived from the customs of feast days, market days, and the carnival. On these occasions, normal social controls were relaxed, and people could let their hair down and have a bit of fun. Thus tendencies towards deviant behaviour were structured into the rhythm of social life, and recognised on the yearly calendar. Similarly, giving time-outs a place in the modern community's calendar of events allows occasional deviant activity to be accommodated into the community norms, and the boundaries of norm breaking to be preserved.

The street is the most common venue for time-out events, allowing people to congregate in large numbers in public areas. Prominent events for Australian youth are New Year's Eve celebrations, Sydney's gay Mardi Gras, 'footie finals week' (in Melbourne), Melbourne Cup day (all states), special outdoor events hosted by radio stations, and events like Schoolies' Week. Such carnival occasions provide opportunities for young people to become influenced by crowd processes, and to behave in ways that are sometimes antisocial.

Sport has been marketed to the masses by grafting the time-out concept onto events like football or cricket matches, so that spectators are conscious of the rhythm – when the next game is, how critical the result is. Thus the events of being in a crowd at 'the footie' become for the ardent fans their peak experiences in the week – when youth can do something free from the controls customarily imposed over their everyday lives. One of Robins' (1984) hooligan respondents explained the nature of his commitment to football in this way: 'The game? I can't miss it now. I've been going for too long . . . It's cos football's in my blood and it always will be' (p. 54).

Schoolies' Week

The first week after leaving school at the end of November is a recent example of a time-out event in Australia, known as Schoolies' Week. It is regarded as an opportunity for adolescents to celebrate their escape from the confines of school life with a high-spirited 'final party' with their schoolmates before they go their separate ways. Its history is uncertain, but it has become so established in the holiday areas of Queensland (the Gold Coast and the Sunshine Coast) that travel agents around the land publish colourful travel brochures, urging that bookings be made many months ahead. The significance of the event can be appreciated when young people travel to these holiday strips from as far away as Melbourne and spend $500 for their week's accommodation, apart from their airfares and daily expenses.

The phenomenon of large numbers of Schoolies flocking to the tourist 'strips' in Queensland, all looking to 'let their hair down' and have a good time, has been presented by the news media as an invasion: a time of lawlessness, loutish behaviour, unruliness, and alcohol and drug abuse. The popular image which has been generated is that Schoolies' Week is a week-long drinking party, when hordes of unruly teenagers who are drunk, cheeky, and ill-behaved crowd the main streets and public spaces of the major seaside resorts. Through the juxtaposition of news headlines ('Schoolie fury erupts': Brisbane *Courier Mail*, 23 November 1994) and emotive language (e.g., 'three-night rampage'; 'public safety', 'street brawl', 'police call for back-up') with picture 'grabs' of carousing or fighting young people and property damage, the media erect a demonology around the leisure behaviour of young people, accompanied by urgings for greater policing and control. One resident in a letter to the editor called Schoolies the 'cockroaches of society', and urged they be banned from the coast.

True, some young people do regard Schoolies' Week as a week of continual drinking and rowdyism, but it is an exaggeration to say that most school leavers are disorderly. It is true that each year sees brawls and disorderly behaviour when thousands of young people crowd into the coastal centres. Thousands of Schoolies and older 'hangers-on' gathered one evening in late November 1993 on the beach area at Maroochydore, on Queensland's Sunshine Coast. When the night's revelries had abated, there was a mess of bottles, cans, foodstuff, and broken glass on the rocks and beach. At the Gold Coast in November 1994, police made thirty-two arrests of youth on one night. However, the direct involvement of Schoolies in offensive behaviour may be judged by reports stating that only six of those detained by police were under the age of 18. Most were in their twenties, and were described by police as 'yobbos', 'older riff-raff', and 'hangers-on', attracted to the scene by the opportunity to make trouble within the anonymity of the crowd.

Youth revelry or riot?

An example of crowd unruliness at a carnival event is the revelry which accompanied the New Year's Eve celebrations in the little seaside town of Byron Bay, southeast of Brisbane, in 1993/4. Contributing to the carnival atmosphere were two organised entertainments: a beach rock concert, and a dance hosted by a local hotel, the mood at both events assisted by the consumption of considerable quantities of alcohol. Transition from fun to crowd disorder was triggered by an incident at a hotel where some young drinkers were refused admission, and a fight erupted. When police intervened they were attacked with bottles. Other signs that the theshold from fun to disorder had been crossed were seen in the free-fall stunts of revellers who swan-dived from the roofs of nearby buildings into the swelling crowd gathered in the main street. When some young people were injured from their falls, police had great difficulty in getting those in the crowd to cooperate with them and make room so that ambulance workers could reach the injured. Later, a water main was deliberately broken, creating a fountain in the main street. This drew further crowd conflict when the police tried to plug the water main by parking their 'paddy wagon' on top of the broken pipe. Youths jumped on top of the van and attempted to overturn it; others chanted 'Let's kill the coppers' as they hurled stones and bottles.

In the following days, the police sergeant in charge dismissed national newspaper reports that rioters had taken control of the town: 'At no stage do I believe it was a riot – just straight-out yobboism. There was no massive damage to shops [although] police were rained with bottles and had to use force to control people.' This incident, involving many young people who had travelled to the town for the express purpose of having a good time at New Year, is an example of the spontaneity and unpredictability of the behaviour of people in mass crowds, where horseplay and high spirits, assisted by liberal quantities of alcohol, can suddenly turn into nastiness and violence.

CROWDS AS A CONTEXT FOR APPRENTICESHIP IN ANTISOCIAL BEHAVIOUR

These accounts of crowd behaviour illustrate how mass crowd participation enrols youth in apprenticeships in antisocial behaviour. They prompt the question, 'Does membership in a crowd change the behaviour of an individual, or does the aggressive and violent individual seek out the crowd?' Reicher (1987) reminds us of the important role of actions in mass crowd behaviour. Unlike in groups, where communication can occur through discussion and deliberation, the acquisition of norms in crowd situations can only occur by induction. Membership of the crowd is established through individuals behaving in conformity with what they perceive to be the norms of the group, and their own actions provide information to others as to the attributes of the crowd. Actions such as clapping, singing, and chanting become criterial attributes for identifying the actors as members of the crowd. In an antisocial crowd, chanting racial abuse or 'cops are pigs', rhythmic hand-clapping, throwing bottles, and hurling stones are all forms of action which serve as markers of crowd identification.

Moreover, the absence of any formal group structure in the crowd means that the actions of a mere handful of people can be interpreted as an example of appropriate behaviour, and act as a catalyst for similar behaviour from other crowd members. In this way, normative influence emerges from collective actions, rather than residing in some previously agreed set of values. The norms guiding behaviour in these fluid social situations have been called 'emergent norms'. Turner and Killian (1957) suggested in their 'emergent norm theory' that the social processes within the crowd may cause norms to alter suddenly and in an apparently unpredictable manner.

The conditions for the emergence of antisocial behaviour in the New Year's Eve street crowd in Byron Bay relate to the effect of new norms emerging from the situation. Participation of some young people in antisocial behaviour within a crowd environment offered a norm which projected an illusion of homogeneity among crowd members. In the Byron Bay incident the actions of police with the 'paddy wagon' appeared to heighten crowd identity. When a small group within the crowd began chanting 'Kill the coppers', the chant was taken up by others, because the actions occurred against the backdrop of crowd behaviour. Faced with dissonance provoked by the extreme outbursts of a few, individual crowd members appeared to be ready to assume that others around them were a homogeneous group, and so may have adopted attitudes which were offensive to them as individuals. Thus behaviour which would not normally be tolerated by people as individuals becomes included into the norms of the crowd and taken to be acceptable.

Deindividuation

These intragroup theories of social identification still do not provide an entirely satisfactory explanation of why riots erupt in one situation but not in others. They provide a motivational rationale for hooliganism, but seem to need some way of accounting for the 'threshold' restraints on the group norms present in a situation, and why these thresholds are crossed in some circumstances and not in others. Engagement in public forms of antisocial behaviour has been explained psychologically in terms of the weakening of self-control as a consequence of submergence of individual identity in that of the crowd. As most crowds assemble with some commonly held beliefs and attitudes, there exists a degree of willingness among members to become immersed in the crowd, with consequences for the lowering of their inhibitions about engaging in socially unacceptable behaviour. Prentice-Dunn and Rogers (1989) explain the process of crowd influence in their 'differential self-awareness theory', which incorporates the concepts of anonymity and deindividuation (see Box 7.1). They argue that the maintenance of self-awareness, at both the personal and the public level, is crucial to avoiding antisocial acts. Social situations such as those found in mass crowds reduce personal accountability or diffuse personal responsibility by arousing group identity and lowering the person's self-awareness.

The crowd context of football hooliganism

From the social identity perspective, it would seem that the milling of the crowd of football fans after a match, and their marching along the streets looking for rival fans, are a necessary phase for deindividuation and accentuating the crowd's identity as a fighting group. In the milling and marching, crowd members are able to recognise one another and sense their unity; and they are engaged in a process of mutual stimulation – of becoming submerged in the crowd in preparation for a fight. The importance of this preparatory phase is twofold: it promotes group cohesiveness and reduces private self-awareness, as group norms of behaviour can emerge and are made more prominent. Conformity to group norms is achieved through 'the mutually perceived similarity between self and ingroup others, produced by the formation and salience of shared social category memberships' (Turner, 1991, p. 160).

Box 7.1 Model of deindividuation through group submergence

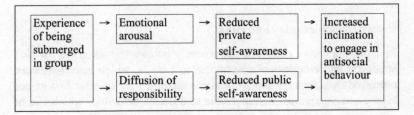

Buford's (1991) account of life in a fighting gang describes a street battle where the supporters used the term 'It had gone off' to mark a shift in the group climate, defining a sudden reduction of inhibition to engage in antisocial behaviour, as if 'some kind of threshold had been crossed'. The change was instigated by the action of one member of the 200-strong fighting gang who smashed a shop window. The effect of this single act by one supporter was to escalate the level of violence. According to Buford, a tremor seemed to go through the people around him, and their walking pace increased, as if they scented excitement. He records that 'on one side of that boundary had been a sense of limits, an ordinary understanding – even among this lot – of what you didn't do' (Buford, 1991, p. 88). With the removal of these normative controls, the crowd was in a situation with few limits, where things rapidly became very violent. The expression 'It had gone off' suggests an image of release like that of a coiled spring, or the blow of pent-up energy from a volcano.

Having experienced the emotional release of crowd violence and crowd vandalism, memories of the sense of group cohesiveness provide a powerful basis for group belonging. This motivation appears in J. Allan's (1989) report of his experiences as an Aberdeen Casual in the mid-1980s. One of his pals, reflecting on why they fought at football, saw it simply in terms of group action: 'I do it because I love it. I love steaming into the away boys. It's magic. It's just magic fun' (Allan, 1989, p.134). While it seems incongruous for anyone to claim it is fun getting punched, kicked, and hit with rocks and bottles by hostile young men, Allan (1989, pp. 135, 78) points out that the excitement and thrill are extremely powerful in the hyped-up state which he experienced when 'in the thick of the action'. The feelings aroused by group violence were like 'an ecstasy pill'. A similar testimony to the hypnotic power of the immediate situation is found in Buford's (1991) first-hand account of hooliganism; he quotes a young man after an episode of street violence saying that 'he was very, very happy and could not remember ever being so happy' (p. 88). A distinction is made between the typical excitement felt where there is danger present, and the more personal 'pure elemental pleasure' which he himself experienced in the crowd, arising not from random violence but from 'the very particular workings of the violence of numbers' (Buford, 1991, p. 219).

Crowd dynamics: play and ritual

In exploring crowd antisocial behaviour, a noteworthy feature is the play structures and elements of playfulness in crowds, which have long been remarked by observers and participants alike. It may seem at first glance highly imaginative and irresponsible to describe behaviour which can be obscene, destructive, or aggressive as play, because play has acquired attributes of innocence through its association with the very young. However, as an attribute of adult behaviour 'play' is not always innocent; for example, witness the phrases 'play hardball', 'play to win', 'play it safe'. Tannenbaum as early as 1938 linked delinquent behaviour with aspects of public play.

'Play' is the insider's definition of the situation, not the outsider's; it is a meaning shared by the players and their audience. Fun, mischief, and excitement may all be features of the young delinquent's initial definition of the situation, reflected in expressions like 'playing truant', 'having a bit of a laugh', 'playing silly buggers'. Play episodes are triggered by the presence of an audience sympathetic to the play makers, by the emergence of a repetitive pattern in the sequence of events, and by the existence of play objects which may be spontaneously introduced into a play sequence; for example, garbage bins as vaulting objects, drink cans as missiles, and garbage lids as shields. Thus onlookers will not understand such behaviour unless they take the viewpoint of a group member. The more typical response of onlookers to actions of this kind by members of a crowd is to interpret such behaviour as deviant, loutish, childish, a nuisance, or a disturbance, rather than attempt to understand it from the insider's perspective. That is, 'official' attention requiring intervention, correction, control, and suppression is preferred over dismissing the behaviour as 'a bit of high-spirited fun'. Thus play and the larrikin role are keys to understanding many forms of group antisocial behaviour.

Insider vs. outsider views of a biker crowd 'riot'

An example of the differences between insider and outsider perceptions of a crowd situation is found in a remarkable study by Cunneen *et al.* (1989) of a biker 'riot' at the Easter motor-cycle races at Bathurst, Australia, in 1985. They conducted an ethnographic analysis of the events across the four-day period, using twenty-two participant observers. These methods allowed them to focus on the lived experiences of the crowd and their interactions with police. They concluded that different and clearly articulated theories of the event were held by the politicians, the police, the media, and the bikers themselves, which constituted 'a conscious and elaborated struggle over the definition of the event' (p. 8).

There were noticeable mood changes in the motor-cycle crowd. After the day's races were completed, campers relaxed, talked, laughed, drank, lit fires, and began to engage in physical contests which transformed the evening into an 'informal carnival' (p. 88). Riders competed in performing 'doughnuts' encircled by a 'bullring' of urgers; others engaged in cockfights, multiple pillion riding (up to four on a bike), climbing light poles via human pyramids, and ceremonial bike burnings (of old bikes). The activities were clearly forms of play and 'spontaneously constructed entertainment', according to Cunneen *et al.* (1989, p. 92), but they were not interpreted in this way by the police.

Shortly after 8 p.m. on the Saturday, a police loudspeaker warned the crowd of about 1000 young people to 'go home, if you don't want to get arrested'. This was greeted by chants and the throwing of flares and lighted toilet rolls, and the police compound became the centre of a bullring where the crowd carried on acting as they had before. At precisely 8.08 p.m., five buses arrived, carrying squads of special police (TRG) who had been stationed about a kilometre away and kept separate from the day's activities. These police were in riot gear. Their arrival and assault on the crowd were filmed by three television crews who had set up their equipment in readiness. Over the next two hours, which constituted the height of the conflict, the observers noted several features of crowd behaviour which are at odds with the concepts of a mindless mob intent on rioting; these included the following:

> A kiosk in police territory continued selling beer to biker patrons for two hours after the riot started, with customers walking through the police controlled areas to buy their beer before returning to the riot zone.
>
> In an area which was a target for police baton charges, a young man found a set of keys, held them up, and began walking among the people who were throwing bricks and bottles, calling out, 'Who lost their keys?'
>
> While the frontline crowd members were heckling police and throwing bricks and occasional Molotov cocktails, there were others who sat round their campfires on the hill, talking and drinking as if nothing was happening.
>
> (Cunneen *et al.*, 1989, pp. 88–89)

A further notable feature of the riot was its ritual pattern. Police would move away from the police compound to charge the crowd, who would retreat 30 to 40 metres, and advance as the police regrouped. This pattern of attack–retreat–regroup–attack, which was coordinated by police whistles in a cycle of between 2 and 10 minutes and continued for some hours, was not lost on the rioters themselves. One young man called to a researcher as he ran past: 'It's a game and a half, isn't it!' Another shouted, 'This is great value. Great entertainment.' After more than an hour had passed, voices were heard shouting out, 'Half time. Change sides'; and later, 'The second half has just started and the police need some *#!* replacements!' The conclusions of the research team were that the riot emerged out of the play ethos associated with the carnival context. While the violence was real, and there were many serious injuries, the actions of the biker people can be seen as reflecting crowd dynamics and not as the coordinated plans of organised gangs or clubs. In the observers' view, 'their collective actions were made possible by the institutional game framework which had been constructed' (Cunneen *et al.*, 1989, p. 103).

TOWARDS AN EXPLANATION OF HOOLIGANISM AND CROWD DISORDER

The insider accounts of football gangs are not romanticising thuggery, vandalism, and bestial behaviour. But while they give the lie to the popular image of mindless violence committed by Neanderthals, the focus of the accounts on the immediate context of group behaviour leaves important questions unanswered. What remains unresolved is whether these hooligans and yobbos are always violent, or whether their violence only occurs when they are associated with others. What is at issue is how crucial is the group basis to their antisocial behaviour in contrast to the role of individual temperament. To resolve this question Murphy *et al.* (1990) draw upon the explanations of the hooligan lads themselves, who deny that they are nutters or terrace drifters with marginal connections to the football. According to their informants, football spectatorism enables them to be part of a collective which provides scope for action, excitement, and recognition, embodied in a masculine 'aggro' culture.

That there has been a considerable amount of fighting at football games and in the streets is hard to deny; but it is less easy to make the inference of unpredictable violence. The idea of creative mischief appears in discussions by football supporters themselves, suggesting that hooligans may display many elements of the larrikin style. For example, Buford (1991, p. 116) quotes one of his subjects arguing that 'you've got to see the humour. You can't have violence without a sense of humour.' According to Marsh *et al.* (1978) the hooligan role is viewed by many of the football fans themselves as an entertainment one, challenging the authorities and outwitting them, stirring, and engaging in outrageous and often coarse practical jokes. Rather than referring to the thug image beloved of the media, the hooligan label is reserved by the fans for those who show inventiveness in their disorderly behaviour, and who know what they can get away with. Marsh *et al.* (1978) comment: 'To see hooligans as destructive is to miss the subtlety of their actions' (p. 72).

Group identification and hooliganism

Branscombe and Wann (1992) have proposed a model of arousal of spectator aggression in which a critical determinant of hostility is the degree of identification with the team. This point is also emphasised in social identity theory (e.g., Tajfel and Turner, 1979; Turner *et al.*, 1987), which states that people's behaviour appears to be influenced by social category membership to different degrees according to the extent to which they identify with the social type. People who are highly identified with the team are prepared to queue longer for tickets than are other fans. They are more concerned about the team's performance and more affected by its successes and failures. It is the highly identified fan who is 'one-eyed' and whose feelings are polarised towards outgroups of fans. The sense of identification with a crowd of like-minded supporters is not an abstract concept; it grows from ongoing relations between place and identity. The custom of following a team and being a regular part of the crowd means that the supporters are not a sea of anonymous faces, but are known to one another. The extroverts in the crowd establish their own personality, through wit and humour, banter and barracking.

The salience of hooligan group identification is strengthened by controls which define the territory of groups and accentuate the symbolic importance of the ends at football or the Hill at Sydney cricket matches. When enclosures acquire a special meaning, it is expected that yobbo behaviour at a cricket or football match will be found in this defined space. Segregation of supporters increases group cohesion and mutual social influence by the phenomenon of group polarisation, where those who share a particular value position endorse that value more strongly following the opportunity to express it. Team identification and social categorisation as a supporter, and segregation in a defined area, all assist the work of group socialisation through which the hooligan identity emerges. Thus, the creaation of designated areas in the interests of crowd control contributes to increasing self-categorisation, a key element in the process of establishing a social identity. The yobbos know where their mates will be.

Intergroup relationships may be expressed in various ways. Some of these find expression in actions intended to hurt, frighten, annoy, or humiliate others. In Ward's youthful experiences of being a football supporter in the 1970s (Ward, 1989), identification was easy and swift: it was based on the fan's accent and wearing the right scarf. 'If you turned up and had the team colours then you were part of the gang. It mattered not one iota that you had never seen the guy standing next to you. If trouble started, you were expected to bale him out and vice versa' (Ward, 1989, p. 8). Intergroup hostility is a means of boosting group identity. Aggression towards opposing fans may restore collective self-esteem, and appears to be greater following a team loss (Branscombe and Wann, 1992). Ward recalls the sense of frustration following his team's Cup round defeat, and how he solved this by catching a couple of rival fans after the game, and belting the daylights out of them. It may not 'totally exorcise the pain, but it sure does stop you feeling as lousy as you did previously', he wrote (Ward, 1989, p. 53).

These actions towards those identified as the outgroup have an entirely different function for those who are the ingroup: they bolster the sense of group solidarity and group belongingness, thus reinforcing their socially offensive behaviour. Ward (1989, p. 181) refers to the excitement, the desire just to be part of it at age 15, and the feeling of belonging and sense of importance that is associated with 'steaming in', as the crowd of visiting fans mass together and surge forward to take the end of the home fans, 'punching and kicking all in front of you'. Personal identity seems to be linked to group identity through the marker characteristics of scarves and accents and confirmed though joint action, e.g., chanting together 'Arsenal! Arsenal!', marching out of the railway station together 'like young gladiators', and fighting together. Group violence supplies social recognition and group embeddedness. One of Buford's informants claimed that the violence 'makes us somebody. Because we're not doing it for ourselves. We're doing it for something greater – for us. The violence is for the lads' (Buford, 1991, p. 118).

Attachment and identity

The insider accounts of hooligan experiences enable us to gain some understanding of the function which group violence serves in social bonding. It is not too far fetched to link this intense nature of the bonding with others, which occurs through the regular association of youths on the terraces, to notions of attachment described in the work of Bowlby (1969) and Hirschi (1969), given the claims by hooligans themselves that friendships established through this process continue over many years. Allan reports that he felt the depth of friendship most acutely in times of extreme fear, for example on 'a cold November night in a dingy back street when you are confronted by superior numbers of rival fans coming at you' (J. Allan, 1989, p. 180). Similarly, Ward (1989) recalls as a hooligan the 'great feeling going down the terrace with a few hundred behind you making a few hundred back off' (p. 181). The feelings appear as intensely felt intimacy between friends, where the common experience bonds them together and gives a sense of group identity. Buford records how the fighting was seen by the hooligans as a once-in-a-lifetime experience, where they had 'been through something important' together, and as a consequence declared, 'We'll never split up. We'll be mates for life' (Buford, 1991, p. 117).

BULLIES, BOVVER BOYS, AND INTERGROUP HOSTILITY

The rituals and rules of disorder which have been noted in crowd behaviour also exist, in somewhat different forms, in the hostile behaviour of adolescent cliques and street gangs. The rituals of threat, bullying, and harassment are as much about asserting the group's identity and exacting fear and respect as they are concerned with actual violence. They represent the expression of group power, coercion, and dominance over others, intended to invoke a sense of powerlessness in those who are bullied or harassed, and produce feelings of dominance and control in those doing the harassing. Taunting and baiting of others are almost always done from the security of a group base; it is rare to find the same actions occurring when a member of the hostile group is alone.

School stand-over groups

Group bullying finds expression at high school in the victimisation of younger students by older and bigger students. A form of group activity of recent times is for a gang of boys to obtain new trainers from schoolboys by physical threat. Some boys are reported to have been stripped of their jackets, trousers, and watch as well. In the 1970s we found the most prevalent power game among Queensland students for establishing dominance over students new to school involved 'stand-over' tactics by year-nine and year-ten boys to extract money. The practice was known as 'jewing' or 'scunging', where the victor acquired status as tough, and the loser was labelled as soft or weak (Power and Cotterell, 1979). The threats by older boys usually occurred when a boy was on his own. Although the older boys threatened to bash the year eight if he did not comply, at most times the threats were verbal ones, which some boys were prepared to challenge. However, some attacks did occur. One boy was punched and kicked by a group of year-ten boys because he would not give them money. For others, the menace in the threats was enough to create apprehension; the realists took the view that: 'When Year 9's jew off a Year 8, they say "your money or your life" and mean it.' Not surprisingly, given this intimidation, many yielded to the threats. One respondent admitted giving money every time he was approached. He described the pattern of coercion and his code of silence in these words: 'One kid I know, I give him money. He says, How much have you got today? I say, some. And he feels your pocket. I don't like giving him any, but you can't dob in' (Power and Cotterell, 1979, p. 227).

'Stirring' is another form of harassment of individual students which was popular among anti-school groups. In general, their victims were different in some way – in physical appearance or from an ethnic minority, or viewed as someone who was 'an easy mark'. Adolescents admitted to bullying practices:

> Tony and I just pick out someone to stir. (*Why?*) Just to annoy them. We pick on kids who will react, just for the fun of it.

> A lot of the class pick on Jeffrey. (*Why?*) We pick on kids who annoy us by being stupid or a nuisance or saying something that's not true.

> (Power and Cotterell, 1979, p. 256)

Graffiti gangs

In Australia many of the antisocial street gangs are graffiti gangs, or have evolved from these; they will travel considerable distances on the trains in order to claim their territory. They are the archetypal antisocial group: they work at night, often alone or in pairs rather than as a group, and thrive on illegal activity, defacing buildings and public property. The Melbourne graffiti gangs (see Daley, 1989) have names which sound like those of heavy metal rock bands (e.g., Claim to Fame, Dead on Arrival), and a distinctive characteristic is the tendency for youth to make the group name and its initials consistent with a three-part rhythm; for example, Time for Crime (TFC), Transit Wrecking Crew (TWC), Plenty Bad Apples (PBA), In Full Effect (IFE), and Major Crime 3 (MC3). An exception to the rhythmical formula is the largest gang, which has called itself 3174 after the postcode for its recruitment area. This gang is reputed to be the most hostile youth gang in Melbourne. Core members are solidly built 16–18-year-olds who have their hair dreadlocked, wear a blue bandana tied around their neck or forehead, and often bear scars on their faces and knuckles.

Graffiti is a means of gang identification. Many members are loners who are not even aware of the others in their gang. The aim is to display one's 'tag', or signature, as widely as possible. Such display, particularly when it is 'got up' in forbidden areas such as private premises or on public signs, is a mark of status. Graffiti gangs (known as 'crews' or 'posses') claim achievements for 'tagging' trains from end to end, and leaving their tags on buildings and equipment inside high-fenced areas. Some even take videos of their work in order to brag about their achievements (see Box 7.2).

Gang rivalry occurs over claims to territory for displaying their art, rather than as a piece of turf. Assertion of gang identity by placing a signature or tag on a wall is often met with resistance and even provocation by other groups. The act of tagging another 'bomber's' (artist's) 'piece' of work (an action known as 'capping' or 'slashing') is interpreted as an insult and a challenge to physical conflict, because it encroaches on another

Box 7.2 Taking a painted path to a jail cell

Graffiti was their labour of love and their urge to paint took them on a Christmas road trip from Melbourne to Queensland. They left their tag THC and filmed themselves at work. It was that footage that eventually helped provide evidence when police finally caught up with them.

(Brisbane *Courier-Mail*, 11 March 1995)

gang's territory and is a mark against its reputation. Police in 1994 reported increased expressions of hostility towards them in the graffiti pieces which were appearing in Brisbane. They also noted an increase in clashes between rival crews, often expressed in 'aerosol fights', but occasionally including violent battles with bats and hammers.

Inside an antisocial adolescent gang

Fighting and vandalism are a major part of 'doing nothing' in street-corner culture (see Corrigan, 1976). They are exciting and take little organisation, and are often ritual events which relieve the tedium of having nothing to do. For some youth, like the Banyo Mob, an outer-suburban Brisbane gang, the railway stations and surrounding areas serve as meeting places. Trains are a means of mobility for gang members, who may travel long distances to meet. Boarding a train is easy to do without a rail ticket, and youth either travel for free inside, or ride on the outside of the train, in what is known as 'siding'. Most evenings, gang members assemble on the platform and wait for a train to see who will arrive on it, and then plan their night's activities. These are mainly drinking parties, held in the park of a nearby sports ground or in a vacant building near the railway station. The parties have no other purpose than to allow friends to meet and drink in a venue where they are free from hassling by the police. At one of these parties, windows were removed from the house and smashed, and some of the boys became involved in fights. The brawling among members of the gang resulted in several boys having facial cuts and black eyes, yet the antagonists seemed to hold no long-term resentment, and actually hugged one another when later talking to the fieldworkers.

The Banyo youths justified their drinking and breaking-and-entering as the need to get into trouble to have some fun. One boy said that if they feel hungry at night and there is no shop open, out of an impulse they break in for a feed. Break-ins also offer opportunities for vandalism; in the gang's area of activity, most of the shops and halls had been broken into several times, with damage to property, and theft of cigarettes, money, and Scratchit gambling tickets. Car break-ins are also common, either for 'hot-wiring' or for petrol-sniffing. For example, one Thursday about midnight four older teenage boys in the gang broke into a car to sniff petrol for fun. They took turns to go to the petrol tank and take a huge sniff, after which they fell on the roadway and rolled around laughing. This routine continued for almost an hour: walking up to the car, breathing in the petrol fumes, falling over, and rolling around on each other laughing.

The motivation to engage in vandalism, burglary, car theft, drinking, and fighting appeared directly linked to the sense of boredom and idleness in the lives of these young people. From conversations across several weeks with youth on the station late at night, a similar theme was voiced – of nothing to do, or not enough to do. The fieldworkers' notes report the 'sheer boredom' felt by these young people, associated with long hours of sitting around together with nothing exciting to do, a depressing feeling which became perceptible to the observers themselves through continued contact with the gang.

The eruption of aggression

Aggressive events can erupt without any warning signs and are notoriously difficult to diagnose without knowledge of the context and of the protagonists. At most times, aggression among antisocial youth is directed towards others in the gang, and many incidents seem to occur unpredictably. There are examples of young people being assaulted after asking an acquaintance for a smoke, or after accidentally bumping into a friend, or even just being present when a friend was angry or drunk. The most common location for group attack is the street, often near a pub or a railway station. Most fighting is done with fists and boots rather than weapons, but this does not reduce the savagery of the encounters. Because the violence erupts with no apparent warning, teachers and those working with youth may overlook or ignore information which suggests that the conflict is an ongoing one. What appears to be an unprovoked attack may be retaliation for some earlier injury or insult, or an escalation of a continuing feud, including one based on ethnic rivalry.

An incident with the Banyo Mob is illustrative of the speed at which violence can erupt. A group of girls were poking fun at Bevan, a large youth in his twenties who was frequently drunk. Suddenly a fight erupted, with the girls punching Bevan and spitting on him. Jonno, the 14-year-old delinquent gang leader, launched into the fight, slapping Bevan around the head, and kicking and kneeing him in the face, the groin, and the spine when he had his back turned. Some of the other boys attempted to stop Jonno, because they could see that Bevan was drunk. They told Bevan to get home, and he limped off. Later, the observers learned that the girls' fight with Bevan had been triggered by him spitting at a girl who teased him. The ferocious involvement of Jonno remained unexplained.

A study of homeless Australian young people by Alder (1991) reports that 60 per cent had been physically assaulted in the past year, many suffering injuries serious enough to require hospital treatment. The predominant form of violence encountered by young males was attacks by groups of strangers: for example, being set upon by a group coming out of the pub; being attacked when walking down the street by a group intent on beating up anyone they met; or straying into the territory of another group, and being belted up for it. These attacks frequently occurred when the youth was on his own. The violence was thought by the victim to be unprovoked, but Alder suggests that among these youth, violence often erupts out of a situation where 'aggro' is present, often implicitly – for example, in defence against trespass on one's personal space in a 'squat', or in response to an assertive remark like 'watch what you're doing', where the aggressor decides to teach the victim a lesson for 'mouthing off'. This is not meant to deny the possibility that the victim is an innocent party who is picked on by strangers looking for the opportunity for some 'aggro', but it directs attention at the *intergroup context* of these aggressive encounters.

Perhaps because these street youths are insecure, they are highly sensitive to any behaviour which may be perceived as a challenge or threat. The grounds for the attack may be trivial to an outsider, but in a street culture where aggressive masculinity is prized, 'males are in a situation where little things mean a lot' (Alder, 1991, p. 11), and any threat to status and reputation is a threat to identity. A member of a Melbourne gang, the Lebanese Tigers, declared, 'If I'm walking in the street and someone calls me a wog, I don't care how many of them there are – I'll fight those words' (Guilliatt, 1984b).

Thus males more commonly express their insecurity in confrontation, belligerent display, and physical assault, and they view any defence by the victim as further provocation, to be dealt with in violent reprisal. The possibility that aggressive youth learn the advantages of 'doing one's block' is raised by studies of Chicano gangs. They refer to the value of 'locura', which means going crazy or wild. It has been noted that gang members periodically act like nutters, as a deliberate ploy to bolster their tough image or to coerce others to agree with them or do them favours. To Farrington *et al.* (1982, p. 333) these aggressive attitudes and behaviours are 'elements of a socially deviant lifestyle'.

Territorial defence

Like other adolescent cliques, those comprising gangs are often based on neighbourhood association. The locality may offer more than a source of recruitment of gang members; it can also give rise to gang identity, because being anchored in a particular locality gives stability and cohesion to the membership. Local affiliations may be based upon street alliances and even linked to family and clique groupings. Physical territory becomes symbolically important for accentuating the group's identity as distinct from other groups. For example, Murphy *et al.* (1990) refer to the strong attachment to their local territory among the Kingsley lads, to the extent that venturing far from the Kingsley estate, except as a gang, was perceived as dangerous and exciting, and likely to involve conflict with other youth. They comment that 'areas beyond the estate were seldom viewed in terms of the potential they offered for leisure exploration' (p. 145).

Accordingly, intergroup relations are determined by definitions of group boundaries. In the streets the dynamics of intergroup conflict may be understood in terms of intrusions into the group's personal space – the invisible zone or territory surrounding the group. The identity of the group extends out into the surrounding public space, and the zone increases in size when the group is larger. Protection of this invisible zone from invasion may even contribute to differentiating the group from others and bonding the members together. Knowles (1989) reports that pedestrians will change their path to avoid entering the space adjoining a group in the street, and that they show signs of stress if forced to cross the group's space. This reaction of passers-by suggests that the shared space which constitutes the immediate territory of the group is more than symbolic; trespass into that space by strangers has psychological significance.

In situations where intergroup competition is sharpened by religious and cultural differences, people are more conscious of their membership of a particular ethnic group. A great deal of conflict between Australian young people from different ethnic backgrounds is precipitated by name-calling intended to provoke a reaction. In Adelaide, groups of Italian-Australians who hang around together in the inner city, dressed in a 'bodgie' style (imitating the tough, street look of American film stars such as James Dean), are provoked into fighting by jeers and ethnic taunts, such as being called 'wogs' by groups of Anglo-Australians, Aboriginal-Australians, or Greeks. Rivalry between ethnic groups goes beyond the activities of stereotyping to the contesting of group space or territory. Gangs go into the city and wander about looking for excitement. One teenager stated:

> You'll go to town and you'll find the Greeks on that side, and the Italians on that side, and you can spot them out. This side of town, you've got

Italian street gangs . . . and if you're Greek on this side of town, well, you're not really lucky!

(Foote, 1992, p. 29)

Both girls and boys from the Italian community acknowledged that the groups offered a means of identity as 'a tough bloke', conferred by the group and maintained by rivalry and physical conflict. The gang members see their behaviour as reacting to earlier incidents, 'just sticking up for each other'. Thus, when one of their number has been casually walking down-town and has been 'jumped' by a group of other boys who appear 'out of nowhere', the gang will 'group together and hit him who hit him' (Foote, 1992, p. 30).

The acts of intergroup hostility are accepted fatalistically as a necessary means of establishing 'respect', where younger boys 'look up to us', and older boys are forced to accept the group's legitimate right to belong. Cohen (1990, p. 16) remarked that 'The ability of gangs to provide their members with enhanced identity is always part of the explanation of gangs.' For these Adelaide youths, their existence and having 'arrived' in terms of a group identity is bound up with having a space of their own in the city. Acceptance is conditional on the groups asserting themselves continually, in order to win such a piece of territory – against hostile resistance not only from rival gangs but from the local traders and the police as well.

LEARNING AN AGGRESSIVE LIFESTYLE

Social learning theorists (e.g., Cairns *et al.*, 1988; Dishion *et al.*, 1991; Patterson *et al.*, 1989; Snyder *et al.*, 1986) see aggressive coping styles developing into hooligan lifestyles through a system of reciprocal re-inforcement, well captured in the notion of coercive interaction cycles. According to the Patterson group, parents are important in training children to adopt antisocial patterns of conduct, through inconsistent and inept reinforcement of positive as well as antisocial behaviour in childhood. Snyder *et al.* (1986) monitored the changing influences of parents and peers in three age groups of boys, 9–10 years, 12–13 years, and 15–16 years. Their research found moderately strong correlations between association with deviant peers and parenting practices such as inept discipline and lack of parental monitoring. The social environment of peers was particularly powerful in adolescence for enhancing deviant behaviour. In their view, the parental environment is important in preventing antisocial behaviour in so far as parental supervision narrows access to deviant peers, whereas lack of monitoring widens it. The relation between the environments of parents and peers is best appreciated in terms of the convoy model. Peer influence grows where the parent environment fails to teach social skills, self-control, and socially appropriate ways of behaving, thus allowing the child and adolescent greater access to deviant peers, who furnish opportunities for direct training in antisocial behaviour.

Peers as convoys supporting aggression

We have seen in Chapter 4 the link between rejection and aggression. By the end of childhood, youngsters who were rejected by conventional peer groups and playmates team up with others of like mind. The experience of social rejection and feelings of exclusion assist in devaluing the activities and prosocial behaviour of normal children for these youngsters, and pre-dispose them to adopt antisocial values and to seek out others who have antisocial attitudes like their own. Two processes, differential association and mutual reinforcement, co-occur. At the friend level, pairs of friends become more and more like each other, or sever the relationship (see Kandel, 1978a). Within the friendship clique, coercive processes operate (Dishion, 1990), shaping each adolescent's behaviour style so that antisocial behaviour is reinforced. The group context would appear then to facilitate the expression of aggressive forms of antisocial behaviour, just as the group context fosters a great deal of delinquent behaviour in general (e.g., Akers *et al.*, 1979; Cairns *et al.*, 1988; Caspi *et al.*, 1993; Emler *et al.*, 1987; Henggeler, 1989; Patterson *et al.*, 1989). The group provides models and reinforcers to the individual member's behaviour because of its ex-clusive relationship with the adolescent (Akers *et al.*, 1979).

Cairns *et al.* (1988) and Dishion (1990) provide helpful interpretations of the association between peer rejection and aggression by recognising the important role of the social network. They point out that the aggressive adolescents may not be broadly popular, but they are not rejected by all; they find friends among others who have similar aggressive styles of interaction. Having been excluded from prosocial groups, or having been made unwelcome because of their aggressive manner, they shop around for others to mix with, and these tend to be antisocial people like themselves. Through differential association, therefore, the social networks which take shape in early adolescence include cohesive clusters where aggression is the basis of peer popularity. These aggressive coalitions serve as social convoys, affording opportunities through the security of numbers for ado-lescents to practise behaving aggressively towards others, and providing models and reinforcers which strengthen their aggressive tendencies.

A longitudinal study by Thornberry *et al.* (1993) highlights the role of gangs as convoys for delinquency; being a member of an antisocial group facilitates the display of antisocial behaviour, particularly physical aggression against others. They found that during periods when adolescents were active in a gang they had higher rates of violence against others than did non-gang members; and in periods when they were not active in the gang, their rates of assault were much lower, and comparable with those of youth who were not in gangs. This study confirms that the group context itself facilitates antisocial behaviour, over and above the antisocial coping styles typical of these adolescents.

Group membership not only facilitates aggression and vandalism by modelling and reciprocal reinforcement of behaviour, but also motivates individuals to express these behaviours through the arousal of shared beliefs. Identification with the group has motivational force: it binds group members together with relatively strong group ties, while differences between the ingroup and the outgroup are accentuated (see Kawakami and Dion, 1993; Wilder and Shapiro, 1991). The proximity of other potentially threatening groups, or situations of intergroup conflict, heighten each gang member's group consciousness, and make each more sensitive to perceived threat and lack of respect from others.

Where the intergroup conflict has an ongoing history, people exhibit what Hewstone (1990, pp. 313, 329) calls 'intergroup attributional bias', explaining away any negative behaviour of their own group as error or an exception. Ingroup stereotyping is 'motivationally driven'. They exaggerate the similarities within their group, and the level of group consensus, often by stereotyping other groups as different from them. Viewing their own group positively in comparison to other groups (for example, we are good sports, but they are cheats; we fight fair, they carry knives) is a means of bolstering their own group's identity. It also provides the seeds of intergroup hostility when the stereotypes employed in group differentiation are contested by another group.

At the same time as ingroup members are absolved from any responsibility for wrong-doing, members of the outgroup are seen to behave in the ways expected of them. These attribution patterns were found by Hunter *et al.* (1991) in a study of attitudes of Catholic and Protestant university students in Northern Ireland. Both groups were much more likely to attribute violence by the outgroup to stable internal causes (such as personality characteristics), whereas violence committed by their own group was explained by external causes (such as circumstances, actions of others requiring self-defence).

EDUCATION AND CURBING HOOLIGANISM

What is the role of community agencies and educational institutions in responding to adolescents' social needs and teaching youth about society's notions of responsible public behaviour? The stance taken here seeks to recognise that both a community policing aspect and community education are necessary. Illustrations are given from the follow-ups to events reported in the chapter: the Easter biker meet, which was transferred from Bathurst to Phillip Island in Victoria, the following year's New Year's Eve experiences in the seaside town of Byron Bay, and Schoolies' Week in 1994 on the Sunshine Coast. These are outlined to illustrate how crowd behaviour can be managed by prior planning and community cooperation so that antisocial behaviour at the level of the crowd is minimised.

When the Easter races of the Australian Grand Prix were relocated to Phillip Island in late 1988, a violence prevention strategy was devised by Veno and Veno (1990), which was aimed at reducing boredom, excessive alcohol consumption, and crowd rowdiness. Its emphasis was on *biker self-policing* and the theme that bikers are responsible people. The authors wrote articles in biker magazines on this theme prior to the meet; consulted with camping area managers about camping standards; arranged a rally for bikers to travel to the site, supported by police to provide right of way; and instituted a media watch to confront journalists who attempted to stir spectators. There were also ongoing consultations with the police and the posting of an observer with police operations to influence in a subtle way the style of policing in response to biker crowd behaviour. Attendance statistics showed that over 240,000 people attended the meet over three days, and there was less crowd disorder than at the previous New Year's Eve celebration in the same area which had attracted one-twentieth that number. The authors modestly concluded that 'by all measures and accounts, the violence prevention strategy was effective' (Veno and Veno, 1990, p. 16).

Following the riotous behaviour at Byron Bay on New Year's Eve 1993/4, a committee was established by the townspeople, business owners, and police to control any influx of yobbo elements into the seaside town the following New Year's Eve. An entry-control policy was decided, which declared the town would be off-limits to any visiting motor vehicle from dawn on New Year's Eve 1994, and this was publicised widely in the months before the Christmas period. No alcohol would be permitted to be brought into the town, and the regulation was administered by police, assisted by members of the local community. For example, arrangements were made for all vehicles to be stopped 5 kilometres from the town, and passengers bused to the town for a small charge, if they did not want to walk. Alcohol-free entertainment was provided in the town. These drastic measures were highly successful in curbing hooliganism for the 1994/5 New Year's Eve occasion, because of the determination and united stance of the townspeople.

Both education and community management were applied to improve Schoolies' Week experiences on the Queensland Sunshine Coast. These are outlined to illustrate how the recognition of different crowd elements and distinctive motivations among Schoolies can lead to better policing and better community relations with young people. First, a network of police, community health and welfare workers, and representatives of service clubs was established more than six months before Schoolies' Week 1994 to liaise with local businesspeople and to plan 'diversionary' entertainment and activities for Schoolies. Known as the Drug Awareness Network, it was able to obtain funding assistance for its work from the National Drug Education unit. The network devised a programme of activities which was later advertised to intending Schoolies by helpers walking the streets and distributing leaflets containing information about forthcoming events. Local newspapers also carried details of these events. The network devised a motto which caught the spirit of the community, endorsing the fun elements of Schoolies' Week, with printed T-shirts bearing the logo, 'Pressure off, Party on!' Second, local businesses were enlisted to promote and support the principle of alcohol-free entertainment, and a commitment was made by the local council to maintain clean and litter-free streets and beaches. The leaflets distributed to Schoolies contained vouchers offering deals on food and recreation. In addition, a special deal was arranged with the cinema complex for a half-price movie night; two alcohol-free night-club parties were organised at a recognised disco, whose liquor licence was suspended for these occasions; and the last day of the scheduled week saw the staging of a surf carnival and free barbecue for Schoolies, based on the (correct) assumption that many would probably have run out of money, and the free meal would prove an attraction. Third, an education programme was mounted by motel operators and also by local schools to encourage young people to act responsibly: they listed the rules the Schoolies were to observe in caring for the facilities in their places of accommodation, and warned them to avoid situations where strangers could gatecrash their rooms and create damage. Some motel operators also provided transport so that young people could travel easily and at no expense to the events provided by the network programme. The programme was generally successful in reducing antisocial behaviour and fostering a holiday atmosphere, but young people commented that more activities should be organised during the week in future.

CONCLUSION

This chapter has explored the group basis of various kinds of antisocial behaviour: group fighting, 'aggro', and bullying, as well as crowd disorder and vandalism in public places. It shows not only that groups exert influences on antisocial behaviour by modelling and direct reinforcement, but also that membership of a group affects the way in which people interpret events around them. In what has been described in this chapter, it is implied that gang activities are a response to boredom, and that engaging in fights, vandalism, and other delinquent activities fosters group solidarity and enhances group identity. However, the corollary that a solution to young people's boredom is the provision of organised activities is not necessarily true. Boredom is an undifferentiated state of apathy. It is not just having nothing to do: it is also not wanting to take up the options for activity which are presently available. There is also a suggestion from the fieldnotes on the Banyo Mob that boredom arises from young people's lack of satisfying social relationships. There is a hint from their positive responding to the fieldworkers that these youth appear at times to sense the disjuncture between their desire for purpose and meaning, and their failure to achieve it in their chosen lifestyle. Contact with interested, non-judgmental adults offers social relationship experiences which these youth clearly value. They remain resistant, however, to following the directions offered to them. In this mindset, the provision of activities or an organised youth club will not 'solve' the problem of boredom among these street youth, as long as the facilities are *provided for* them.

By contrast, joint planning with young adult bikers by police and community members at Phillip Island, and the concerted involvement of a range of community agents in planning for the recreational needs of youth in Schoolies' Week, including the direct organisation of events and activities by adults, proved successful and was widely appreciated. It is these issues of connecting youth with adults in meaningful ways which are the subject matter of the concluding chapters.

Part III
Social support

Part III

Social support

Introduction

In exploring social relations in adolescence, it would be relatively easy to focus exclusively on peer relations and thus to overlook the continuing and developmentally important relationships which young people have with adults. Previous sections have discussed social network structures and contents of social exchange and influence in social relations, in various settings important to young people. The chapters in this concluding part adopt a more holistic approach to attachment and social identity than has been followed so far, and focus explicitly on the influence of social settings in fostering positive relations between adolescents and adults. They retrieve the concept of social provisions (Weiss, 1974) and the way these are expressed in schools and organised groups when these deliberately seek to operate as supportive environments for the social development of young people.

The educative importance of connecting to adults is underlined in a statement from the Carnegie Council on Adolescent Development (1989, p. 37), namely that 'Every student needs at least one thoughtful adult who has the time and takes the trouble to talk with the student about academic matters, personal problems, and the importance of performing well.' Youth organisations and schools provide settings where young people can widen the network of social ties with others, so as to interact with those their own age and also with unrelated adults. A second beneficial effect of contacts with adults is that adolescents can become connected to, and identified with, adult society. From a social identity perspective, the establishment of ties between participants in an organised group fosters the development of a group consciousness, which strengthens into membership loyalties. The individual becomes 'bonded into' the club or organisation.

Although youth organisations are major sources of structured leisure-time activities for young people, and provide key social venues for establishing friendships with others of a similar age, there is little research on the effects of youth–adult contact on adolescents' social development.

A recent review of research on adolescence in North America (Feldman and Elliott, 1990, p. 493) concluded that there was 'a notable absence' in the existing literature of any systematic assessment of the influence of organised youth activities on adolescent development. One of the difficulties in seeking to arrive at such an assessment is the lack of theory on the value of youth participation in clubs, team sports, and cultural groups (see Brown, 1988), especially theory which describes how participation in the activities of organised groups may influence and enhance social and personality development. What is more disturbing is the neglect by theorists and researchers of the supportive function which embeddedness in a youth group, school club, or voluntary organisation can achieve. Most writings view social relationships as individual ties, when it is clear that there is a powerful set of *individual–group* ties in human experience. These relationships are captured in the language of social integration, inclusion, connectedness, and social identity, terms which refer to the individual's relational standing with a community or social group. Previous chapters have examined in detail the social consequences of being alienated from school and rejected by the group; this part is concerned with processes of inclusion, acceptance, membership, and community, and the importance of schools and organised youth groups in making these experiences of connectedness possible for young people.

The environment of schools and youth organisations comprises a variety of social niches, which differ in the extent to which they match with individuals to provide the fit which releases satisfaction and emotional growth. The task of those who wish to ensure that such niches are developmentally supportive is to take account of the needs of all members. Button (1974) described the major needs of adolescents as the need for companionship and affection, the need for security, the need to be somebody and have significance, and the need for adventure and new experience. These needs are stated in a way which accommodates the attachment and identity themes in expressive forms: of adventure seeking and having significance to others. A supportive environment for youth is not therefore a cottonwool protection of youth from new experience; it is the provision of sufficient acceptance, reassurance, and security to give youth the confidence to seek out and respond to challenge, to venture and develop their powers.

8 Social relations and support in adult-organised settings

The theme which is developed in this chapter is the role of youth organisations in connecting youth to the wider society, building attachment, commitment, and a sense of place in the community. Youth organisations are valuable in structuring informal social relationships between adults and young people, as well as in widening the contacts among youth themselves. Becoming a member of a youth club is a social experience. The club structure, meeting place, and activities afford opportunities to make new social contacts, form new friendships, acquire different values. Youth organisations provide a means for young people to meet adults in leader and helper roles. These roles are highly prescribed and scripted, which restricts the opportunity for close interaction and adult intrusiveness into the world of young people, and thus respects their right to privacy. Nevertheless, the formal helping structure within the club allows adults and older youth to communicate via their role as leader, coach, or counsellor that the young person matters. These relationships contribute a sense of being connected to significant others, and a shared belonging in the group which gradually evolves into a personal community (Hirsch, 1981). As the individual's needs for acceptance and recognition are met, association with the group or club becomes a rewarding experience; through interaction with others in the club, and absorbing the club traditions, the newcomer becomes invested into its organisational culture.

SOCIAL INTEGRATION PROCESSES IN YOUTH ORGANISATIONS

Let us examine the social psychological functions of membership in a youth group, and how the organisation structures social relations. When a young person begins attending a youth club or joins a sports team, s/he becomes subject to the small-group processes described in Chapters 2 and 3. These are directed at integrating the new member into the club through adopting the club's norms and building loyalty to its traditions. There is a series of tests which each newcomer must pass in order to become a member; but these are not seen as mechanisms for exclusion. They are markers of the new recruit's increasing compatibility with the group and signal the newcomer's progression in commitment. For example, in well-established youth organisations, new applicants for membership are given a status in the organisational hierarchy (e.g., nipper, tenderfoot) and assigned to a section or cell group within the club or organisation, where others in that cell group take responsibility for explaining the norms and traditions and assisting the newcomer to fit in.

Membership of a youth organisation introduces adolescents not only to the activities which are provided but to the roles which constitute the organisational structure. Through participation in the activities, individuals learn to recognise and perform the particular roles and learn the unwritten social rules which characterise the organisation. This Parsonian concept of the individual being shaped by the prevailing norms and values of the social system, so that her/his behaviour conforms with its demands, meets resistance from current scholars as being overly deterministic. But the distinction between learning a set of role behaviours and robot-like compliance to outside demands is well illustrated in the research on behaviour settings (e.g., Barker, 1968; Schoggen, 1989). This research shows that people conform to the standing pattern of behaviour which is scripted in a setting such as a debate, choir practice, or netball game, but the style of their behaviour remains highly individual.

The connection between setting structures, activities, and the roles and relationships which flow from these is seen in the sport of netball. This is the most popular sport in Australia in terms of the level of participation, with over half a million women and teenage girls playing it each weekend. Teenage girls are attracted to netball not only by the appeal of the sport but by the opportunities provided by the structure of the sports clubs for young people to connect with adults. On a typical Saturday at Faulkner Park, which is the location of the Western Brisbane Netball Association's competition facilities, teams are playing from 11.30 a.m. to 5 p.m. on the twelve netball courts. The grading of players into age levels and ability levels provides a structure of progression in the sport, and the presence of senior games at the same venue provides a bridge between junior and senior teams so that teenagers can observe more skilled players. Adults and experienced players are involved as officials, umpiring games and ensuring that rules and standards of play and dress are maintained. There is a learning aspect to the sport to which adults provide assistance: teenagers learn the finer points of the game from participation and also from observing the moves in other games, noting the relation between technique and strategy on the one hand, and court dominance on the other. Adults also act as coaches, training junior players and instructing them in team tactics. One 13-year-old girl attributed her involvement in netball to the coach, who made training 'great fun'. Older teenagers valued the opportunity through the sport to meet new people outside their school group and neighbourhood, and through playing in a team to maintain friendships with them.

Team sports, unlike individual sports and non-sport encounters, direct the attention of players beyond the events of winning or losing an individual game, to build them into the structure of the club's organisation and its traditions. A significant feature of bonding the members of a sporting team together is what Fine (1988) describes as 'the creation of collective meaning'. In addition to the use of home ground, and the regalia of club colours and player strip, there is emphasis on the ladder of progress, which links each individual game within 'the season' so that players are not only focused on winning a particular game but also aware of their participation in the team's (and the club's) 'evolving history'. Team bonds are built from members participating in the collective act of making meaning from the games played. Top teams will recall games where they narrowly defeated a strong team, or convincingly won against another team; particular team members will acquire legendary stature from some feat of skill (or luck), events which Fine (1988, p. 311) notes 'have lengthy referential afterlives'. This aspect of social anchoring to the group through tale-telling is as old as history; it is the basis of the Beowulf saga and the corroboree, and is perhaps best expressed in the St Crispin's Day speech of Shakespeare's King Henry before the battle of Agincourt.

♦ ADULTS IN ADOLESCENTS' SOCIAL NETWORKS

The function of voluntary organisations may be appreciated in social network terminology as social structures containing ties between members. When a young person joins a club, s/he gains access to a new social world. Of particular importance is the role of organised groups in linking young people to unrelated adults, and, through the relationships formed, in helping youth to gain benefit from adults' supportive influence in their lives. The proportion of unrelated adults reported in the social networks of American youth varies from about 10 per cent (e.g., Blyth *et al.*, 1982) to 13–15 per cent for adult friends and acquaintances (Scritchfield and Picou, 1982). In the latter study, teachers and school counsellors comprised a further 13–14 per cent, and peers were a relatively small proportion, whereas the Blyth *et al.* study found that 40 per cent of the network were peers.

Organised settings may be more important in European countries than in North America as venues for enhancing adolescents' opportunities for social contact with non-related adults, and for these adults to become in time significant members of their social network. Bo's research (Bo, 1989) found that Norwegian youth have greater numbers of unrelated adults in their networks and are more likely to know them through membership of organised groups, and also through contact with their parents' friends. Youth who generally met their friends at organised settings nominated over one-third more significant adults and over one-half more peers than those who met their friends on street corners and in other hangouts. Moreover, they tended to have either large or small configurations of significant adults, and those who had few adults in their network did not seem to 'compensate' for the lack of adults by having greater numbers of peer associates. Membership of voluntary groups was related to higher academic performance and better school adjustment, whereas membership of neighbourhood cliques or gangs was related to lower academic performance and lower adaptation to school.

Socialisation and support functions

Some researchers (e.g., Hendry *et al.*, 1992; Hurrelmann, 1990b) have investigated the roles adults play which contribute to the fulfilment of adolescents' developmental tasks. These studies describe the influence of adults from a reference group perspective rather than as actual persons, because the method of eliciting the groups draws attention to their roles, and does not identify them as named members of the social network. For example, Hurrelmann (1990b) provided German adolescents with a checklist of representative persons from their social network and asked them to indicate which kind of person they would turn to for help in resolving two hypothetical problem situations. He found that where the problem was of a personal nature, informal sources of support (parents, friends, relatives) were likely to be sought out; but where the problem was scholastic, teachers were ranked ahead of relatives as potential sources of help. Reliance on informal (strong tie) support rather than formal (weak tie) support with personal problems is understandable; the threshold of social risk is higher for a person who turns for help to people outside the network of close ties.

Reported contacts with significant others in relation to the two types of problem situation were also examined. The likelihood of adolescents seeking support from various significant others showed a decline in proportion to the lessening closeness of the relationship tie. Teachers were found to fulfil a role as a significant other for some adolescents, well ahead of that performed by other helping professions. For the personal problem, contacts with unrelated adults were reported by only 6 per cent of respondents. Other studies also confirm that contact with unrelated adults is less likely for personal matters. The exchanges with adult non-kin reported by Norwegian youth (Cochran and Bo, 1989) rarely included interactions which were extensive enough to be described as emotional support. They would be more accurately described as 'pleasant social exchanges' and 'dropping in'. Nevertheless, they serve as social mechanisms for linking young people into the wider community.

Using a different method, Hendry *et al.* (1992) asked adolescents at Scottish secondary schools to describe the relationship functions of significant others. Adolescents who were in their first year (ages 11–12) or in their fourth year (ages 15–16) nominated two persons who were significant to them – one from within their family and one who was unrelated to them – and were asked to describe their mentoring characteristics by means of a checklist. The researchers found that adults (mostly teachers and group leaders) were chosen as a significant non-family member by 34 per cent of the respondents, the remainder choosing predominantly same-sex friends. This choice of adult non-kin is clearly higher than that recorded in other studies using methods which did not focus so directly on actual persons known to the young person.

The most important mentoring functions identified for the family members named were enabler, believer, teacher, supporter, and role model. The characteristics of the unrelated adults which young people endorsed were similar to those of family members; for example, believer, enabler, and teacher featured prominently. The teachers who were nominated were described as challenging, while the youth group leaders nominated were distinctively seen as role models. The supporter function was endorsed only for friends. When younger adolescents were compared with older ones, only the believer characteristic maintained its importance across the age groups.

The coach relationship with young people

In sport, the coach sometimes occupies a central role in a person's development. The coach's significance was noted at recent testimonial dinners in Sydney, where former star Rugby League players took the opportunity to say how their lives were influenced by particular coaches. Players from Sydney's Eastern Suburbs premiership team of 1974 recalled how their coach Jack Gibson was available to players when they needed help; one quipped that in the interests of the players, he was 'out at all hours, never home, and sending his wife insane'. At the time, many were 'young blokes from the country', naive about city ways, and they benefited from the coach teaching them what life was all about; viz., 'Work hard, persevere, and you'll do alright; otherwise, get back on the bus and go home.'

Staging of the world gymnastic championships in Brisbane in 1994 prompted news stories about the mentor role of Frank Vig, the Hungarian gymnast known as the 'father' of the sport in Queensland. Vig helped hundreds of young people develop their skills, several becoming Olympians. The respect of these athletes is seen as they continue to refer to him as *Mr* Vig. An Olympian recalled in the press how he was 'always there at the "Y" [the YMCA] – he was a minder for us all. I could never have gone as far as I did in the sport without his help.' Such influences tend to be more appreciated by people in retrospect, and are notable when the report is by an outstanding achiever. We can only speculate whether the reports of elite sportspersons are indicative of the experiences of lesser players, or whether elite players had greater opportunity to develop special relationships with their coach. Gottlieb (1991) reports that boys who were regarded as highly competitive and successful preferred the help of adults who were experts, and prized the attention of coaches. However, boys whom he described as outsiders occupied a different social niche: they did not participate in school or community activities and rarely sought the help of teachers or other adults.

Evidence that coaches themselves place a good deal of importance on social development comes from a survey by Gould and Martens (1979) of the attitudes of over 400 volunteer coaches of youth sports in the Midwest of the USA. The coaches gave priority to providing good leadership and promoting the youngster's well-being. When asked to list the topics which should be included in a coaching clinic, a majority of coaches rated as highly important such personal development aspects as motivating youngsters, encouraging sporting behaviour, and teaching young people to be good losers.

Developing close trusting relationships

How does a relationship develop to become significant? What are the attributes of such a relationship? They include trust, respect, open acceptance of the other (Carl Rogers' 'unconditional positive regard'), and the kind of genuineness in normal social interaction which has validity. Some suggest that a relationship between an adolescent and an adult person becomes significant when the adult communicates the idea that the adolescent matters as a person. This is evident in the testimonies of sportspeople already mentioned. Rosenberg and McCullough (1981) suggested that it is through adolescents' relations with social network members, and being included in an actively functioning network, that young people see themselves as mattering, as being somebody. Recognition comes from the simple experience of being accepted as part of a network. Membership of the club or youth organisation itself confers a sense of belonging and identity, so that being a member of the 'Y' is a characteristic one shares with the champions, the Olympians, the great coaches. And membership makes these adults accessible and potential influences.

From the adult's perspective, there may be no conscious enlistment of the adolescent into her/his 'admiration society'. More often than not, it is through a chance remark or incident that the adult comes to realise that her/his relationship with a particular young person is significant, that the young person depends on her/him to take appropriate action and be available when needed, and that her/his actions and attention have made a difference to that young person's life. These relations are characterised by equality rather than formal role patterns, and depend, says Gottlieb (1991), on the successful pairing of an attentive adult with a young person who needs to be recognised, within a freely chosen relationship. For example, Gottlieb and Sylvestre (1994, p. 21) describe the interpersonal relations between young people and adults who are significant to them as 'marked by informality, spontaneity, acceptance, and sustained interaction', which developed when the adult responded to the youth as someone who was 'capable of mature dialogue'. The qualities are summarised in Box 8.1.

YOUTH WORK AND YOUTH ORGANISATIONS

Modern youth work and youth organisations had their origins in the activities of churches and voluntary organisations in the eighteenth and nineteenth centuries. These bodies were concerned with providing structures

Box 8.1 Features of effective support from an adult or non-age peer

---

The adult or non-age peer:

1 has the benefit of distance from the tensions of peer network, to provide more balance and objectivity;
2 is able to consider the young person's ideas, problems, and worries on their merits, free of any family history;
3 is able to be straight, and focus directly on the young person's personal weaknesses in order to encourage self-understanding and self-correction;
4 knowing the adult world view, is able to interpret the reactions and views of adults to the young person;
5 has a reality-based perspective, arising out of experience with similar personal difficulties;
6 provides a model of an effective person who can manage to integrate experiences and regulate conflicting demands on her/his life.

through which adults could reach youth and connect them to the orderly world of adult responsibility and citizenship. They sought to develop citizens and mould character, so that young people would acquire habits of diligence and self-control, rather than congregate in groups, separate from adult society, aimlessly whiling away their time. Over the ensuing years, the meanings associated with youth work have widened beyond the religious and educational focus of the early organisations such as the Sunday school (begun in the 1780s) and the YMCA (begun in 1844). Gradually, the emphasis on promoting moral behaviour and character development has enlarged to recognise the educational validity of leisure and recreational goals; and the focus has shifted towards social relaxation and personal development for individuals to obtain greater enjoyment from non-work time. For example, the YMCA began as a Bible class and Christian education programme, but soon widened its activities so as to include physical education in the gymnasium, cultural activities, and skill development in team games. Thus what began as religious organisations have expanded to include physical and cultural activities, and education and personal development objectives.

The clubs and societies were designed not only to structure the time of young people but to bring them within the reach and surveillance of adults. In this respect, the youth organisations have long sought to address the 'drift' away from adult contact into peer company, because of the antisocial consequences of such associations. This concern with structuring youth leisure time is roundly criticised by some radical sociologists like Nava (1984) and White (1990) as being reformist and welfarist; but they miss the point of the educational benefits that can flow to young people, as to other age groups, from the community provision of structured recreational activities. Structured forms of recreation yield greater satisfaction than unstructured leisure, as the research of Csikszentmihalyi and Larson (1984) has shown. Intensive monitoring of adolescents' leisure experiences found that it was the highly structured activities, rather than the passive and unstructured ones like reading and watching TV, which gave the most intrinsically rewarding leisure experiences to adolescents. Activities conducted within an organised framework allow youth to develop skills, and much skill learning involves adults as teachers or mentors. Most modern youth organisations provide some opportunity for the learning and mastery of skills, as they always have; these may range from learning bushcraft and first aid in the Scouts or Guides to using light effectively in a photography club, or playing goalie in a sports team.

Youth organisations contain a great deal of diversity, which is often obscured by attempts at generalisation. A survey of national youth organisations in Britain by Thomas and Perry (1975) classified them into the following categories: federations of clubs; uniformed organisations; church coordinating bodies for youth; bodies with a wide age range but including a youth sector; service organisations; and stand-alone groups which operate in several sites. Attempts to categorise different types of youth work and youth organisations include those by Eggleston (1976) and Smith (1988). Eggleston (1976) distinguished youth organisations in Britain in terms of whether their focus was organisation centred, where the structure was well established and varied little from area to area in its programme or approach, or whether it was client centred, which referred to a more loosely structured approach that reflected local concerns. He detected a shift in British youth work in the 1970s away from an organisation-centred to a client-centred approach, where youth work activities reflected the needs of the local community. Smith (1988) has suggested that approaches to working with youth are driven by several different traditions, the major ones being to promote leisure enjoyment, character building, or social and personal development. Other traditions, such as that of youth rescue, are relatively minor. The reformist element in youth work continues, however, whether this is expressed in the welfare concerns for health and housing or in the concerns for improving young people's use of leisure time. Smith has grouped the various traditions into three forms of expression: a *movement-based form*, arising from the major youth movements such as the Scouts and Boys' Brigade; a *professionalised form*, represented in youth welfare work and recreational leadership; and an *organic form*, concerned with satisfying the leisure interests of members themselves, and characterised by self-government. These forms of expression of the traditions coexist, but the implication which can be drawn from Eggleston's earlier typology, as well as from Smith and other commentators, is that there is an evolution of the forms towards more organic ones, responsive to local concerns.

Declining participation in sport and youth groups

For several decades, observers have noticed a decline in the numbers of young people who participate in youth clubs, or show an interest in the traditional forms of youth organisation. The decline is particularly pronounced among those teenagers over 16 years of age. Evans (1987) notes this is the very age group whose needs have been the concern of the Youth Service in Britain. A strong decline could also be detected by the 1970s in the membership of Rural Youth clubs and Surf Lifesaving clubs in Australia, while older, more established youth organisations such as the Scouts have been experiencing a shrinking youth membership over a longer period. The strongly age-graded nature of the adolescent's world is reflected in the timetable set for joining and leaving organised youth groups;

MacLeod (1982, p. 14) comments that 'efforts to alter that timetable work about as well today as in the 1920s'. Hogan (1968, p. 15) attributed the failure of Scouting to retain the interest of older teenagers, evident in Britain even in the 1940s, to the absence of 'a progressively exacting course of training'. Boys join the Scouts in order to satisfy their desire for adventure, but when the activities are not managed in a progression, boys lose their enthusiasm. MacLeod (1982) notes that past the age of 14 or 15 years, the 'gang-like' activities of camping, firelighting, and bushcraft lose their appeal; he reports that the median age for leaving the Scouts was $14\frac{1}{2}$ years as early as 1921 in the United States, with over three-quarters of boys leaving before the age of 16 years. They become bored by the lack of variety and lack of increasing challenge, and frustrated by the authoritarian aspects of the organisational structure.

Recent studies of adolescent recreation patterns in Australia report an age-related decline in young people's participation in outdoor leisure activities and in individual and team sports across the high-school years, together with a steep increase in social forms of leisure (see, for example, Australian Sports Commission (ASC), 1991; Department of Tourism and Recreation (DTR), 1975; Garton and Pratt, 1987; Jobling and Cotterell, 1990). The decline in participation in sport and active recreation is similar to that noted among youth in other Western countries (e.g., Ewing and Seefeldt, 1990; Hendry, 1983). The trend has been established for some time. A study of the leisure interests and activities of over 9000 Sydney youth undertaken in the late 1960s (Connell *et al.*, 1975) found a decline with age in the popularity of organised sport, matched by a corresponding increase by 17 and 19 years of age in 'sociable interests' and 'mating interests' among males, and in fashion among females. When school leavers were asked to nominate their three most common leisure activities, the girls were hard put to find even three, naming parties, dances, and talking together. Boys nominated talk, sport, and parties and dances. Connell *et al.* (1975, p. 211) made the comment that 'hardly any of them mention spending time in adult-organised clubs'.

Some of the forces affecting participation may be developmental. Hendry (1983, 1989) has developed a focal theory of leisure to explain the changes in leisure patterns observed in studies of British youth, noting that the age-related changes in leisure orientation roughly correspond with different relational concerns which emerge during the adolescent years. This work builds on that of Coleman (1980), who identified a shift in the focus of relationship concerns during adolescence, from concern with heterosexual relations in the early years, to concern with peers and group belonging in mid-adolescence, and later to concerns with autonomy and separation from parents. Thus in the early adolescent period, participation in adult-organised activities and groups helps structure acquaintance with the opposite sex, the focal concern of this period. During middle adolescence, concern with establishing good peer relationships prompts a shift in leisure focus to casual activities, structured by youth themselves. The third focal stage links the pursuit of commercial leisure activities with adolescent strivings for autonomy, as older teenagers increasingly see themselves as being grown up and thus part of the adult world. Hendry (1989) suggests that the timing of these shifts in leisure focus is likely to be influenced by socio-cultural values and by factors in the local environment which affect leisure opportunities.

A focal theory of leisure can be successfully applied to youth leisure interests in countries with different lifestyles and climates. An Australian national study to determine the recreation needs of 12–20-year-olds in Australia (Department of Tourism and Recreation (DTR), 1975) noted a decline in the importance given by young people to organised sports, clubs, and uniformed groups across the teenage years, and an increased interest in casual and commercial activities such as a coffee shop/meeting place, and in leisure places under the control of young people themselves, to 'run the way they want'. While not completely rejecting adult leadership and involvement, young people believed that adults 'have been far too intrusive and assertive'. The kind of structure desired by Australian youth was one with 'just enough organisation', with adults providing help and guidance 'in the spirit of an open and listening partnership and not an anxious and prescriptive proprietorship'. In short, young people expressed the wish to 'be together without being organised into somebody else's scheme or program or premiership contest' (Department of Tourism and Recreation (DTR), 1975, pp. vii–viii). There was also a strong expression of concern by discussants about a desire for a sense of community. The lack of appropriate places for relaxed social interaction with friends, and the lure of pubs and 'drinking scenes' in the absence of alternatives, made young people dismayed. An urgent need was 'to be trusted with places and spaces of their own', with maximum flexibility for adapting to the activities they want to pursue.

Tension concerning the nature of leadership and the controlling role of adults is a factor in the declining popularity of youth organisations which do not allow young people room to develop their own lifestyles, and which want to oversee the leisure time of young people in order to develop 'socially responsible' attitudes and behaviour. A theme in the Australian and British studies is the resistance of many young people to adult-determined forms of recreation, particularly youth groups and competitive sport, which they see as incompatible with their psychological development and lifestyles. Structures which may have been acceptable to young people a generation or two ago have limited appeal to today's generation. The relationships which youth seek with adults are mutually respecting ones; they reject traditional youth organisations as coercive and rule bound, and resent being treated as future citizens when they see this as something they already have become. Thus the drawing power of the youth centre has declined from its being a social venue and reference point for a wide spectrum of the community's young people. The need for satisfying social leisure experiences remains, despite changes in the structures through which it finds expression.

YOUTH CLUBS AND ORGANISED GROUPS IN THE FUTURE

We are interested in ways of structuring the social environment for young people, mindful that the social structures created by previous generations may no longer be acceptable to or appropriate for the youth of today. The challenge to youth work, according to Hurrelmann (1990a), p. 329, is the lack of 'free space' for young people in our highly structured environment. He notes the lack of situations which are 'non-commercial, unorganised, unsupervised, and non-pedagogical' where adolescents could test their limits. The desire of youth to be accepted on their own terms implies that the leadership and control of clubs and organisations should be in the hands of young people themselves, and that this should include the management of finances and facilities as well, although clearly autonomy and respon-sibility go hand in hand. Jones (1987, p. 276) concluded his review of recent approaches to work with juvenile offenders with these words:

> More than anything else, there is a need to give adolescents meaningful roles in society, to create bonds to social institutions, to develop a sense of self-esteem and self-confidence, and to create a stable base from which the risks that promote developmental, psychological, educational and personal growth can be taken.

This statement echoes a common concern with social integration in the literature on youth work; namely that, if young people are to avoid alien-ation and despair, they have to be meaningfully linked to social institutions.

New forms of suburban recreation

Organised youth work continues, but the most appropriate form is not always one where there is a youth club which meets each night or on some other regular basis. Some are adult-supervised monthly activities, like the blue-light discos conducted by the local police, or adult-controlled entertainments, like the Crush Club disco in Hobart, managed by people with experience in youth entertainment. The latter is an alcohol-free night club for teenagers which runs each Friday and Saturday, with quality entertainment and a club atmosphere, where young people can enjoy themselves without worrying about drunken youth harassing them. Some activities are less structured and operate in a more varied manner, usually with adult assistance if not control. For example, Urjadko (1991) describes a multi-pronged youth recreation programme in an outer Melbourne suburb, which incorporates after-hours transport to recreation points for youth, music practice facilities, discount movie tickets, a disco with a no-alcohol cocktail bar, and adventure experiences like a specially designed nine-day Outward-Bound-style course with canoeing, trekking, cycling, and community work. Moreover, students are enlisted as information officers promoting the activities at their schools.

An after-school programme for youth offenders in Townsville described by Carter and Drew (1991) incorporates two components of three hours each per week: a *compensatory curriculum*, aimed at improving self-reliance and self-confidence through positive interactions with caring, competent adults; and a *correctional curriculum*, focused directly on reducing delinquent behaviour by a programme of discussion and analysis of offences. Both curriculums seek to involve youth in fun activities: the discussions and analyses include filming the delinquent episodes and 'stop points' (points for considering possible alternatives and working out the actions needed for the positive alternatives to occur) in the episode, with the author as film director, and others as actors. The film is followed by analysis of alternatives, and further filming of the changes, so that participants see the episodes unfold differently, and gain deeper understanding of means–ends thinking. The compensatory curriculum includes an activities component fortnightly on Saturday afternoons, where youth have participated in abseiling, orienteering, sailing, touch football, and rock climbing.

Group development through wilderness adventure

The origin of outdoor adventure programmes is Outward Bound, founded by two educators, Kurt Hahn and Jim Hogan, who employed the principles of experiential learning to incorporate physical accomplishments and community service into the regular school curriculum. The principle enunciated by Hahn of 'adventure as an ingredient in education' (Hogan, 1968, p. 118) focused on the whole person, and on discovering the unrealised physical and mental strengths of students through the use of experiential modes of learning.

A feature of wilderness adventures is the group context. The nature of adventure pursuits means that people who begin the adventure as strangers must live in close proximity for days on end, encounter unpredictable natural elements, and learn group cooperation in order to achieve their objectives. The group has an interest in each person's success because the group reaps the benefits of each individual's achievement. Ewert and Heywood (1991, p. 593) comment that 'the use of the natural environment as a place to promote and develop groups . . . has become a popular education and management-training technique'. Wilderness adventure can provide participants with intense physical and emotional experiences that are unique to the group: they alone have experienced the peculiar pain and fear of battling the natural elements, and the joy and exhilaration of winning through. The physical challenge and novelty of activities can make demands on participants' commitment to one another, which have the effect of structuring group relationships so that individual members progress rapidly from secondary-level relations to primary-level ones, encountering intense interpersonal experiences of closeness, familiarity, interdependence, and trust. Knowledge that they shared in unique experiences provides a special bond of friendship.

The effects of outdoor challenge on group processes were not fully appreciated at first by those in the Outward Bound schools, as Hogan (1968) acknowledges in his account of its early developments. Initially, the allocation of a new intake of boys at Gordonstoun and Aberdovey to different 'watches' was viewed as a straightforward organisational matter of the kind regularly undertaken in schools. The focus of the challenging experience was directed at the individual's growth of confidence and self-control rather than at group processes. But as time progressed Hogan (1968, p. 72) reported that 'our perspective changed'; instructors came to realise that a process of team building was taking place before their eyes 'which might be much more significant than the grade of badge for which a boy might qualify'. He noted with a sense of wonder that friendships were established among former strangers, these being based upon 'mutual respect arising out of testing situations' (p. 73).

Individual development

Wilderness also has a psychological impact at the individual level. Ewert (1989) describes the nature of outdoor adventure as 'a complex arousal system' (p. 12) which may lead a person at times to peak experience, where the individual is acutely aware of self, fully concentrating on the situation, and the feelings are so intense that there is a sense of transcendence of reality. The idea of peak experience was introduced by Maslow (1962) to describe those moments when people were most fulfilled and most truly themselves, but was applied to outdoor adventure by Csikszentmihalyi (1975). He interviewed people who engaged in demanding outdoor activities like mountain climbing, and found that the intense discipline of mind and body required as they concentrated on the immediate task produced a fusion between the demands of the situation and their smooth responses to it. In this 'flow state', action and awareness, mastery and anxiety are merged.

An interesting characteristic of adventure challenges is what Ewert calls 'the aloneness inherent in the activities' (Ewert, 1989, p. 56). On a rock climb, or kayaking over rapids, the individual is placed in a contest with nature, where, despite the presence and encouragement of others, the challenge is for the individual to perform and requires total focusing on self. There is the necessity of acceptance in order to cope, for example yielding to the force of the rapids, and persisting despite the cold and the pain, because nature does not listen to one's complaints. Moreover, each decision and action has an irrevocable personal consequence. Once you begin the rope descent, or enter the rapids, there is no turning back: you have to 'go through with it', and commit total effort, strength, and concentration. The personal benefits of outdoor challenge include enhanced awareness of one's physiological and emotional states, increased confidence in being able to cope individually in unpredictable situations, and a deep sense of freedom. These benefits are derived from self-control: control of attentional focus on the situation, and control of such emotions as fear, doubt, and panic. They are experiences which are not found in any other recreation activity. Scherl (1989, p. 129) summarises the effects of wilderness in this way: 'One becomes more aware of one's inner capabilities and resources when required to exert self-control and more aware of oneself as an integral part of the transaction.'

CONCLUSION: APPLICATIONS TO ANTISOCIAL YOUTH

Several authorities make it clear that connecting with many young people who are older than 13 or 14 years through formal organisations such as youth centres and youth clubs is difficult. Many of these youth are not club oriented and may be described as 'unattached', preferring to hang around with their friends, mucking about and not doing much. Roberts (1983, p. 177) argues that vulnerable young people need 'places where they can relate to each other without obtrusive supervision or high admission charges . . . They need opportunities to acquire and practise leisure interests and skills . . . to enhance their lifestyles.' Government-funded sports and leisure complexes are unlike the places favoured by these young people for leisure purposes: the amusement arcades, cafés, and pubs; the multi-purpose halls; and the parks with 'kick-about areas'. The community facilities provided for these youth are unstimulating and lack flexibility; they restrict the range of leisure options to traditional uses, and give them little opportunity to control their own environment and develop their own activities.

The problem of how to reach 'unattached youth' is not altogether a new one, as it dates from at least the early 1940s. For example, Macalister Brew (1957, pp. 106, 161) referred to the youth club 'competing in an open field' against commercial forms of entertainment, and saw the value of beginning a youth programme via a teenage canteen to provide a meeting place, which might later develop into a youth club. She lamented the 'regrettable tendency' to measure the success of such work in terms of the rate of transfer into a youth club proper of youth contacted in this way, acknowledging that some young people will remain unattached, and that not all adolescents need to be attached to youth groups.

In this section we discuss programmes which seek to minimise delinquency among antisocial youth by promoting personal competencies. Given the multiplicity of factors which have been identified as contributing to delinquent behaviour, it is unlikely that any programme can be designed with the appropriate mix of experiences to ensure unqualified success. The two models discussed here are community arts and wilderness experiences. Both are concerned with developing personal skills (physical mastery, technical competency) and life skills (emotional control and self-management) through group relations and through taking personal responsibility for solving problems.

Community arts

The community arts model enlists young people in devising an artistic solution to a community concern, using art or live theatre. The complexity of the problem places demands on their imagination and planning, as well as on the technical skills of organisation and execution of the plan. Many of the artists are graffiti exponents, enlisted through the community arts model to direct their energies into socially acceptable art products in approved urban art locations. One of the tasks of the community arts workers is to educate the public to see that graffiti has to be treated differently from vandalism, and to provide sites for artists to display their work legally. These outlets include walls of commercial buildings, construction-site panels, and fence-painting competitions. In some cases, paint and artistic advice are provided free to the artists. Police involved with graffiti groups in New South Wales towns have found that these community-based approaches are highly effective in reducing vandalism.

A project established by the city of Gosnells, near Perth, was successful in establishing good relations with local graffiti artists and in reducing the 'tagging' of public buildings to the point where it was non-existent (O'Doherty, 1991).

For local councils, the community arts model poses a dilemma in respect of promoting self-organised activities for young people, where these involve facilities such as 'a building which young people can have for themselves and run the way they want to' (Department of Tourism and Recreation, 1975, p. 28). The cost of establishing the facilities makes adults reluctant to pass control into the hands of youth. From the viewpoint of youth themselves, the slowness of adults to cede responsibility and control of facilities to them is further complicated by the unwillingness of local authorities to update and modify existing facilities in ways which are appropriate to youth needs. Some local councils in Australia are slow to commit expenditure to the maintenance of recreation facilities like outdoor skateboard bowls, as if damage reflects mistreatment by young people rather than the wear and tear which is a consequence of heavy use. Thus the potential to enlist youth in caring for their community is placed at risk by adult cautiousness, born out of mistrust, or short-sightedness, or a desire to control youth. When graffiti appears, the more reactionary voices are heard declaring, 'See, they don't deserve our good will', as if young people have to earn the right to be treated as citizens.

Outdoor programmes for delinquent youth

The experiential learning emphasis in the Outward Bound schools and their use of adventure settings has been applied to work with antisocial and delinquent youth. Where traditional approaches, including counselling and detention in institutions, have been ineffectual, programmes located in natural environments provide concrete experiences which offer tangible short-term goals and the basis for re-establishing trust in a delinquent youth's dealings with peers and adults. The outdoor adventure programmes have been widely adopted by workers in the juvenile justice arena in New Zealand and Australia in recent years, with considerable evidence of effectiveness, in the short term at least, in reducing juvenile offending. Evaluations of the programmes suggest that the effects diminish after about twelve months, leading experienced workers to recognise that one cannot simply provide a stimulating experience to youth, and then drop them back into their old environment without providing a programme of ongoing support and guidance (e.g., Lyon, 1991).

Not all delinquent youth will benefit from adventure programmes. They have special appeal to those whose deviancy involves risk and challenge;

for example, youth who steal cars. Some suggest that the wilderness 'flow' experience resembles the kind of excitement and adrenalin rush which youth experience from high-speed car chases through the city, and recent attempts to introduce these boys to wilderness adventures have been justified as a way of redirecting their behaviour into socially acceptable situations, which offer excitement and risk through another kind of intensely lived experience (see Mayne, 1993; Pearson, 1991). They are appropriately viewed as interventions which aim to minimise rather than treat delinquency, according to Gullotta and Adams (1982). They promote competency, including physical and technical skills, problem solving, and self-management, through group relations. A key attribute associated with benefits from challenging outdoor experiences is that of trust through partnership (e.g., Ewert and Heywood, 1991; Marx, 1988; Mayne, 1993). Youth have to partner another, or depend on the strengths of another. This relationship is in contrast to street situations which seek to probe the weaknesses of the other in order to enhance one's ego. The building of trust has a reinforcing effect on adult instructors too; at some of the sites in Australia, instructors have volunteered to work for reduced salaries or just for their keep in order to remain involved.

These programmes require time for youth to work through their conflicts. For example, the outdoor programme described by Marx (1988) in Maine, USA, seeks through adventure to provide a concrete, action-oriented form of reality therapy, and to continue the work after youth return from the adventure component. It consists of a series of four-day periods, interspersed with returning to the youth's family. This pattern continues over a four-month schedule. Counselling is held in the home during these returns, to involve parents in the change process and integrate the changes into the local environment. After the challenge phase, follow-up continues through an eight-month community-based programme which contains day-length recreational outings and activities.

The wilderness programme conducted on 80 acres of bushland and gorge country at Tallong, southwest of Sydney, by the Sydney City Mission (see Hill, 1992; Letts *et al.*, 1991) works on a twenty-two-week programme timetable, with a quota of about thirty boys and a staggered intake of four boys every three weeks. The programme does not accept court referrals, only volunteers, and conducts an extensive prior assessment to establish whether it is likely to be appropriate to the needs and problems of each student. There are five phases: exploration (camping and brief wilderness ventures), basic skills (expeditions), work experience (an employment training phase), advanced wilderness skills, and a final phase of community work, which is followed by a nine-day independent expedition.

A criticism sometimes heard is that the adventure challenge approach is male oriented. It is true that males are a large proportion of programme intakes, but this is in part a response to the offender population and staff resources. The largest wilderness adventure project in Australia is Project Hahn in Tasmania, which in a five-year period has enrolled over 500 young people in its challenge courses, about half of whom have been troubled young people, and seventy-five of these were females. A wilderness programme in the Carnarvon Gorge area called Saddler's Springs Education Centre has been catering exclusively for adolescent girls, and focuses on developing their 'bush eyes' for observing animals in the wild, and recognising plants. The nature aspect of wilderness works its own healing and wonder on disturbed and rejected youth, as it does on most of us; I recall the thrill experienced by three 16-year-old boys out camping 'on safari' in a large school group, when I alerted them one night to the wild possums in the trees. As others settled down in the tents oblivious to the night-life outside, these boys found themselves hand-feeding the nocturnal marsupials with pieces of fruit.

Other programmes in Australia have included work placements of youth in island communities and on cattle stations. For example, groups of up to five juvenile offenders are placed in community service projects on Wardang Island in South Australia and linked with the local Aboriginal community. They work for a month renovating shacks, planting trees, fishing, and catching rabbits. Several government departments fund a training farm in north Queensland, which accommodates up to twenty-four young people for a minimum of one month. The central activities of the farm concern the management and care of horses, including catching wild horses (brumbies) and breaking them in. Learning to relate to horses and the distinctive nature of each horse is central: rough treatment will see the animal play up; right treatment will see the horse cooperate and respond with affection. The goal of the farm is to allow young people time to redirect their lives. Various life skills are taught, such as bush skills, carpentry, and cooking, all of which involve working with adults, including accepting criticism. A teacher on the farm said, 'My role is to give these people the confidence to start something and the self-discipline to see it through' (Hill, 1994, p. 82). A teenage girl who worked there for four months stated: 'Petford Training Farm calmed me down and gave me time to think where I was heading' (Hill, 1994, p. 87).

The programmes provide social niches where troubled youth can relate to others, learn skills, and find themselves. Macalister Brew (1957, p. 114) concluded her list of ten 'don'ts' to youth leaders with the following advice:

Don't expect results. We are dealing with the most mercurial quality in
the world, the adventurous yet timid, changeable yet loyal, earnest yet
frivolous, adolescent human being. Often these young people will have
passed out of the group long before the effect of their membership will
be apparent to them or others.

9 Schools as supportive environments

Previous chapters have described the kinds of social influence exerted upon adolescents in different social contexts, and some of the consequences of social rejection, alienation, and susceptibility to peer pressures, including difficulties in adjusting to high school, emotional and social loneliness, and adoption of risk behaviour. Relatively little has been said about young people's resilience, energy, optimism, and hunger for acquiring new competencies. These healthy aspects of personality are present in young people, and are particularly evident when environments allow for the possibility of growth and do not merely focus on control and correction. Responsibility for devising environments which are protective and supportive for adolescents as they build attachment and commitment to social institutions clearly involves schools. The theme of this chapter is prevention of alienation and antisocial behaviour by the creation of a supportive school community.

Semmens (1990) argues that we should endeavour to connect young people to at least one key social institution in a way which respects their growth. The most obvious and central social institution in the lives of young people is the school. Apart from the family, the school is the only agency of society which takes a broad view of the adolescent and deals with the person rather than just the category or the problem. From a social networks perspective, school connects to the other social worlds which adolescents inhabit: the family, the peer group, the local community, and the workplace. In addition to its outward connections with the key institutions of society, the school is itself a social system, containing a variety of settings, which approximate closely to the range of interpersonal situations associated with the wider society. Its settings contain recurring patterns of roles and rules which give order and predictability to social relations. As a key social institution, the school is a source of what Semmens (1990, p. 28) calls 'redemptive pathways' to adulthood.

ALIENATION AND ATTACHMENT REVISITED

Evidence has been presented that susceptibility to risk behaviours such as smoking and alcohol abuse, and proneness to engage in antisocial behaviour, are related to the quality of attachments to parents and to the school (see Dishion *et al.*, 1991; Smith *et al.*, 1989). Liska and Reed (1985) see the connection between weakened attachment to these social institutions and proneness to delinquency as a reciprocally reinforcing process. A similar point is made by Kulka *et al.* (1982), who distinguished two aspects of alienation from school: negative attitudes towards school, the teachers, and other students on the one hand; and lack of involvement in school groups and activities on the other. They suggested that students' attitudes to *school in general* were 'causally antecedent' to their attitudes to teachers and fellow students, and to involvement in school life.

Hurrelmann and Engel (1992) urge that efforts be directed at improving the quality of school, as a central plank in the prevention of antisocial and deviant behaviour. Improvements should focus on 'changing the social climate of school settings in order to develop attachments between the school and the individual student. Schools have to offer opportunities for meaningful involvement' (p. 135). Meaningful involvement includes respecting the autonomy concerns of young people and creating a sense of belonging (Goodenow, 1992, 1993), to stem classroom disaffection as well as respond to their call for a place of their own to run the way they want to. Box 9.1 models the building of attachments, based upon the processes seen as critical in the studies cited in this and previous chapters.

Fragmentation of approaches to at-risk youth

Interventions directed towards at-risk youth have tended to remove them from their regular settings in order to address their problem characteristics in specialised treatment programmes. The agency model continues to attract support, despite its proven inefficacy in reducing misconduct and problem behaviour in and out of school (see Linney and Seidman, 1989) and its low success with delinquent interventions (see Lundman, 1993). The appeal of agency-based control approaches to dealing with delinquents

Box 9.1 Cyclic process of forming attachments

Positive expectations of school → Cooperative behaviour → Approval by teachers → Positive attitudes towards teachers → Increased involvement → Endorsement of commitment to school and other at-risk groups is their focus on a specific group, their short-term programme commitment, and their management within a single agency, which obviates the need to consult with other agencies and is touted as an advantage in ease of delivery of a coherent programme. Semmens (1990) and Linney and Seidman (1989) are among those who condemn the myopia of agency-based approaches, which thrive in a world apart from the key institutions of society, such as the family, the peer group, the school, and voluntary organisations. What the interventions fail to recognise is the nature of the social ecology of youth at risk; and their short-sighted approach is incapable of enlisting the social network in linking the young person into healthy social environments. Amazingly, they bypass the major social institution which all youth attend: the school; and by so doing they devalue the skills and experience of teachers, and deny the validity of the school as a social system connected to the community by historical and emotional ties as well as geographical ones.

In reaction to the narrowness of agency-based interventions, an increasing number of scholars are calling for the adoption of an *ecological perspective* in support provisions for troubled and troublesome children and youth. In health risk areas, inclusion of groups beyond the school, including the family, peers, the media, government agencies, and community organisations, is needed if lasting changes are to occur (see Seidman, 1991; Weissberg *et al.*, 1991). Acknowledging the embeddedness of the school in its community is an early step in valuing and strengthening the web of supportive links between the school and community agencies and groups.

PREVENTION OF ALIENATION BY THE CREATION OF EFFECTIVE COMMUNITY

The concept of *supportive school environments* stresses how students in the school are linked to its organisation, to groups of fellow students, and to a variety of roles and relations with others through activities available at school. To do the hard work in *creating* supportive school environments requires more than a few pious statements about inclusive education or goals for personal and social development. Real structures and programmes have to be devised, which enlist the energies of school staff over the long haul. Design of appropriate environmental settings for assisting lonely, anxious, shy, aggressive, or otherwise antisocial young people must be consciously undertaken, and not be assumed to occur by administrative fiat. Implementation of a supportive environment requires not only a school development plan but an *operational plan* which specifies the actions required and the responsibilities of staff, and allocates sufficient resources for the plan to be implemented.

A central plank of a support philosophy is that it be seen as *pervading* the school environment rather than a separate activity performed in pastoral care groups or by selected members of the school staff, or offered as a special means of overcoming deficiencies in particular students or groups. In explaining their policy for supportive schools, the Tasmanian Department of Education (1988) emphasised that the focus of a supportive school environment is 'care for the present and future well-being of *all* students' (original emphasis), adding that 'student support could be taken as the overarching concept to include these and all other programmes with a student focus' (pp. 48–49).

Developing a sense of community

Structural modifications to schools, which alter the internal organisation in ways that personalise the administrative system and increase the level of control which teachers themselves have over their daily work, are important and worthwhile. But organisational changes are most effective when they grow out of a broader school support policy that is equally concerned with the morale of teachers and with the well-being of students, and not just interested in reducing dropout and behaviour problems. Schools are more than a collectivity of peer crowds competing for status and popularity in the adolescent society. Those schools which strive to establish a sense of *community* among their inhabitants exert positive influences over young people's development. McMillan and Chavis (1986) propose four characteristics of a sense of community, which are sufficiently robust to apply to a geographic community as well as to a school or a relational one not bounded by its locality. They resemble several of Weiss's (1974) provisions of social relationships, such as attachment, reassurance of worth, reliable alliance, and social integration. The characteristics are *membership, reinforcement, influence,* and *shared emotional connection.*

Membership addresses the sense of shared belonging and personal relatedness to a group. Through membership a person is connected to others, identifies with the group or institution, and gains emotional security. Through rules of membership the group imposes boundaries, defining who belongs and who does not. In early adolescence, boundary maintenance is vigorously pursued, in proportion to the value placed on membership. The mutual *reinforcement* which members of a community receive occurs in the form of integration and need fulfilment. Association with the group or institution must be rewarding for the individual members and for the collective; members value the membership of others, and reinforce their membership status, thus integrating them into the group or institution.

Belonging to a community includes the process of *influence*. Influence is reciprocal where membership is genuine and individuals feel that they matter to the group. Cohesiveness and conformity go hand in hand: behaving in conformity with the others validates one's identity as a group member. The fourth feature, *shared emotional connection*, is 'the definitive element of true community', according to McMillan and Chavis (1986, p. 14), and is based on a shared history. The greater the commitment to this history, through investment of energy and time and involvement with other community members, the greater the emotional connection. Participating in the events and activities of the community assists members to become conscious of their roots, helps them to feel a sense of honour and pride, and increases their awareness of shared values.

McMillan and Chavis (1986, p. 14) comment that

> strong communities are those that offer their members positive ways to interact, important events to share and ways to resolve them positively, opportunities to honour members, opportunities to invest in the community, and opportunities to experience a spiritual bond among members.

Schools and colleges can create a strong sense of community through the climate they establish within the normal programme of activities, but they can strengthen the bonds of attachment to the school as an entity through sponsoring school-level events which evoke an awareness of shared history with other members of the school, and which provide entry through school traditions to identification with members from the past.

Coleman (1961) nominated sports competitions ('athletics') as *the only means* by which schools, in his view, could create internal cohesiveness and foster student identification with the school. Such a strategy seeks to build in-group cohesion by responding to an *external* stress. But attachment and cohesiveness can be built on shared experiences arising from the programme of the institution itself. An illustration comes from my own university college, which celebrated Anzac Day (25 April) with a simple ceremony where the principal read two short extracts from the Gallipoli memoirs of a former principal, Dr Merrington; the student club president read 'Lest we forget'; the names were read from the college roll of honour; and the lament 'Flowers of the Forest' was played by the college piper, while the 300 college students stood in respectful silence. The Merrington flag, the only Australian flag to fly at Gallipoli, was displayed throughout the week in the college chapel.

This solemn occasion may be compared with the liveliness of the Bannockburn dinner, celebrated a month later, when the senior men and women of the college and members of the college council attend the dinner in kilts; the haggis is piped in; and all the college stand for the recital of

Burns' address to the haggis. The dinner proceeds, with Highland dancing, pipers, and the singing of familiar Scottish songs. Bursaries are awarded by the college council to students who have made outstanding contributions to college life. Creation of events of this kind, in which membership of a community is celebrated and the bonds among students and friends of the college affirmed, assists social integration and builds attachment.

NICHES FOR FOSTERING HEALTHY RELATIONSHIPS

Of importance is the creation of environmental niches where supportive relationships can be fostered. Niches are miniature environments tailored to the needs of particular individuals. In nature, different species occupy distinctive niches within the physical environment: some birds will feed off the tops of trees while others feed on lower branches. Social niches contain roles and activities which specify the relations between the occupants, and provide reassurance about the limits of these roles and relations. They provide a setting and a structure for adolescent and adult inhabitants to interact within a zone that may well develop beyond traditional role boundaries, so that other legitimate roles, apart from teacher, leader, and behaviour-controller, can emerge, such as guide, adviser, instructor, supporter, appraiser, and collaborator. The value of voluntary organisations lies in the opportunity they provide for structured social interaction and, through this, for youth to gain a sense of connectedness, belonging, affiliation, and identification with the group, team, or club. School administrative arrangements can also shape niches which are specifically designed with certain adolescents in mind. These could include adjustments to the daily class timetable for at-risk students, educational programmes which link with community activities or groups, and the creation of consultative and special support groups with clear roles for students and teachers, including the allocation of additional resources and designated personnel to the setting.

Activities such as bus trips, concerts, camps, and wilderness adventures are forms of time-out events associated with the host environments of schools and voluntary organisations; their value lies in offering niche structures where the traditional roles are suspended or modified (see Box 9.2). For example, the principal of the high school who turns up at the school rowing shed before the start of the regatta is a more accessible figure to students than s/he is likely to be in her/his role as manager of a staff of over 100 teachers and a student population of 1800. Moreover, just as these events and activities are subsets of their larger host environments, lodged within these activities is an array of miniature niches where roles, relations, and interactions are patterned in unique ways to connect youth with others and to communicate significance and mattering. The resulting experiences

Box 9.2 Sponsorship of support in ecological systems

Settings → Activities → Roles → Relations → Support

---

range from sharing in the moment of sunrise after having risen at 4.30 a.m. and hiked in the darkness for an hour; to seeing the transformation worked on the cast at the final rehearsal of the rock eisteddfod, now decked out in the costumes that you have been working on for so long.

Support networks

In order to increase the supportiveness of the school it is helpful to consider how social networks within the school are structured. Elsewhere I reported on the ways a distorted social network, with weak attachments to parents and restricted ties to peers, indicated unhappiness and loneliness at school (Cotterell, 1994). It would seem that designing peer support appropriate for lonely or bereaved adolescents requires an understanding of the networks of peer relations. Similarly, issues such as peer rejection and intergroup conflict require an appreciation of the network structures of the adolescents who are the subject of concern. Within a community there are many open channels of communication among members: the personal networks of individuals are readily known, and the community as a whole is responsive to individual concerns. In a sense, the community 'grapevine' is quick to sense change in the well-being of individual members, much in the way that a spider detects vibrations from a sector of its web. Tracing the turnarounds of youth who were at risk of school failure and dropping out, Gregory (1995, p. 153) noted the presence of determination and a deliberate decision to stop and change their direction, but added that 'they did not do this by themselves'. All of those in the study had at least one person outside the school who believed in them. By offering support and encouragement, this person provided the security necessary for the adolescent to change and move forward in a positive direction. The significant supporters included an uncle, a grandmother, girlfriends, and boyfriends. At the school level, it was only when these young people moved into a smaller school that sufficient attention was given to their needs. Students testified that effective support within the school was identified with 'teachers who know you as a person', or 'counsellors who are always on my back' and did not give up on them (Gregory, 1995, p. 150). The correlates of teacher support were higher academic competence, greater self-regulation, and greater emotional security in dealings with adults and peers at school.

Mini-schools as supportive social niches

Another supportive niche is the mini-school or school-within-a-school. This is a semi-autonomous environment created for new students so that they have a defined territory in the school and a separately organised curriculum. The Carnegie Council on Adolescent Development report (1989) advocates designing school-within-a-school structures as supportive environments for adolescents. The report's authors believe that creation of educational niches within the wider school would allow relations with teachers to be less 'fragmented' than at present, and would make it possible for supports for this age group to be concentrated at a more personal level, so that teachers had the opportunity 'to develop an understanding of students as individuals' (p. 38). Queensland introduced year-eight centres in 1978, where teachers taught the same class for several subjects as a member of a team of specialist year-eight teachers, rather than as subject specialists. Victorian schools had adopted mini-school structures somewhat earlier, so that Evans (1978) found over eighty high schools with units designed to cater for young adolescents. Felner *et al.* (1982) developed an intervention programme based on creating a mini-school structure which was intended to increase the stability of class groups. They found that it allowed peer and teacher support systems to operate effectively, with improved adjustment manifested in better achievement and school attendance.

Certainly the school-within-a-school structures which have been devised in Queensland high schools have had dramatic effects on improving teacher–student relations and strengthening attachments of young adolescents to the school. But the demands on school staff are heavy and unambiguous: work in the year-eight centre for three years, then move out into the regular school environment. This commitment to give the work with year-eight students priority over other teaching interests in the school was a non-negotiable condition of being on the year-eight team, and the contract further required sharing the staff room in the centre, and joint curriculum planning and team teaching.

The practical effects of building institutional attachment and commitment were explored by Evans (1983) in his thesis on the impact of 'transition sub-schools' on the integration of adolescent youngsters into secondary school in Victoria. He selected four schools from forty-one identified as having a mini-school structure, so that each school represented a different approach. Student experiences in each were then monitored over a period of more than a year, and compared with those of students in a traditional secondary school. The transition sub-schools provided opportunities for year-seven students (about 11 years of age) to develop their own separate identity, through location of most of their lessons in a sub-school which they could call their own place with its own regulations, and where they were taught by the same small group of teachers. The mini-structure was seen as a means of integrating newcomers into the school. Evans tested his data on a model of group integration proposed by Crandall (1978), and on the basis of his results proposed a revised model (see Box 9.3).

Evans found that integration proceeded in a sequence of stages rather than being a multi-dimensional simultaneous process. The benefits to students in the mini-school structures were clear. They were more satisfied with school, were more willing to be involved, identified more strongly with it, and exhibited greater values convergence than those in the traditional school. While there was a range of student responses in the different schools, Evans concluded that those in the mini-schools became integrated into school life more rapidly than students in the traditional school.

One of the features of the sub-school structure in these Victorian schools was that it fostered closer relationships between students and their teachers, and this was reflected in student attitudes. Evans noted that 'The more closely staff at Year 7 worked as a team, the more likely it was that their pupils would hold positive attitudes towards the school, and see themselves as part of it' (Evans, 1983, p. 153). Thus there was a connection between the physical and organisational features of the transition sub-schools and their relational quality. The physical arrangements fostered collegial contacts among the staff, which encouraged them to work together as a team. The organisational flexibility allowed teachers to spend more time interacting with students, and to become more responsive to student needs.

In summary, alienation may be reduced by creating a responsive community. The steps towards that goal should respect the following principles, based on Gregory (1995):

1 Make the school structure small and adults within it accessible.
2 Create a school climate which promotes healthy peer relations.
3 Allow students authentic experiences of success in a context which develops self-responsibility.

Box 9.3 Evans' (1983) model of group integration

Satisfaction → Involvement →Identification → Norm convergence

MOTIVATION AND INFLUENCE

Educators find that the concept of motivation, described in terms of motives and needs, is remote from young people's everyday classroom concerns and behaviour, and unable to provide guidance on what kinds of supportive structure teachers need to assemble if students are to be given real help at school. Classrooms are complex social systems which are more easily apprehended by their inhabitants in terms of activities, rules, and roles than in terms of their fundamental educational and developmental purposes. Organisational matters can easily come to dominate the thinking of teachers to such an extent that little attention is directed to the teaching of attitudes and values and the fostering of self-regulated learning: of learning to think and solve problems rather than just to complete the tasks.

Teachers express regret that students do not become engaged and involved in the subject in the way that would transform them into biologists, historians, or chemists. The emotional response of students is frequently one of disaffection, as we have seen, expressing resistance towards the press of busy and irrelevant work. The way the teacher handles student resistance, either viewing it as an attempt by students to adapt to the surface features of classroom life by signalling their independence, or recognising the mismatch between the students' reading of the situation and the teacher's educative goals, has much to do with the teacher's values. The teacher who can sense student frustration and impatience, and link basic work with that which is novel and more challenging by modifying the task system of the classroom, is also effectively modulating the classroom climate, making it more student oriented and responsive to the emotional concerns of classroom life (see Furlong, 1991).

Classrooms as motivational settings

The classroom is not an island, but is nested within the broader system of the school, and the actions of an individual teacher, with the best will in the world, will have limited impact on personal change if the climate of the school is not supportive as well. The language of motivation is often sharply focused on individual–task relations and teacher–student ones, and seldom viewed within its larger social context. Maehr and Midgley (1991, p. 406) urge that attention be given to a 'whole-school focus' in the literature on motivation research, one which seeks to change the school psychological environment and its organisational culture, and believe the time has come for issues of motivation and goals at classroom level to be linked to the broader goals promoted at the level of the school system itself. Such a prospect removes motivation from its association with individual striving and persistence, and links it to the creation of environments where the learner can derive meaning and value from the activities because the school and classroom goals are clear.

Philippi (1994) found her intervention work with potential school drop-outs could be better explained in terms of identifying life tasks when assisting students to set goals and make efforts at school than by an intervention strategy which trained students in goal setting. She explained this in terms of Locke's (1991) notion of the *motivational core*, which must be established or strengthened before a person can gain a sense of commit-ment to goals, or mobilise efforts to achieve them. She concluded, 'The presence of life tasks seemed to mobilise effort and helped provide com-mitment to goals. The successful subjects chose to follow life tasks which they valued, and that provided meaning for their actions' (p. 29). The motivational principle which is exemplified in Philippi's research is cap-tured in Maehr's (1984) theory of *personal investment*, which assumes that the level of investment which people make in certain activities depends upon the meaning which those activities have, derived from three inter-related cognitions: those about *the self*, those about *goals*, and those about *action possibilities*.

Self-concept has been viewed in this book as emerging from group association and social categorisation, from which the adolescent derives a number of social identities. As these identities become formed, individual 'selves' are spawned, containing self-knowledge and beliefs about what is possible for the person, not only in the present but also reaching out into the future (see Markus and Nurius, 1986). These selves are therefore *sense-making* structures, shaped by the individual's association with primary groups. It requires the actions of teachers to translate general life-goals and concerns about community into concrete reality at the classroom level. Teachers are creators of motivational systems through the kinds of relation they establish with their students in terms of assigning meaning to the tasks undertaken. Creating these motivational systems is not easy, because they arise out of teacher–student relations and depend on effective reading of the situation by the teacher, as well as upon good will on all sides. My 16-year-old son recently captured this matching of needs and structure in comments about his basketball coach, who last year seemed so unhelpful to the team, yet in their morning training sessions this year has been a great helper and guide. The difficulty in instituting a supportive relationship is that teachers are initially working with raw, unprocessed material; the matching process is a gradual one, made somewhat easier with semi-processed material, where the parts of the teaching and learning communi-cation system are more closely in tune with one another.

CONCLUSION

The prospecting expedition which is represented in the pages of this book has led us past the charting of structures and assaying of rock-hard concepts to an appreciation of the changing patterns in the social landscapes of young people. Geological analogies have been replaced by biological ones, reflecting the openness and dynamism of social relations and social processes. The guiding theories of attachment and identity focused our attention on the *individual's* relation to others and their place in the social group. In the concluding part of the book the implications of building healthy attachments and identities have directed our gaze more widely, to the key public institutions commissioned with responsibility to create social environments which make it possible for healthy personality to develop. Coleman's work in 1961 on the adolescent society carried the subtitle 'the social life of the teenager and its impact on education'; the institution of the school was viewed as a monolithic structure capable of being subverted by peer subcultures. The present chapter adopted a different view of the school – as a social system which can create environments within its bounds which are responsive to the needs of its adolescent population.

How do educators resolve the dilemma of group life in school? Csikszentmihalyi and Larson (1984) document the importance of time with friends in the daily lives of adolescents; they note that the motivational states identified for activities spent in the company of friends are highly positive, involved, excited, sociable, and free. The positive vibrancy of settings containing friends is in contrast with those where adults are in control, or where adults intervene in a controlling manner, as is common in the settings of the traditional high school. However, many schools are building an organisational culture which respects friendship interaction as a legitimate facet of a school community. They recognise that the informal social structures are a source of social integration and shared emotional connection in a true community, which provide bonds of attachment sufficient to hold a young person into the community.

Rather than peer groups being seen as subversive clusters, affiliation with others in cliques and crowds is regarded as a means of satisfying the adolescent's need for belonging. It is more a matter of social identification than an indication of declining school motivation in the sense Coleman portrayed in his picture of an anti-academic peer subculture. It would be advisable if teachers allowed students room to find their style through affiliation with a peer group without imputing some flow-over to classroom motivation (after all, the research has not yet managed to verify the existence of such a flow-over). The implication is that attention should be given to ways of making classroom environments more compatible with the social identities which students value.

While one must acknowledge the interactive basis of support, namely that support resides naturally in healthy social relations, there are occasions when peer companionship support is inadequate. These include times when adolescents are overly concerned about their lack of acceptance from their peers, and other times when individuals may encounter extremely distressing circumstances where supports must be mobilised to help them. In these instances a formal support structure is needed. However, the assembly of a support group after a problem has arisen is likely to be far less effective than the mobilisation of a pre-existing social group. The presence of existing groups and the hosting of socially integrative events mean that network ties already exist, and the ties provide a platform for extending the relations between the members, in the same way as a set of vines in the jungle provides a lattice connecting the large trees with one another.

The principle which these approaches reflect is one that sees school structures building group cohesion. When practitioners concentrate on developing a durable 'personal community', Gottlieb (1988, p. 520) argues, the effects are more long lasting than those associated with person-centred interventions, because they are supported by the web of ties which constitute the person's social network.

References

Abrams, D., and Emler, N. (1992). 'Self-denial as a paradox of political and regional social identity: findings from a study of 16- and 18-year-olds'. *European Journal of Social Psychology*, 22, 279–295.

Abrams, D., Wetherell, M., Cochrane, S., Hogg, M. A., and Turner, J. C. (1990). 'Knowing what to think by knowing who you are: self-categorization and the nature of norm formation, conformity and group polarization'. *British Journal of Social Psychology*, 29, 97–119.

Adelson, J., and Doehrman, M. (1980). 'The psychodynamic approach to adolescence'. In J. Adelson (ed.), *Handbook of Adolescent Psychology* (pp. 99–116). New York: Wiley.

Akers, R. L., Krohn, M. D., Lanza-Kaduce, L., and Radosevich, M. (1979). 'Social learning and deviant behaviour: a specific test of a general theory'. *American Sociological Review*, 44, 636–655.

Alder, C. (1991). 'Victims of violence: the case of homeless youth'. *Australian and New Zealand Journal of Criminology*, 24, 1–14.

Allan, G. (1989). *Friendship: Developing a sociological perspective*. London: Harvester Wheatsheaf.

Allan, J. (1989). *Bloody Casuals: Diary of a football hooligan*. Edinburgh: Northern Books.

Allen, J. P. (1989). 'Social impact of age mixing and age segregation in school: a context-sensitive investigation'. *Journal of Educational Psychology*, 81, 408–416.

Alpert, B. (1991). 'Students' resistance in the classroom'. *Anthropology and Education Quarterly*, 22, 350–366.

Ammaniti, M., Ercolanti, A. P., and Tambelli, R. (1989). 'Loneliness in the female adolescent'. *Journal of Youth and Adolescence*, 18, 321–329.

Andersson, B. E. (1992). 'The contradictory school' (paper presented at the Fourth Biennial Meeting of the Society for Research in Adolescence, March, Washington, DC).

Angus, L. (1981). 'The sweathogs: definitions of unacceptable pupils' (paper presented at the AARE Annual Conference, November, Armidale).

Angus, L. (1984). 'Student attitudes to teachers and teaching'. *Unicorn*, 10, 240–250.

Anthony, K. H. (1985) 'The shopping mall: a teenage hangout'. *Adolescence*, 20, 307–312.

Armsden, G. C., and Greenberg, M. T. (1987). 'The inventory of parent and peer attachment: individual differences and their relationship to psychological well-being in adolescence'. *Journal of Youth and Adolescence*, 16, 427–454.

Asher, S. R., and Dodge, K. A. (1986). 'Identifying children who are rejected by their peers'. *Developmental Psychology*, 22, 444–449.

Asher, S. R., Parkhurst, J. T., Hymel, S., and Williams, G. A. (1990). 'Peer rejection and loneliness in childhood'. In S. Asher and J. Coie (eds), *Peer Rejection in Childhood* (pp. 253–273). Cambridge: Cambridge University Press.

Atkinson, R. (1988). 'Respectful, dutiful teenagers'. *Psychology Today*, October, pp. 22–23, 26.

Aumair, M., and Warren, I. (1994). 'Characteristics of juvenile gangs in Melbourne'. *Youth Studies Australia*, 13(2), 40–44.

Australian Government (1990). *Tobacco in Australia: A summary of related statistics*. Canberra: Department of Community Services and Health.

Australian Sports Commission (ASC) (1991). *Sport for Young Australians*. Canberra: Australian Sports Commission.

Balk, D. E. (1983). 'Adolescents' grief reactions and self-concept perceptions following sibling death: a case study of 33 teenagers'. *Journal of Youth and Adolescence*, 12, 137–161.

Balk, D. E. (1990). 'The self-concepts of bereaved adolescents: sibling death and its aftermath'. *Journal of Adolescent Research*, 5, 112–132.

Balk, D. E. (1991). 'Death and adolescent bereavement: current research and future directions'. *Journal of Adolescent Research*, 6, 7–27.

Bank, S. P., and Kahn, M. D. (1982). *The Sibling Bond*. New York: Basic Books.

Barker, R. G. (1968). *Ecological Psychology*. Stanford, CA: Stanford University Press.

Barker, R. G., and Gump, P. V. (eds) (1964) *Big School, Small School*. Stanford, CA: Stanford University Press.

Barnes, J. A. (1954). 'Class and committee in a Norwegian island parish'. *Human Relations*, 7, 39–58.

Bauman, K. E., and Fisher, L. A. (1986). 'On the measurement of friend behaviour in research on friend influence and selection: findings from longitudinal studies of adolescent smoking and drinking'. *Journal of Youth and Adolescence*, 15, 345–353.

Bean, J. P. (1985). 'Interaction effects based on class level in an explanatory model of college student dropout syndrome'. *American Educational Research Journal*, 22, 35–64.

Berndt, T. (1979). 'Developmental changes in conformity to peers and parents'. *Developmental Psychology*, 15, 608–616.

Berndt, T. (1982). 'The features and effects of friendship in early adolescence'. *Child Development*, 53, 1447–1460.

Berndt, T. (1989). 'Obtaining support from friends during childhood and adolescence'. In D. Belle (ed.), *Children's Social Networks and Social Supports* (pp. 308–329). New York: Wiley.

Berndt, T., and Perry, T. (1986). 'Children's perceptions of friendships as supportive relations'. *Developmental Psychology*, 22, 640–648.

Berndt, T., Hawkins, J., and Hoyle, S. (1986). 'Changes in friendship during a school year: effects on children's and adolescents' impressions of friendship and sharing with friends'. *Child Development*, 57, 1284–1297.

Bernstein, S. (1964). *Youth on the Streets: Work with alienated youth groups*. New York: Assocation Press.

Bessant, J. (1994). 'Naughty, immoral and depraved: making young female offenders visible'. *Youth Studies Australia*, 13(2), 45–50.

Bigelow, B., and La Gaipa, J. (1975). 'Children's written descriptions of friendship: a multidimensional analysis'. *Developmental Psychology*, 11, 857–858.

Billy, J. O., and Udry, J. R. (1985). 'Patterns of adolescent friendship and effects on sexual behavior'. *Social Psychology Quarterly*, 48, 27–41.

Blyth, D. A., Simmons, R. G., and Bush, D. (1978). 'The transition into early adolescence: a longitudinal comparison of youth in two educational contexts'. *Sociology of Education*, 51, 149–162.

Blyth, D. A., Hill, J. P., and Smyth, C. K. (1981). 'The influence of older adolescents on younger adolescents: do grade-level arrangements make a difference in behaviors, attitudes, and experiences?'. *Journal of Early Adolescence*, 1, 85–110.

Blyth, D. A., Hill, J. P., and Thiel, K. S. (1982). 'Early adolescents' significant others: grade and gender differences in perceived relationships with familial and non-familial adults and young people'. *Journal of Youth and Adolescence*, 11, 425–450.

Bo, I. (1989). 'The significant people in the social networks of adolescents'. In K. Hurrelmann and U. Engel (eds), *The Social World of Adolescents* (pp. 141–165). Berlin: Walter de Gruyter.

Bott, E. (1957/1971). *Families and Social Networks* (2nd edn). London: Tavistock.

Bowlby, J. (1969). *Attachment and Loss* (Vol. 1). *Attachment*. Harmondsworth: Penguin.

Bowlby, J. (1974). *Attachment and Loss* (Vol. 2). *Separation, Anxiety and Anger*. New York: Basic Books.

Bowlby, J. (1984). *Attachment and Loss* (Vol. 3). *Loss* (2nd edn). Harmondsworth: Penguin.

Boyer, E. L. (1987). *College: The undergraduate experience in America*. New York: Harper and Row.

Brake, M. (1985). *Comparative Youth Culture*. London: Routledge.

Branscombe, N. R., and Wann, D. L. (1992). 'Role of identification with a group, arousal, categorisation processes, and self-esteem in sports spectator aggression'. *Human Relations*, 45, 1013–1033.

Brennan, T. (1982). 'Loneliness at adolescence'. In L. A. Peplau and D. Perlman (eds), *Loneliness: A sourcebook of current theory, research and therapy* (pp. 269–290). New York: Wiley.

Broadbent, R. (1994). 'Young people's perceptions of their use and abuse of alcohol'. *Youth Studies Australia*, 13(3), 32–35.

Brown, B. B. (1988). 'The vital agenda for research on extracurricular influences: a reply to Holland and Andre'. *Review of Educational Research*, 58, 107–111.

Brown, B. B. (1989). 'The role of peer groups in adolescents' adjustment to secondary school'. In T. J. Berndt and G. W. Ladd (eds), *Peer Relationships in Child Development* (pp. 188–215). New York: Wiley.

Brown, B. B., and Lohr, M. J. (1987). 'Peer group affiliation and adolescent self-esteem: an integration of ego-identity and symbolic interaction theories'. *Journal of Personality and Social Psychology*, 52, 47–55.

Brown, B. B., Clasen, D. R., and Eicher, S. A. (1986a). 'Perceptions of peer pressure, peer conformity dispositions, and self-reported behaviour among adolescents'. *Developmental Psychology*, 22, 521–530.

Brown, B. B., Eicher, S. A., and Petrie, S. (1986b). 'The importance of peer group ("crowd") affiliation in adolescence'. *Journal of Adolescence*, 9, 73–96.

Brown, P. (1987). *Ordinary Kids*. London: Tavistock.

Buford, B. (1991). *Among the Thugs*. London: Secker and Warburg.

Buhrmester, D., and Furman, W. (1987). 'The development of companionship and intimacy'. *Child Development*, 58, 1101–1113.

Buhrmester, D., and Furman, W. (1990). 'Perceptions of sibling relationships during middle childhood and adolescence'. *Child Development*, 61, 1387–1398.

Bukowski, W., Newcomb, A., and Hoza, B. (1987). 'Friendship conceptions among early adolescents: a longitudinal study of stability and change'. *Journal of Early Adolescence*, 7, 143–152.

Button, L. (1974). *Developmental Group Work with Adolescents*. London: University of London Press.

Cairns, R. B., Cairns, B. D., Neckerman, H. J., Gest, S. D., and Gariepy, J. L. (1988). 'Social networks and aggressive behavior: peer support or peer rejection?'. *Developmental Psychology*, 24, 815–823.

Campbell, A. (1984). *The Girls in the Gang*. London: Blackwell.

Canter, D. (1986). 'Putting situations in their place: foundations for a bridge between social and environmental psychology'. In A. Furnham (ed.), *Social Behaviour in Context* (pp. 208–239). New York: Allyn and Bacon.

Carnegie Council on Adolescent Development (1989). *Turning Points: Preparing America's youth for the 21st century*. New York: Carnegie Corporation.

Carter, A., and Drew, N. (1991). 'A community driven response to juvenile offending'. In J. Vernon and S. McKillop (eds), *Preventing Juvenile Crime* (proceedings of AIS Conference, July 1989, pp. 144–150). Canberra: Australian Institute of Criminology.

Cartwright, D. (1951). 'Achieving change in people. Some applications of group dynamics theory'. In W. W. Charters and N. L. Gage (eds), *Readings in the Social Psychology of Education*. Boston: Allyn and Bacon.

Cartwright, D., and Zander, A. (eds) (1960). *Group Dynamics: Research and theory*. Evanston, IL: Row Peterson.

Cartwright, D., and Zander, A. (eds) (1968). *Group Dynamics: Research and theory* (2nd edn). London: Tavistock.

Caspi, A., Lynam, D., Moffit, T. E., and Silva, P. A. (1993). 'Unraveling girls' delinquency: biological, dispositional, and contextual contributions to adolescent misbehavior'. *Developmental Psychology*, 29, 19–30.

Chassin, L., Presson, C., Bensenberg, M., Corty, E., and Sherman, S. (1981). 'Predicting adolescents' intentions to smoke cigarettes'. *Journal of Health and Social Behavior*, 22, 445–455.

Chassin, L., Presson, C., and Sherman, S. (1989). '"Constructive" vs. "destructive" deviance in adolescent health-related behaviors'. *Journal of Youth and Adolescence*, 18, 245–262.

Cicirelli, V. (1989). 'Feelings of attachment to siblings and well-being in later life'. *Psychology and Aging*, 4, 211–216.

Claes, M. (1992). 'Friendship and personal adjustment during adolescence'. *Journal of Adolescence*, 15, 39–55.

Claes, M. (1994). 'Friendship characteristics of adolescents referred for psychiatric treatment'. *Journal of Adolescent Research*, 9, 180–192.

Clark, M. L. (1991). 'Social identity, peer relations, and academic competence of African-American adolescents'. *Education and Urban Society*, 24, 41–52.

Cochran, M. M., and Bo, I. (1989). 'The social networks, family involvement and pro- and anti-social behavior of adolescent males in Norway'. *Journal of Youth and Adolescence*, 18, 377–398.

Cohen, A. K. (1955). *Delinquent Boys: The culture of the gang*. Glencoe, IL: Free Press.

Cohen, A. K. (1990). 'Foreword and overview'. In C. R. Huff (ed.), *Gangs in America* (pp. 7–21). Newbury Park, CA: Sage.

Cohen, S. (1973). *Folk Devils and Moral Panics*. St Albans: Paladin.

Coie, J. D. (1990). 'Toward a theory of peer rejection'. In S. Asher and J. Coie (eds), *Peer Rejection in Childhood* (pp. 365–401). Cambridge: Cambridge University Press.

Coie, J. D., and Dodge, K. A. (1983). 'Continuities and changes in children's social status: a five-year longitudinal study'. *Merrill-Palmer Quarterly*, 29, 261–282.

Coie, J. D., and Kupersmidt, J. B. (1983). 'A behavioral analysis of emerging social status in boys' groups'. *Child Development*, 54, 1400–1416.

Coie, J. D., Dodge, K. A., and Kupersmidt, J. B. (1990). 'Peer group behavior and social status'. In S. Asher and J. Coie (eds), *Peer Rejection in Childhood* (pp. 17–59). Cambridge: Cambridge University Press.

Coleman, J. C. (1974). *Relationships in Adolescence*. London: Routledge and Kegan Paul.

Coleman, J. C. (1980). *The Nature of Adolescence*. London: Methuen.

Coleman, J. S. (1961). *The Adolescent Society*. New York: Free Press.

Conger, J. J., and Petersen, A. C. (1984). *Adolescence and Youth* (3rd edn). New York: Harper.

Connell, W., Stroobant, R., Sinclair, K., Connell, R., and Rogers, K. (1975). *12 to 20: Studies of city youth*. Sydney: Hicks Smith.

Corrigan, P. (1976). 'Doing nothing'. In S. Hall and T. Jefferson (eds), *Resistance through Rituals* (pp. 103–105). New York: Holmes and Meier.

Costanzo, P. R. (1970). 'Conformity development as a function of self-blame'. *Journal of Personality and Social Psychology*, 14, 366–374.

Costanzo, P. R., and Shaw, M. E. (1966). 'Conformity as a function of age level'. *Child Development*, 37, 967–975.

Cotterell, J. L. (1991). 'The emergence of adolescent territories in a large urban leisure environment'. *Journal of Environmental Psychology*, 11, 25–41.

Cotterell, J. L. (1992). 'School size as a factor in adolescents' adjustment to the transition to secondary school'. *Journal of Early Adolescence*, 12, 28–45.

Cotterell, J. L. (1994). 'Analyzing the strength of supportive ties in adolescent social supports'. In F. Nestmann and K. Hurrelmann (eds), *Social Networks and Social Support in Childhood and Adolescence* (pp. 257–267). Berlin: Walter de Gruyter.

Cotterell, J. L., and Schoggen, P. (1986). 'Studying the ecology of adolescent life in small communities' (paper presented at 4th National Development Conference, August, Sydney).

Cotterell, J. L., Davern, T., Pemberton, M., and Attwood, A. (1994). 'Social network influences on adolescent plans' (paper presented at the Australian Human Development Association Conference, July, Melbourne).

Covington, M. V., and Omelich, C. L. (1988). 'I can resist anything but temptation: adolescent expectations for smoking cigarettes'. *Journal of Applied Social Psychology*, 18, 203–227.

Crandall, R. (1978). 'The assimilation of newcomers into groups'. *Small Group Behavior*, 9, 331–336.

Csikszentmihalyi, M. (1975). *Beyond Boredom and Anxiety*. San Francisco: Jossey-Bass.

Csikszentmihalyi, M., and Larson, R. (1984). *Being Adolescent*. New York: Basic Books.

Cuban, L. (1992). 'What happens to reforms that last? The case of the junior high school'. *American Educational Research Journal*, 29, 227–251.

Cunneen, C., Findlay, M., Lynch, R., and Tupper, V. (1989). *Dynamics of Collective Conflict: Riots at the Bathurst bike races*. Sydney: Law Book Co.

Cusick, P. A. (1973). *Inside High School*. New York: Holt, Rinehart and Winston.

Cutrona, C. E. (1982). 'Transition to college: loneliness and the process of social adjustment'. In L. A. Peplau and D. Perlman (eds), *Loneliness: A sourcebook of current theory, research and therapy* (pp. 291–309). New York: Wiley.

Cutts-Dougherty, K., Eisenhart, M., and Webley, P. (1992). 'The role of social representations and national identities in the development of territorial knowledge: a study of political socialisation in Argentina and England'. *American Educational Research Journal*, 29, 809–835.

Daley, P. (1989). 'The chill-out boys'. *Age*, Melbourne, 17 September, 8.

Davies, B. (1991). 'Long term outcomes of sibling bereavement'. *Journal of Adolescent Research*, 6, 83–96.

Davies, L. (1978). 'The view from the girls'. *Educational Review*, 30, 103–109.

de Jong-Giervald, J. (1989). 'Personal relationships, social support, and loneliness'. *Journal of Social and Personal Relationships*, 6, 197–221.

Denholm, C., Horniblow, T., and Smalley, R. (1992). 'The times they're still a'changing: characteristics of Tasmanian adolescent peer groups'. *Youth Studies Australia*, 11(2), 18–25.

Department of Tourism and Recreation (DTR) (1975). *The Recreational Priorities of Australian Young People* (Youth Say Project). Canberra: Australian Government Publishing Service.

Deutsch, M., and Gerard, H. B. (1955). 'A study of normative and informational social influences upon individual judgment'. *Journal of Abnormal and Social Psychology*, 51, 629–636.

Diaz, R., and Berndt, T. (1982). 'Children's knowledge of a best friend: fact or fancy?'. *Developmental Psychology*, 18, 787–794.

Dielman, T. E. (1994). 'School-based research on the prevention of adolescent alcohol use and misuse: methodological issues and advances'. *Journal of Research on Adolescence*, 4, 271–293.

Dishion, T. (1990). 'The peer context of troublesome child and adolescent behaviour'. In P. Leone (ed.), *Understanding Troubled and Troublesome Youth* (pp. 128–153). London: Sage.

Dishion, T., Patterson, G., Stoolmiller, M., and Skinner, M. (1991). 'Family, school, and behavioral antecedents to early adolescent involvement with anti-social peers'. *Developmental Psychology*, 27, 172–180.

Dodge, K. A. (1983). 'Behavioral antecedents of peer social status'. *Child Development*, 54, 1386–1399.

Dodge, K. A., Coie, J. D., and Brakke, N. P. (1982). 'Behavior patterns of socially rejected and neglected preadolescents: the roles of social approach and aggression'. *Journal of Abnormal Child Psychology*, 10, 389–410.

Douvan, E., and Adelson, J. (1966). *The Adolescent Experience*. New York: Wiley.

Doyle, W. (1986). 'Content representation in teachers' definitions of academic work'. *Journal of Curriculum Studies*, 18, 365–379.

Duck, S. (1975). 'Personality similarity and friendship choices by adolescents'. *European Journal of Social Psychology*, 5, 351–365.

Dunphy, D. C. (1963). 'The social structure of urban adolescent peer groups'. *Sociometry*, 26, 230–246.

Dunphy, D. C. (1969). *Cliques, Crowds and Gangs*. Melbourne: Cheshire.

Dunphy, D. C. (1972). *The Primary Group: A handbook for analysis and field research*. New York: Appleton-Century-Crofts.

East, P. L. (1989). 'Early adolescents' perceived interpersonal risks and benefits: relations to social support and psychological functioning'. *Journal of Early Adolescence*, 9, 374–395.

Eccles, J. S., and Midgley, C. (1989). 'Stage/environment fit: developmentally appropriate classrooms for early adolescents'. In R. E. Ames and C. Ames (eds), *Research on Motivation in Education* (Vol. 3, pp. 139–186). New York: Academic Press.

Eder, D. (1985). 'The cycle of popularity: interpersonal relations among female adolescents'. *Sociology of Education*, 58, 154–165.

Eder, D., and Hallinan, M. (1978). 'Sex differences in children's friendship'. *American Sociological Review*, 43, 237–250.

Eggleston, S. J. (1976). *Adolescence and Community*. London: Arnold.

Eiser, J. R., Morgan, M., and Gammage, P. (1987). 'Belief correlates of perceived addiction in young smokers'. *European Journal of Social Psychology*, 11, 375–385.

Eiser, J. R., Morgan, M., Gammage, P., Brooks, N., and Kirby, R. (1991). 'Adolescent health behaviour and similarity-attraction: friends share smoking habits (really), but much else besides'. *British Journal of Social Psychology*, 30, 339–348.

Emler, N., Reicher, S., and Ross, A. (1987). 'The social context of delinquent conduct'. *Journal of Child Psychology and Psychiatry*, 28, 99–109.

Engel, U., Nordlohne, E., Hurrelmann, K., and Holler, B. (1987). 'Educational career and substance use in adolescence'. *European Journal of Psychology of Education*, 11, 365–374.

Ennett, S. T., and Bauman, K. E. (1991). 'Mediators in the relationship between parental and peer characteristics and beer drinking by early adolescents'. *Journal of Applied Social Psychology*, 21, 1699–1711.

Entwistle, D. R. (1990). 'Schools and the adolescent'. In S. S. Feldman and G. R. Elliott (eds), *At the Threshold: The developing adolescent* (pp. 197–224). Cambridge, MA: Harvard University Press.

Evans, K. (1987). 'Participation of young adults in youth organisations in the United Kingdom: a review'. *International Journal of Adolescence and Youth*, 1, 7–31.

Evans, M. J. (1978). 'Some aspects of school procedures in primary to post-primary school transition' (occasional paper, Burwood State College). Burwood, Victoria.

Evans, M. J. (1983). 'The integration into secondary school of pupils in transition from primary to secondary schooling' (unpublished Ph.D. thesis, Monash University).

Everhart, R. B. (1982). 'The nature of "goofing off" among junior high school adolescents'. *Adolescence*, 17, 177–187.

Ewert, A. W. (1989). *Outdoor Adventure Pursuits: Foundations, models, and theories*. Columbus, OH: Publishing Horizons.

Ewert, A. W., and Heywood, J. (1991). 'Group development in the natural environment: expectations, outcomes, and techniques'. *Environment and Behavior*, 23, 592–615.

Ewing, M. E. and Seefeldt, V. (1990). *American Youth and Sports Participation*. East Lansing: Youth Sports Institute of Michigan State University.

Fanos, J. H., and Nickerson, B. G. (1991). 'Long-term effects of sibling death during adolescence'. *Journal of Adolescent Research*, 6, 70–82.

Farrington, D. P., Berkowitz, L., and West, D. J. (1982). 'Differences between individual and group fights'. *British Journal of Social Psychology*, 21, 323–333.

Feldman, S. S., and Elliott, G. R. (eds) (1990). *At the Threshold: The developing adolescent*. Cambridge, MA: Harvard University Press.

Felner, R. D., Ginter, M., and Primavera, J. (1982). 'Primary prevention during school transitions: social support and environmental structure'. *American Journal of Community Psychology*, 10, 277–290.

Fine, G. A. (1988). 'Team sports, seasonal histories, significant events: Little League baseball and the creation of collective meaning'. *Sociology of Sport Journal*, 2, 299–313.

Finn, J. D. (1989). 'Withdrawing from school'. *Review of Educational Research*, 59, 117–142.

Fischer, C. S. (1982). *To Dwell among Friends: Personal networks in town and city*. Chicago: University of Chicago Press.

Fischer, C. S., Jackson, R. M., Stueve, C. A., Gerson, K., Jones, L. M., and Baldessare, M. (1977). *Networks and Places: Social relations in the urban setting*. New York: Free Press.

Fisher, S., and Hood, B. (1987). 'The stress of the transition to university: a longitudinal study of psychological disturbance, absent-mindedness and vulnerability to homesickness'. *British Journal of Psychology*, 78, 425–441.

Flay, B., Koepke, D., Thomson, S., Santi, S., Best, A., and Brown, K. (1989). 'Six year follow-up of the first Waterloo school smoking prevention trial'. *American Journal of Public Health*, 79, 1371–1376.

Foote, N. N. (1951). 'Identification as the basis for a theory of motivation'. *American Sociological Review*, 16, 14–21.

Foote, P. M. (1992). 'Like, I'll tell you that happened from experience: perspectives on Italo-Australian youth gangs in Adelaide'. *Youth Studies Australia*, 11(2), 26–32.

Foshee, V., and Bauman, K. E. (1994). 'Parental attachment and adolescent cigarette smoking initiation'. *Journal of Adolescent Research*, 9, 88–104.

Freeman, L. (1992). 'The sociological concept of "group": an empirical test of two models'. *American Journal of Sociology*, 98, 152–166.

Friesen, D. (1968) 'Academic–athletic–popular syndrome in the Canadian high school society'. *Adolescence*, 3, 39–52.

Furlong, A. (1989). 'Psychological well-being and the transition from school'. *British Journal of Education and Work*, 3, 49–55.

Furlong, V. J. (1991). 'Disaffected pupils: reconstructing the sociological perspective'. *British Journal of Sociology of Education*, 12, 293–307.

Furman, W., and Buhrmester, D. (1985). 'Children's perceptions of the personal relationships in their social networks'. *Developmental Psychology*, 21, 1016–1024.

Galambos, N., and Silbereisen, R. (1987). 'Substance use in West German youth: a longitudinal study of adolescents' use of alcohol and tobacco'. *Journal of Adolescent Research*, 2, 161–174.

Garton, A. F., and Pratt, C. (1987). 'Participation and interest in leisure activities by adolescent school children'. *Journal of Adolescence*, 10, 341–351.

Gaskell, G., and Smith, P. (1986). 'Group membership and social attitudes of youth: an investigation of some implications of social identity theory'. *Social Behaviour*, 1, 67–77.

Gerber, R. W., and Newman, I. M. (1989). 'Predicting future smoking of adolescent experimental smokers'. *Journal of Youth and Adolescence*, 18, 191–201.

Gilbert, J. (1986). *A Cycle of Outrage: America's reactions to the juvenile delinquent in the 1950s.* New York: Oxford University Press.

Gill, R. (1991). 'Scenes from a mall'. *Sunday Age*, Melbourne, 2 June.

Giordano, P., Cernkovich, S., and Pugh, M. (1986). 'Friendship and delinquency'. *American Journal of Sociology*, 91, 1170–1201.

Glynn, T. J. (1981). 'From family to peer: a review of transitions of influence among drug-using youth'. *Journal of Youth and Adolescence*, 10, 363–383.

Goodenow, C. (1992). 'Strengthening the links between educational psychology and the study of social contexts'. *Educational Psychologist*, 27, 177–196.

Goodenow, C. (1993). 'Classroom belonging among early adolescent students: relationships to motivation and achievement'. *Journal of Early Adolescence*, 13, 21–43.

Gottlieb, B. H. (1988). 'Support interventions: a typology and agenda for research'. In S. Duck (ed.), *Handbook of Personal Relationships* (pp. 519–541). New York: Sage.

Gottlieb, B. H. (1991). 'Social supports in adolescence'. In M. E. Colten and S. Gore (eds), *Adolescent Stress: Causes and consequences* (pp. 281–306). New York: McGraw-Hill.

Gottlieb, B. H., and Sylvestre, J. C. (1994). 'Social support in the relationships between older adolescents and adults'. In F. Nestmann and K. Hurrelmann (eds), *Social Support in Childhood and Adolescence* (pp. 53–73). Berlin: Walter de Gruyter.

Gould, D., and Martens, R. (1979). 'Attitudes of volunteer coaches toward significant youth sport issues'. *Research Quarterly*, 50, 369–380.

Gregory, L.W. (1995). 'The "turnaround" process: factors influencing the school success of urban youth'. *Journal of Adolescent Research*, 10, 135–164.

Guilliatt, R. (1984a). 'Street gangs I: the Sandy Boys'. *Age*, Melbourne, 5 September, 11.

Guilliatt, R. (1984b). 'Street gangs II: the Lebanese Tigers'. *Age*, Melbourne, 8 September, 11.

Gullotta, T. P., and Adams, G. R. (1982). 'Minimizing juvenile delinquency: implications for prevention programs'. *Journal of Early Adolescence*, 2, 105–117.

Hagedorn, J. M. (1990). 'Back in the field again: gang research in the nineties'. In C. R. Huff (ed.), *Gangs in America* (pp. 240–259). Newbury Park, CA: Sage.

Hansell, S. (1981). 'Ego development and peer friendship networks'. *Sociology of Education*, 54, 98–106.

Hansen, D.A. (1989). 'Lesson evading and lesson dissembling: ego strategies in the classroom'. *American Journal of Education*, 97, 184–208.

Harford, T., and Grant, B. (1987). 'Psychosocial factors in adolescent drinking contexts'. *Journal of Studies on Alcohol*, 48, 551–557.

Harkins, S. G., and Szymanski, K. (1989). 'Social loafing and social facilitation'. In C. Hendrick (ed.), *Review of Personality and Social Psychology* (Vol. 9, pp. 167–188). Beverly Hills, CA: Sage.

Harris, A., and Sheehan, M. (1995). 'Taking the hiccups out of alcohol education'. *Youth Studies Australia*, 14(1), 41–45.

Harvey, J. H., Orbuch, T. L., Weber, A. L., Merbach, N., and Alt, R. (1992). 'House of pain and hope: accounts of loss'. *Death Studies*, 16, 99–124.

Harvey, S., and Simpson, L. (1989). *Brothers in Arms: The inside story of two bikie gangs*. Sydney: Allen and Unwin.

Hendry, L. B. (1983). *Growing Up and Going Out*. Aberdeen: Aberdeen University Press.

Hendry, L. B. (1989). 'The influence of adults and peers on adolescents' lifestyles and leisure-styles'. In K. Hurrelmann and U. Engel (eds), *The Social World of Adolescents* (pp. 245–263). Berlin: Walter de Gruyter.

Hendry, L. B., Roberts, W., Glendinning, A., and Coleman, J. C. (1992). 'Adolescents' perceptions of significant individuals in their lives'. *Journal of Adolescence*, 15, 255–270.

Henggeler, S. W. (1989). *Delinquency in Adolescence*. Newbury Park, CA: Sage.

Hewstone, M. (1990). 'The "ultimate attribution error"? A review of the literature on intergroup causal attribution'. *European Journal of Social Psychology*, 20, 311–335.

Hill, C. (1992). 'Bush medicine'. *Australian Geographic*, 27 (July–September), 30–41.

Hill, J. P., and Holmbeck, G. N. (1986). 'Attachment and autonomy during adolescence'. In G. J. Whitehurst (ed.), *Annals of Child Development* (Vol. 3, pp. 145–189). Greenwich, CT: JAI Press.

Hill, P. (1994). 'A crop of dreams'. *Australian Geographic*, 34 (April–June), 76–89.

Hirsch, B. J. (1981). 'Social networks and the coping process: creating personal communities'. In B. H. Gottlieb (ed.), *Social Networks and Social Support* (pp. 149–170). Beverly Hills, CA: Sage.

Hirsch, B. J. and Dubois, D. L. (1989). 'The school–nonschool ecology of early adolescent friendships'. In D. Belle (ed.), *Children's Social Networks and Social Supports* (pp. 260–274). New York: Wiley.

Hirsch, B. J., and Dubois, D. L. (1992). 'The relation of peer social support and psychological symptomatology during the transition to junior high school: a two-year longitudinal study'. *American Journal of Community Psychology*, 20, 333–347.

Hirsch, B. J., and Renders, R. (1986). 'The challenge of adolescent friendship: a study of Lisa and her friends'. In S. E. Hobfoll (ed.), *Stress, Social Support, and Women* (pp. 17–27). Washington, DC: Hemisphere.

Hirschi, T. (1969). *Causes of Delinquency*. Berkeley, CA: University of California Press.

Hobfoll, S. E., and Stokes, J. P. (1988). 'The process and mechanics of social support'. In S. W. Duck (ed.), *Handbook of Personal Relationships* (pp. 497–517). New York: Wiley.

Hogan, J. M. (1968). *Impelled into Experiences: The story of the Outward Bound schools*. Wakefield: Educational Productions.

Hogan, N. S., and Greenfield, D. B. (1991). 'Adolescent sibling bereavement symptomatology in a large community sample'. *Journal of Adolescent Research*, 6, 97–112.

Hogg, M. A., and Abrams, D. (1988). *Social Identifications*. London: Routledge.

Hogg, M. A., Abrams, D., and Patel, Y. (1987). 'Ethnic identity, self-esteem, and occupational aspirations of Indian and Anglo-Saxon British adolescents'. *Genetic, Social, and Psychology Monographs*, 113, 487–508.

Holden, E., and Dwyer, P. (1992). 'Making the break: leaving school early' (working paper 8, Youth Research Centre, Melbourne University).

Hollingshead, A. (1949). *Elmtown's Youth.* New York: Wiley.

Homel, P., and Flaherty, B. (1986). 'Alcohol use by Australian secondary school students'. *Journal of Drug Issues*, 16, 199–207.

Horowitz, R., and Schwartz, G. (1974). 'Honor, normative ambiguity and gang violence'. *American Sociological Review*, 39, 238–251.

Hughes, J. (1989). *Australian Words and their Origins.* Melbourne: Oxford University Press.

Hundleby, J. D., and Mercer, G. W. (1987). 'Family and friends as social environments and their relationship to young adolescents' use of alcohol, tobacco, and marijuana'. *Journal of Marriage and the Family*, 49, 151–164.

Hunter, J. A., Stringer, M., and Watson, R. P. (1991). 'Intergroup violence and intergroup attributions'. *British Journal of Social Psychology*, 30, 261–266.

Hurrelmann, K. (1990a). 'Health promotion for adolescents: preventive and corrective strategies against problem behaviour'. *Journal of Adolescence*, 13, 231–250.

Hurrelmann, K. (1990b). 'Parents, peers, teachers and other significant partners in adolescence'. *International Journal of Adolescence and Youth*, 2, 211–236.

Hurrelmann, K., and Engel, U. (1992). 'Delinquency as a symptom of adolescents' orientation toward status and success'. *Journal of Youth and Adolescence*, 21, 119–138.

Jackson, A. W. and Hornbeck, D. W. (1989). 'Educating young adolescents: why we must restructure middle grade schools'. *American Psychologist*, 44, 831–836.

Jessor, R. (1992). 'Risk behaviour in adolescence: a psychosocial framework for understanding and action'. *Developmental Review*, 12, 374–390.

Jessor, R. L. and Jessor, S. (1977). *Problem Behaviour and Psychosocial Development: A longitudinal study of youth.* New York: Academic Press.

Jobling, I. F., and Cotterell, J. L. (1990). 'Adolescent leisure: sport and physical recreation'. In P. C. L. Heaven and V. J. Callan (eds), *Adolescence: An Australian perspective* (pp. 184–197). Sydney: Harcourt Brace Jovanovich.

Johnson, F., and Aries, E. (1983). 'Conversational patterns among same-sex pairs of late-adolescent close friends'. *Journal of Genetic Psychology*, 142, 225–238.

Jones, D. (1991). 'Friendship satisfaction and gender: an examination of sex differences in contributions to friendship satisfaction'. *Journal of Social and Personal Relationships*, 8, 167–185.

Jones, D. W. (1987). 'Recent developments in work with young offenders'. In J. C. Coleman (ed.), *Working with Troubled Adolescents* (pp. 265–279). London: Academic Press.

Jones, R., and Thornburg, H. (1985). 'The experience of school transfer: does previous relocation facilitate the transition from elementary to middle-level educational environments?'. *Journal of Early Adolescence*, 5, 229–237.

Jones, W. H., Freemon, J. E., and Goswick, R. A. (1981). 'The persistence of loneliness: self and other determinants'. *Journal of Personality*, 49, 27–48.

Kagan, D. (1990). 'How schools alienate students at risk: a model for examining proximal classroom variables'. *Educational Psychologist*, 25, 105–125.

Kahn, R. L., and Antonucci, T. (1980). 'Convoys over the life course: attachments, roles, and social support'. In P. B. Baltes and O. G. Brim (eds), *Life-span Development and Behavior* (Vol. 3, pp. 253–286). New York: Academic Press.

Kandel, D. (1978a). 'Homophily, selection, and socialisation in adolescent friendships'. *American Journal of Sociology*, 84, 427–436.

Kandel, D. (1978b). 'Similarity in real-life adolescent friendship pairs'. *Journal of Personality and Social Psychology*, 36, 306–312.

Kandel, D., Kessler, R., and Margulies, R. (1978). 'Antecedents of adolescent initiation into stages of drug use'. *Journal of Youth and Adolescence*, 7, 13–40.

Kawakami, K., and Dion, K. L. (1993). 'The impact of salient self-identification on relative deprivation and action intentions'. *European Journal of Social Psychology*, 23, 525–540.

Kenny, M. E. (1987). 'The extent and function of parental attachment among first-year college students'. *Journal of Youth and Adolescence*, 16, 17–29.

Kimmel, D., and Weiner, I. (1985). *Adolescence: A developmental transition*. Hillsdale, NJ: Lawrence Erlbaum.

Kinney, D. A. (1993). 'From nerds to normals: the recovery of identity among adolescents from middle school to high school'. *Sociology of Education*, 66, 21–40.

Klein, M. W. (1971). *Street Gangs and Street Workers*. Englewood Cliffs, NJ: Prentice-Hall.

Knowles, E. (1989). 'Spatial behavior of individuals and groups'. In P. B. Paulus (ed.), *Psychology of Group Influence* (2nd edn, pp. 53–86). Hillsdale, NJ: Lawrence Erlbaum.

Kobak, R. R., and Sceery, A. (1988). 'Attachment in late adolescence: working models, affect regulation, and representations of self and others'. *Child Development*, 59, 135–146.

Kon, I., and Losenkov, V. (1978). 'Friendship in adolescence: values and behavior'. *Journal of Marriage and the Family*, 40, 143–155.

Kulka, R. A., Kahle, L. R., and Klingel, D. M. (1982). 'Aggression, deviance, and personality adaptation as antecedents and consequences of alienation and involvement in high school'. *Journal of Youth and Adolescence*, 11, 261–279.

Kupersmidt, J. B., Coie, J. D., and Dodge, K. A. (1990). 'The role of poor peer relations in the development of disorder'. In S. Asher and J. Coie (eds), *Peer Rejection in Childhood* (pp. 274–305). Cambridge: Cambridge University Press.

Kwakman, A., Zuiker, F., Schippers, G., and de Wuffel, F. (1988). 'Drinking behaviour, drinking attitudes, and attachment relationship of adolescents'. *Journal of Youth and Adolescence*, 17, 247–253.

La Gaipa, J. and Wood, H. D. (1981). 'Friendships in disturbed adolescents'. In S. Duck and R. Gilmour (eds), *Personal Relationships 2: Personal relationships in disorder* (pp. 169–189). London: Academic Press.

Lasley, J. R. (1992). 'Age, social context, and street gang membership: are "youth" gangs becoming "adult" gangs?'. *Youth and Society*, 23, 434–451.

Laursen, B. (1995). 'Conflict and social interaction in adolescent relationships'. *Journal of Research on Adolescence*, 5, 55–70.

LeBon, G. (1896/1908). *The Crowd: A study of the popular mind*. London: Unwin.

Lempers, J. and Clark-Lempers, D. (1992). 'Young, middle, and late adolescents' comparisons of the functional importance of five significant relationships'. *Journal of Youth and Adolescence*, 21, 53–96.

Lempers, J., and Clark-Lempers, D. (1993). 'A functional comparison of same-sex and opposite-sex friendships during adolescence'. *Journal of Adolescent Research*, 8, 89–108.

Letts, R., Hazleton, P., and Carter, M. (1991). 'Tallong wilderness program'. In J. Cianchi (ed.), *Proceedings of First National Symposium on Outdoor/Wilderness Programs for Offenders* (pp. 133–139). Canberra: Adult Corrective Services, Australian Capital Territory Government.

Leventhal, H., Keeshan, P., Baker, T., and Wetter, D. (1991). 'Smoking prevention: toward a process approach'. *British Journal of Addiction*, 86, 583–587.

Levin, I., and Stokes, J. P. (1986). 'An examination of the relation of individual difference variables to loneliness'. *Journal of Personality*, 54, 717–733.

Lewis, C. S. (1960). *The Four Loves*. London: Harcourt Brace Jovanovich.

Lewis, G. H. (1989). 'Rats and bunnies: core kids in an American mall'. *Adolescence*, 24, 881–889.

Lindsay, P. (1984). 'High school size, participation in activities, and young adult social participation: some enduring effects of schooling'. *Educational Evaluation and Policy Analysis*, 6, 73–83.

Lindsay, W. (1987). 'Social skills training with adolescents'. In J. C. Coleman (ed.), *Working with Troubled Adolescents* (pp. 107–122). London: Academic Press.

Linney, J. A. and Seidman, E. (1989). 'The future of schooling'. *American Psychologist*, 44, 336–340.

Lipsitz, J. (1980). *Growing Up Forgotten*. New Brunswick, NJ: Transaction Books.

Liska, A. E., and Reed, M. D. (1985). 'Ties to conventional institutions and delinquency: estimating reciprocal effects'. *American Sociological Review*, 50, 547–560.

Locke, E. A. (1991). 'The motivation sequence, the motivation hub, and the motivation core'. *Organisational Behaviour and Human Decision Processes*, 50, 288–299.

Lundman, R. J. (1993). *Prevention and Control of Juvenile Delinquency* (2nd edn). New York: Oxford University Press.

Lyon, D. (1991). 'Outdoor programs within a probation service context in New Zealand'. In J. Cianchi (ed.), *Proceedings of the First National Symposium on Outdoor/Wilderness Programs for Offenders* (pp. 25–37). Canberra: Adult Corrective Services, Australian Capital Territory Government.

Macalister Brew, J. (1957). *Youth and Youth Groups*. London: Faber and Faber.

McDougall, W. (1921). *The Group Mind*. London: Cambridge University Press.

MacLeod, D. (1982). 'Act your age: boyhood, adolescence and the rise of the Boy Scouts of America'. *Journal of Social History*, 16(2), 3–20.

McMillan, D.W., and Chavis, D.M. (1986). 'Sense of community: a definition and theory'. *Journal of Community Psychology*, 14, 6–23.

McNeil, J. N., Silliman, B., and Swihart, J. J. (1991). 'Helping adolescents cope with the death of a peer: a high school case study'. *Journal of Adolescent Research*, 6, 132–145.

Maehr, M. L. (1984). 'Meaning and motivation: toward a theory of personal investment'. In R. E. Ames and C. Ames (eds), *Research on Motivation in Education* (Vol. 1, pp. 115–144). New York: Academic Press.

Maehr, M. L., and Midgley, C. (1991). 'Enhancing student motivation: a school-wide approach'. *Educational Psychologist*, 26, 399–427.

Marcos, A. C., Bahr, S. J., and Johnson, R. E. (1986). 'Test of a bonding/association theory of adolescent drug use'. *Social Forces*, 65, 135–161.

Margulies, R., Kessler, R., and Kandel, D. (1977). 'A longitudinal study of onset of drinking among high-school students'. *Journal of Studies on Alcohol*, 38, 879–912.

Markus, H., and Nurius, P. (1986). 'Possible selves'. *American Psychologist*, 41, 954–969.

Markus, H., and Ruvolo, A. (1989). 'Possible selves: personalised representations of goals'. In L. A. Pervin (ed.), *Goal Concepts in Personality and Social Psychology* (pp. 211–242). Hillsdale, NJ: Lawrence Erlbaum.

Marsh, P., Rosser, E., and Harre, R. (1978). *The Rules of Disorder*. London: Routledge.

Martinson, I. M., and Campos, R. G. (1991). 'Adolescent bereavement: long-term responses to a sibling's death from cancer'. *Journal of Adolescent Research*, 6, 54–69.

Marx, J. D. (1988). 'An outdoor adventure counselling program for adolescents'. *Social Work*, 33, 517–520.

Maslow, A. H. (1962). *Toward a Psychology of Being*. Princeton, NJ: Van Nostrand.

Mayne, R. (1993). 'Open-air repairs'. *Bulletin*, 31 August, 20–21.

Meichenbaum, D. (1977). *Cognitive Behaviour Modification: An integrative approach*. New York: Plenum Press.

Meighan, R. (1977). 'The pupil as client: the learner's experience of schooling'. *Educational Review*, 29, 123–135.

Meuss, W. (1994). 'Psychosocial problems and social support in adolescence'. In F. Nestmann and K. Hurrelmann (eds), *Social Networks and Social Support in Childhood and Adolescence* (pp. 241–255). Berlin: Walter de Gruyter.

Milardo, R. M. (1992). 'Comparative methods for delineating social networks'. *Journal of Social and Personal Relationships*, 9, 447–461.

Milgram, S., and Toch, H. (1969). 'Collective behaviour: crowds and social movements'. In G. Lindzey and E. Aronson (eds), *The Handbook of Social Psychology* (2nd edn, Vol. 4, pp. 507–610). Reading, MA: Addison-Wesley.

Miller, W. B. (1975). *Violence by Youth Gangs and Youth Groups as a Crime Problem in Major American Cities* (report to the National Institute for Juvenile Justice and Delinquency Prevention). Washington, DC.

Mitchell, J. C. (ed.) (1969). *Social Networks in Urban Situations*. Manchester: Manchester University Press.

Mitic, W. (1990). 'Parental versus peer influence on adolescents' alcohol consumption'. *Psychological Reports*, 67, 1273–1274.

Montemayor, R., and van Komen, R. (1980). 'Age segregation of adolescents in and out of school'. *Journal of Youth and Adolescence*, 9, 371–381.

Montemayor, R., and van Komen, R. (1985). 'The development of sex differences in friendship patterns and peer group structure during adolescence'. *Journal of Early Adolescence*, 5, 285–294.

Moorhouse, H. F. (1991). 'Football hooligans: old bottle, new whines?'. *Sociological Review*, 39, 489–502.

Moreland, R. L., and Levine, J. M. (1982). 'Socialization in small groups: temporal changes in individual–group relations'. *Advances in Experimental Social Psychology*, 15, 137–192.

Morgan, M., and Grube, J. W. (1991). 'Closeness and peer group influence'. *British Journal of Social Psychology*, 30, 159–169.

Mosbach, P., and Leventhal, H. (1988). 'Peer group identification and smoking: implications for intervention'. *Journal of Abnormal Psychology*, 97, 238–245.

Murphy, P., Williams, J., and Dunning, E. (1990). *Football on Trial: Spectator violence and development in the football world*. London: Routledge.

Musgrave, P. W. (1985). 'Some methodological, substantive, and theoretical aspects'. In P. Fensham (ed.), *Alienation from Schooling* (pp. 286–302). Melbourne: Routledge and Kegan Paul.

Nash, R. (1973). 'Clique formation among primary and secondary school children'. *British Journal of Sociology*, 24, 303–313.

National Board of Employment, Education and Training (NBEET) (1993). *In the Middle: Schooling for young adolescents*. Schools Council, Canberra: AGPS.

Nava, M. (1984). 'Youth work provision, social order, and the question of girls'. In A. McRobbie and M. Nava (eds), *Gender and Generation* (pp. 85–111). London: Macmillan.

Newman, B., and Newman, P. (1976). 'Early adolescence and its conflict: group identity versus alienation'. *Adolescence*, 11, 261–274.

Newman, B., and Newman, P. (1986). *Adolescent Development*. Columbus, OH: Charles Merrill.

Nightingale, E. O., and Wolverton, L. (1993). 'Adolescent rolelessness in modern society'. *Teachers College Record*, 94, 472–486.

Nisbet, J. D., and Entwistle, N. J. (1969). *The Transition to Secondary School*. London: London University Press.

Nurmi, J. E. (1991). 'How do adolescents see their future? A review of the development of future orientation and planning'. *Developmental Review*, 11, 1–59.

O'Brien, J., Goodenow, C., and Espin, O. (1991). 'Adolescents' reactions to the death of a peer'. *Adolescence*, 26, 431–440.

O'Doherty, M. (1991). 'Positive responses to youthful graffiti'. In J. Vernon and S. McKillop (eds), *Preventing Juvenile Crime* (proceedings of AIS Conference, July 1989, pp. 177–184). Canberra: Australian Institute of Criminology.

Oetting, E. R., and Beauvais, F. (1987a). 'Common elements in youth drug abuse: peer clusters and other psychosocial factors'. *Journal of Drug Issues*, 17, 133–151.

Oetting, E. R., and Beauvais, F. (1987b). 'Peer cluster theory, socialisation characteristics, and adolescent drug use: a path analysis'. *Journal of Counselling Psychology*, 34, 205–213.

Offer, D., and Offer, J. (1975). *From Teenager to Young Manhood: A psychological study*. New York: Basic Books.

O'Hagan, F. J. (1976). 'Gang characteristics: an empirical survey'. *Journal of Child Psychology and Psychiatry and Allied Disciplines*, 17, 305–314.

Ostrov, E., and Offer, D. (1978). 'Loneliness and the adolescent'. *Adolescent Psychiatry*, 6, 34–50.

Palmonari, A., Pombeni, M. L., and Kirchler, E. (1990). 'Adolescents and their peer groups: a study on the significance of peers, social categorization processes and coping with developmental tasks'. *Social Behaviour*, 5, 33–48.

Parker, J. G., and Asher, S. R. (1993). 'Friendship and friendship quality in middle childhood: links with peer group acceptance and feelings of loneliness and social dissatisfaction'. *Developmental Psychology*, 29, 611–621.

Parkhurst, J. T., and Asher, S. R. (1992). 'Peer rejection in middle school: subgroup differences in behavior, loneliness, and interpersonal concerns'. *Developmental Psychology*, 28, 231–241.

Parsons, T. (1963). 'On the concept of influence'. *Public Opinion Quarterly*, 27, 37–92.

Patrick, J. (1973). *A Glasgow Gang Observed*. London: Eyre Methuen.

Patterson, G., DeBaryshe, B., and Ramsey, E. (1989). 'A developmental perspective on antisocial behaviour'. *American Psychologist*, 44, 329–335.

Pearson, B. (1991). 'Outdoor adventure camps: personal development through challenge'. In J. Vernon and S. McKillop (eds), *Preventing Juvenile Crime* (Proceedings of AIS Conference, July 1989, pp. 159–168). Canberra: Australian Institute of Criminology.

Pearson, G. (1983). *Hooligan: A history of respectable fears*. London: Macmillan.

Peplau, L. A., and Perlman, D. (eds) (1982). *Loneliness: A sourcebook of current theory, research, and therapy*. New York: Wiley.

Peplau, L. A., Micelli, M., and Morasch, B. (1982). 'Loneliness and self-evaluation'. In L. A. Peplau and D. Perlman (eds), *Loneliness: A sourcebook of current theory, research, and therapy* (pp. 135–151). New York: Wiley.

Perlman, D., and Joshi, P. (1989). 'The revelation of loneliness'. In M. Hojat and R. Crandall (eds), *Loneliness: Theory, Research, and Applications* (pp. 63–76). London: Sage.

Philippi, M. (1994). 'Goal setting to increase educational motivation in at risk adolescents' (unpublished M.Psych.Ed. dissertation, University of Queensland).

Planalp, S., and Benson, A. (1992). 'Friends' and acquaintances' conversations 1: Perceived differences'. *Journal of Social and Personal Relationships*, 9, 483–506.

Poole, M. E. (1983). *Youth: Expectations and transitions*. Melbourne: Routledge and Kegan Paul.

Power, C. N., and Cotterell, J. L. (1979). *Students in Transition*. Adelaide: School of Education, Flinders University.

Power, C. N., and Cotterell, J. L. (1981). *Changes in Students in the Transition from Primary to Secondary School*. Canberra: Australian Government Publishing Service.

Prentice-Dunn, S., and Rogers, R. (1989). 'Deindividuation and the self-regulation of behavior'. In P. B. Paulus (ed.), *Psychology of Group Influence* (pp. 87–109). Hillsdale, NJ: Lawrence Erlbaum.

Pulkkinen, L. (1983). 'Youthful smoking and drinking in a longitudinal perspective'. *Journal of Youth and Adolescence*, 12, 253–283.

Pulkkinen, L., and Narusk, A. (1987). 'Functions of adolescent drinking in Finland and the Soviet Union'. *European Journal of Psychology of Education*, 11, 311–326.

Raphael, B. (1983). *The Anatomy of Bereavement*. New York: Basic Books.

Raphael, B. (1988). 'Youth health – who cares?'. *Youth Studies*, 8(1), 27–32.

Reicher, S. (1987). 'Crowd behaviour as social action'. In J. Turner (ed.), *Rediscovering the Social Group: A self-categorization theory* (pp. 171–203). Oxford: Blackwell.

Renshaw, P. D., and Brown, P. J. (1993). 'Loneliness in childhood: concurrent and longitudinal predictors'. *Child Development*, 64, 1271–1284.

Roberts, K. (1983). *Youth and Leisure*. London: Allen and Unwin.

Robins, D. (1984). *We Hate Humans*. London: Penguin.

Rook, C. (1899). *The Hooligan Nights*. London: Grant Richards.

Rook, K. S. (1984). 'Promoting social bonding: strategies for helping the lonely and socially isolated'. *American Psychologist*, 39, 1389–1407.

Rook, K. S. (1987). 'Social support versus companionship: effects on life stress, loneliness, and evaluations by others'. *Journal of Personality and Social Psychology*, 52, 1132–1147.

Roscoe, B., and Skomski, G. (1989). 'Loneliness among late adolescents'. *Adolescence*, 24, 947–955.

Rosenberg, M., and McCullough, B. C. (1981). 'Mattering: inferred significance and mental health among adolescents'. *Research in Community and Mental Health*, 2, 163–182.

Rosenthal, D. A., and Hrynevich, C. (1985). 'Ethnicity and ethnic identity: a comparative study of Greek-, Italian-, and Anglo-Australian adolescents'. *International Journal of Psychology*, 20, 723–742.

Rubenstein, C., and Shaver, P. (1982). 'The experience of loneliness'. In L. A. Peplau and D. Perlman (eds), *Loneliness: A sourcebook of current theory, research, and therapy* (pp. 206–223). New York: Wiley.

Salzinger, L. L. (1982). 'The ties that bind: the effect of clustering on dyadic relationships'. *Social Networks*, 4, 117–145.

Samuel, L. (1984). 'And words will often hurt me'. *Education News*, 18(9), 21–23.

Sanford, S., and Eder, D. (1984). 'Adolescent humor during peer interaction'. *Social Psychology Quarterly*, 47, 235–243.

Savin-Williams, R. (1980). 'Dominance hierarchies in groups of middle to late adolescent males'. *Journal of Youth and Adolescence*, 9, 75–85.

Scherl, L. M. (1989). 'Self in wilderness: understanding the psychological benefits of individual–wilderness interaction through self-control'. *Leisure Sciences*, 11, 123–135.

Schoggen, P. (1989). *Behavior Settings*. Stanford, CA: Stanford University Press.

Schultz, N. R., and Moore, D. (1989). 'Further reflections on loneliness research'. In M. Hojat and R. Crandall (eds), *Loneliness: Theory, research, and applications* (pp. 37–40). London: Sage.

Schwendinger, H., and Schwendinger, J. S. (1985). *Adolescent Subcultures and Delinquency*. New York: Praeger.

Scritchfield, S., and Picou, J. (1982). 'The structure of significant other influence on status aspirations: black–white variations'. *Sociology of Education*, 55, 22–30.

Seeman, M. (1959). 'On the meaning of alienation'. *American Sociological Review*, 24, 783–791.

Seidman, E. (1991). 'Growing up the hard way: pathways of urban adolescents'. *American Journal of Community Psychology*, 19, 173–201.

Selnow, G. W., and Crano, W. D. (1986). 'Formal vs informal group affiliations: implications for alcohol and drug use among adolescents'. *Journal of Studies on Alcohol*, 47, 48–52.

Semmens, R. (1990). 'Delinquency prevention: individual control or social development'. *Youth Studies*, 9(3), 23–29.

Shaver, P., and Hazan, C. (1989). 'Being lonely, falling in love: perspectives from attachment theory'. In M. Hojat and R. Crandall (eds), *Loneliness: Theory, research, and applications* (pp. 105–124). London: Sage.

Shaver, P., Furman, W., and Buhrmester, D. (1985). 'Transition to college: network changes, social skills and loneliness'. In S. Duck and D. Perlman (eds), *Understanding Personal Relationships: An interdisciplinary approach* (pp. 193–220). London: Sage.

Sherif, M. (1936). *The Psychology of Social Norms*. New York: Harper and Bros.

Sherif, M., and Sherif, C. (1964). *Reference Groups*. New York: Harper and Row.

Silbereisen, R. K., Noack, P., and Eyferth, K. (1986). 'Place for development: adolescents, leisure settings, and developmental tasks'. In R. K. Silbereisen, K. Eyferth, and G. Rudinger (eds), *Development as Action in Context: Problem behavior and normal youth development* (pp. 87–107). New York: Springer- Verlag.

Simons, R. L., Conger, R. D., and Whitbeck, L. B. (1988). 'A multistage social learning model of the influences of family and peers upon adolescent substance abuse'. *Journal of Drug Issues*, 18, 293–315.

Simpura, J. (1985). 'Drinking: an ignored leisure activity'. *Journal of Leisure Research*, 17, 200–211.

Smith, D. M. (1985). 'Perceived peer and parental influences on youths' social world'. *Youth and Society*, 17, 131–156.

Smith, E. A. (1963). *American Youth Culture: Group life in teenage society*. New York: Free Press.

Smith, G. (1975). 'Kids, cops and conflict: a participant-observation study'. *Australian and New Zealand Journal of Sociology*, 11, 21–27.

Smith, G. R., and Gregory, T. B. (1987). 'The contrasting social climates of two high schools in the same town'. In B. J. Fraser (ed.), *The Study of Learning Environments* (Vol. 3, pp. 50–59). Perth: Curtin University.

Smith, M. (1988). *Developing Youth Work*. Milton Keynes: Open University Press.

Smith, M., Canter, W., and Robin, A. (1989). 'A path analysis of an adolescent drinking behaviour model derived from problem behaviour theory'. *Journal of Studies on Alcohol*, 50, 128–142.

Smith, M. D. (1983). *Violence and Sport*. Toronto: Butterworths.

Snyder, J., Dishion, T. J., and Patterson, G. R. (1986). 'Determinants and consequences of associating with deviant peers during pre-adolescence and adolescence'. *Journal of Early Adolescence*, 6, 29–43.

Stacy, A. W., Sussman, S., Dent, C. W., Burton, D., and Flay, B. R. (1992). 'Moderators of peer social influence in adolescent smoking'. *Personality and Social Psychology Bulletin*, 18, 163–172.

Stattin, H., Gustafson, S., and Magnusson, D. (1989). 'Peer influences on adolescent drinking'. *Journal of Early Adolescence*, 9, 227–246.

Tajfel, H. (1978). 'Social categorisation, social identity, and social comparison'. In H. Tajfel (ed.), *Differentiation between Social Groups* (pp. 61–76). London: Academic Press.

Tajfel, H. (1981). *Human Groups and Social Categories*. Cambridge: Cambridge University Press.

Tajfel, H., and Turner, J. (1979). 'An integrative theory of social conflict'. In W. Austin and S. Worchel (eds), *The Social Psychology of Intergroup Relations* (pp. 33–48). Monterey, CA: Brooks-Cole.

Takahashi, K., and Majima, N. (1994). 'Transition from home to college dormitory: the role of preestablished affective relationships in adjustment to a new life'. *Journal of Research on Adolescence*, 4, 367–384.

Tannenbaum, F. (1938). *Crime and the Community*. New York: Columbia University Press.

Tanner, D. (1990). 'Gender differences in topical coherence: creating involvement in best friends' talk'. *Discourse Processes*, 13, 73–90.

Tasmanian Department of Education (1988). 'Supportive school environments'. *Tasmanian Education Gazette*, 22, April, 46–50.

Taylor, S. (1980). 'School experience and student perspectives: a study of some effects of secondary school organisation'. *Educational Review*, 32, 37–52.

Thomas, M., and Perry, J. (1975). *National Voluntary Youth Organisations*. London: PEP Social Science Institute.

Thornberry, T., Krohn, M. D., Lizotte, A., and Chard-Wierschem, D. (1993). 'The role of juvenile gangs in facilitating delinquent behaviour'. *Journal of Research in Crime and Delinqency*, 30, 55–87.

Tolson, J. M., and Urberg, K. A. (1993). 'Similarity between adolescent best friends'. *Journal of Adolescent Research*, 8, 274–288.

Trommsdorff, G. (1986). 'Future time orientation and its relevance for development as action'. In R. K. Silbereisen, K. Eyferth, and G. Rudinger (eds), *Development as Action in Context* (pp. 121–136). Berlin: Springer-Verlag.

Turner, J. (1991). *Social Influence*. Milton Keynes: Open University Press.

Turner, J., Hogg, M., Oakes, P., Reicher, S., and Wetherell, M. (1987). *Rediscovering the Social Group: A self-categorization theory*. Oxford: Blackwell.

Turner, R., and Killian, L. (eds) (1957). *Collective Behavior*. Englewood Cliffs, NJ: Prentice-Hall.

Ullah, P. (1987). 'Self-definition and psychological group formation in an ethnic minority'. *British Journal of Social Psychology*, 26, 17–23.

Urberg, K. (1992). 'Locus of peer influence: social crowd or best friend'. *Journal of Youth and Adolescence*, 21, 439–450.

Urberg, K., Shyu, S., and Liang, J. (1990). 'Peer influence in adolescent cigarette smoking'. *Addictive Behaviors*, 15, 247–255.

Urjadko, V. (1991). 'Community based initiatives in crime prevention'. In J. Vernon and S. McKillop (eds), *Preventing Juvenile Crime* (Proceeding of AIS Conference, July 1989, pp. 169–175). Canberra: Australian Institute of Criminology.

Van Knippenberg, A. (1991). Book review of *Social Identifications* (Hogg and Abrams). *British Journal of Social Psychology*, 30, 271–272.

van Roosmalen, E. H., and McDaniel, S. A. (1989). 'Peer group influence as a factor in smoking behavior of adolescents'. *Adolescence*, 24, 801–816.

Veno, A., and Veno, E. (1990). 'Primary prevention of violence: the 1989 Australian Grand Prix'. *Criminology Australia*, 1(4), 14–16.

Verkuyten, M. (1991). 'Self-definition and ingroup formation among ethnic minorities in the Netherlands'. *Social Psychology Quarterly*, 54, 280–286.

Vigil, J. D. (1990). 'Cholos and gangs: culture change and street youth in Los Angeles'. In C. R. Huff (ed.), *Gangs in America* (pp. 116–128). Newbury Park, CA: Sage.

Vinsel, A., Brown, B., Altman, I., and Foss, C. (1980). 'Privacy regulation, territorial displays and effectiveness of individual functioning'. *Journal of Personality and Social Psychology*, 39, 1104–1115.

Waddell, N., and Cairns, E. (1986). 'Situational perspectives in Northern Ireland'. *British Journal of Social Psychology*, 25, 25–31.

Walker, J. (1988). *Louts and Legends*. Sydney: Allen and Unwin.

Ward, C. (1989). *Steaming In: Journal of a football fan*. London: Simon and Schuster.

Wehlage, G. G., and Rutter, R.A. (1986). 'Dropping out: how much do schools contribute to the problem?'. *Teachers College Record*, 87, 374–392.

Weinraub, M., Brooks, J., and Lewis, M. (1977). 'The social network: a reconsideration of the concept of attachment'. *Human Development*, 20, 31–47.

Weiss, R. S. (1973). *Loneliness: The experience of emotional and social isolation*. Cambridge, MA: MIT Press.

Weiss, R. S. (1974). 'The provisions of social relationships'. In Z. Rubin (ed.), *Doing unto Others* (pp. 17–26). Englewood Cliffs, NJ: Prentice-Hall.

Weiss, R. S. (1982). 'Issues in the study of loneliness'. In L. A. Peplau and D. Perlman (eds), *Loneliness: A sourcebook of current theory, research, and therapy* (pp. 71–80). New York: Wiley.

Weiss, R. S. (1989). 'Reflections on the present state of loneliness research'. In M. Hojat and R. Crandall (eds), *Loneliness: Theory, research, and applications* (pp. 1–16). London: Sage.

Weissberg, R.P., Caplan, M., and Harwood, R.L. (1991). 'Promoting competent young people in competence-enhancing environments: a systems-based perspective on primary prevention'. *Journal of Consulting and Clinical Psychology*, 59, 830–841.

Wellman, B. (1981). 'Applying network analysis to the study of support'. In B. H. Gottlieb (ed.), *Social Networks and Social Support* (pp. 171–200). Beverly Hills, CA: Sage.

Wellman, B. (1988). 'Structural analysis: from method and metaphor to theory and substance'. In B. Wellman and S. D. Berkowitz (eds), *Social Structures: A network approach* (pp. 19–61). Cambridge: Cambridge University Press.

Wellman, B. (1992). 'Men in networks: private communities, domestic friendships'. In P. Nardi (ed.), *Men's Friendships* (pp. 74–114). Newbury Park, CA: Sage.

Werebe, M. (1987). 'Friendship and dating relationships among French adolescents'. *Journal of Adolescence*, 10, 269–289.

White, R. (1990). *No Space of their Own*. Melbourne: Cambridge University Press.

Wilder, D. A., and Shapiro, P. (1991). 'Facilitation of outgroup stereotypes by enhanced ingroup identity'. *Journal of Experimental Social Psychology*, 27, 431–452.

Wildermuth, N. L. (1990). 'Loneliness in adolescence: why it occurs and what to do about it'. In P. L. Heaven and V. J. Callan (eds), *Adolescence: An Australian perspective* (pp. 255–269). Sydney: Harcourt Brace Jovanovich.

Wilks, J. (1987). 'Drinking among teenagers in Australia: research findings, problems and prospects'. *Australian Drug and Alcohol Review*, 6, 207–226.

Williams, K., Harkins, S. and Latane, B. (1981). 'Identifiability as a deterrent to social loafing: two cheering experiments'. *Journal of Experimental Social Psychology*, 40, 303–311.

Wittenberg, M. T., and Reis, H. T. (1986). 'Loneliness, social skills, and social perception'. *Personality and Social Psychology Bulletin*, 12, 121–130.

Yablonsky, L. (1959). 'The delinquent gang as a near-group'. *Social Problems*, 7, 109–117.

Young, J. E. (1982). 'Loneliness, depression and cognitive therapy: theory and applications'. In L. A. Peplau and D. Perlman (eds), *Loneliness: A sourcebook of current theory, research, and therapy* (pp. 379–405). New York: Wiley.

Youniss, J., and Smollar, J. (1985). *Adolescent Relations with Mothers, Fathers, and Friends*. Chicago: University of Chicago Press.

Zisman, P., and Wilson, V. (1992). 'Table hopping in the cafeteria: an exploration of "racial" integration in early adolescent social groups'. *Anthropology and Education Quarterly*, 23, 199–220.

Name index

Subject index